John Barron

FOR ME!

The Long Road to the White House

NEW
SOUTH

To my wife, my family, and to Ursa

A New South book

Published by
University of New South Wales Press Ltd
University of New South Wales
Sydney NSW 2052
AUSTRALIA
www.unswpress.com.au

© John Barron 2008
First published 2008
The special Obama victory edition 2008

National Library of Australia
Cataloguing-in-Publication entry

Author: Barron, John.
Title: Vote for me: the long road to the White House/John Barron.
ISBN: 978 1 921410 86 4 (pbk.)
Notes: Includes index.
Subjects: Presidents – United States – Election.
        Elections – United States.
        Political campaigns – United States.
        Communication in politics – United States.
        Mass media – Political aspects – United States.
        Political psychology.
Dewey Number: 324.973

Internal design Di Quick
Author photo Thomas Gallane
Cover design Peter Long
Printer Ligare

Vote for Me!

JOHN BARRON is an Australia-based journalist and
documentary maker. He presents a daily national news
and current affairs program on ABC NewsRadio. John
has followed American politics for many years and has
reported on several US Presidential elections. In 2004
he covered George W. Bush's re-election from the US
for radio and television. He has been closely following
the 2008 campaign since it started in the cornfields of
Iowa in 2007. He is making a documentary on the 2008
election with his wife, film-maker Rebecca Glenn, with
whom he lives in Sydney.

# ★ Contents

Preface vi

Acknowledgments ix

1 A Whole Lotta Shakin' Going On 1

2 Grassroots 25

3 You Watch, We Decide 43

4 Get Out the Vote 69

5 Hard Yards in the Granite State 89

6 George McGovern's Dog 111

7 Follow the Money 135

8 The South and the North 152

9 Leadership 165

10 A Warm Bucket of Ambition 181

11 The Fall 204

12 The End of the Road 227

Index 246

★ Preface

I have been interested in US Presidential politics for about as long as I can remember. I grew up hearing the word 'Watergate' on the radio without really knowing what it was all about. Then Jimmy Carter had a likeable cartoon face that often came on the television after *The Goodies*, but he wasn't very good and he lost to an old man who made movies a long time ago. I don't know why I was interested then, except that it seemed very important. It still does. After all, decisions made in the White House affect the lives of billions of people around the world, including Australians.

My first attempt at being a journalist was haranguing an American exchange student in my first year of high school by repeatedly asking him the question that was dominating the news that year: 'Who do you think will win the 1984 Democratic Presidential nomination?'

I'm not sure what annoyed him most – my attempted American newscaster accent or the invisible microphone I shoved into his face each morning – but whichever it was, he would respond by punching my arm.

Almost a quarter of a century later, while working on this book and a documentary film, I found myself asking pretty much the same question of a former Presidential candidate who ran for the 1984 Democratic nomination and who was also the target of the Watergate break-in. I'm happy to say that Senator George McGovern didn't punch me in the arm – maybe it helps to have a real microphone.

The 2008 Presidential election was arguably the most competitive and wide open in eight decades. Not since 1928 had there been no President or Vice President from either party standing, although some say that in 1952 President Harry Truman hardly sought re-election even though he did appear on the ballot in early primaries.

The men and one woman who sought the nomination of the Democratic and Republican parties throughout the long campaign season of 2007/08 were also the most diverse list of potential Presidents ever. They included an African-American, a white woman, a Latino, a Mormon, a former Southern Baptist preacher, an Italian-American, a former prisoner of war and a vegan who says he has seen a UFO.

Some you have almost certainly heard of: Barack Obama, John McCain, Hillary Clinton and Rudy Giuliani. Others, perhaps not: Bill Richardson, Mike Huckabee, Mitt Romney, Fred Thompson, Joe Biden and Chris Dodd. And if you've heard of Tom Tancredo, Dennis Kucinich, Mike Gravel, Tommy Thompson, Sam Brownback, Alan Keyes, Jim Cox or Duncan Hunter, you suffer the same obsession that has afflicted me for many years.

The Presidential primaries in the first half of 2008 attracted record voter turnout, particularly on the Democratic side. The amount of money spent on the campaigns also set new records, as did the candidates' ability to raise money – especially online. It was also a remarkable primary election process because the two candidates seen as the most likely favourites, Rudy Giuliani and Hillary Clinton, both failed to win their party's Presidential nomination. It became a contest between the first black man ever nominated by a major political party and the oldest-ever first-time nominee.

This is the story of a historic election: how it happened, why it happened, the people who made the system the way it is, and those who would like to see it changed.

★ Acknowledgments

I usually skip this part of a book, unless I know the author and think I might be mentioned. I never have been – I don't know many authors. I would, however, like to thank a number of people who I now expect to thank me should they write a book: Benython Oldfield of Zeitgeist Media Group, who on hearing we were making a documentary film on the US election, suggested I write a book as well – without your inspiration and guidance this book would never have happened.

Thanks go to Bruce Wolpe, who suggested I go to Iowa to meet some potential Presidents.

Thank you as well to Phillipa McGuinness at UNSW Press for your enthusiasm for the subject and the book, and to my editor Sarah Shrubb, who carefully tweaked, polished, clarified and otherwise improved my words. (Note: she left that last compliment intact.)

Thanks also go to Julian Morrow and Geraldine Brooks for saying nice things on the cover.

And thank you to YOU – who have either just bought this book, or are reading this because you have time to kill in a bookshop. Buy it and go get a coffee, or carefully put it back on the shelf and don't leave any smudgy finger-marks on it – it will be on the remainder table soon enough.

Thank you to the many fine men and women across the US who agreed to be interviewed for this project, from the Presidential candidates all the way up to Jerry the Iowa Fair hog-keeper. Special thanks go to our wonderful American friends Bob and Wendy Wheeler, the delightful Gloria and Alan Mills, and to the many others who invited a couple of Aussies with a notebook, camera and grubby boots into their homes – sorry about the rug.

Thank you to Sue and Leigh Dyson for your support of the film, and by extension, this book.

And thanks too, to all of our friends who were so engaged and encouraging - in particular Rogan Jacobson and Dr Claire Hooker, who were there in Boston in 2004 to see the start of a long road, and my 'little brother' and friend, the indestructible Cielo Ellis-Vega.

To the family I was given (John W. Barron, Ann Barron, Sarah Barron and Emma Barron) and the one I gained (Doctors Odile and Andrew Glenn, and Asher and Louisa Mitchell), thank you for believing, encouraging and caring as you do.

And finally, to my wife Rebecca Glenn, whose talent inspires and whose love makes all things seem possible.

1 A Whole Lotta Shakin' Going On

Iowa, August 2007: The Presidential candidate is sweating in the 40°C heat of a typically humid summer's day. It's not just a few beads of perspiration that can be dabbed away with a handkerchief, but a steady trickle from somewhere above his hairline, down his forehead onto his cheeks, where they merge into salty streams that fall from the candidate's jowls onto the rapidly darkening collar of his navy blue cotton shirt. It seems strange to see an aspiring President sweat: the unselfconscious way in which he lets the perspiration flow brings to mind an ageing heavyweight fighter trying to get into shape for one last bout, or maybe fat Elvis from a particularly sultry concert in Hawaii in the mid-1970s. The latter effect is enhanced by the chunky gold ring on one of his chubby fingers.

The Presidential candidate is Bill Richardson, the 59-year-old

Latino former Democratic Party Congressman, UN Ambassador and now Governor of the state of New Mexico. He's on the soapbox at the Iowa State Fair, which is held in the capital, Des Moines, each August. The fair was the inspiration for the 1950s Broadway musical *State Fair*, by Rodgers and Hammerstein. Each summer, about one in three Iowans can be found here, and five months ahead of the crucial caucus vote, where there are Iowans, there are plenty of would-be Presidents like Bill Richardson.

He smiles a smile amplified by the deep tan of his skin and some probably very expensive dental work: 'I want to say thank you to everyone in Iowa who's shaken my hand and said hello.' Richardson knows a bit about hand-shaking. In 2002 he set a world record of 13,392 hand-shakes in 8 hours while campaigning in New Mexico. 'This is the essence of how we elect our President,' Richardson tells the crowd. 'Grassroots, hand-shaking, meeting people directly. Iowa should make the decision on the next President – not the smarty-pants set in Washington.' The cheer from the hundred or so Iowans sitting on hay bales around the State Fair Soap Box says they agree. 'I'm running for President because I believe we need to bring this country together,' he beams, flashing the dental work.

The lengthy US Presidential election cycle, which runs once in every four years, starts with a caucus vote in the largely rural corn and pork producing mid-western state of Iowa, about 10 months before the nation's general election in November. Here members of the two major American parties, the Republicans and the Democrats, start the process of deciding which two candidates will face off in the Presidential election. Some states hold 'primary'-style elections where party members simply go to a local polling station and cast a secret ballot for their preferred candidate out of the list of nominees – the whole process takes just a few minutes. Other states, such as Iowa, hold a 'caucus', which is more like a town hall meeting where party members indicate who they favour, then argue the pros and cons of their candidate for several hours before a final show of hands vote is taken. It's very public, sometimes very heated, and someone can arrive intending to support one candidate and leave as a delegate sworn to another. This makes opinion polls taken before the caucus quite unreliable.

But even though they're all talking or thinking about particular candidates, both the primary voters and caucus-goers are in fact electing delegates to their party's state or national convention, and it is those delegates who will then vote for the actual Presidential nominee. These delegates are allocated on a per capita basis, so more populous states such as California, Florida and New York have many more delegate votes than states like Iowa.

That's why it was decided in the early 1970s that small states such as Iowa and New Hampshire, and more recently Nevada and South Carolina, would be allowed to vote earlier in the primary and caucus process (which can take up to five months). This was seen as a way to ensure that their interests would not be ignored by candidates altogether.

Today, Iowa's caucus is still five months away, but the campaigning is already in full swing. Governor Richardson is among eight Democrats and nine Republicans seeking to become America's 44th President. All the candidates converge on Iowa during August 2007. For the Republicans there's an important Straw Poll of support for candidates in the college town of Ames, and for the Democrats there's the first official debate, in Des Moines.

I'm here to film an independent documentary with my wife Rebecca, who is also a journalist and screenwriter. We both reported on the 2004 Presidential election for the ABC and wanted to find out more about how this remarkable, convoluted and super-expensive process of selecting candidates and then a President works. During that bitter battle between Republican President George W. Bush and Democratic Senator John Kerry we'd been surprised at the level of passion, engagement and idealism we'd seen – considering that only about 50 per cent of adult Americans vote. In 2004 we'd arrived just three days before the election; this time we wanted to see where it all begins – more than a year out from the Presidential poll, here in Iowa.

The Iowa caucuses give this state of fewer than 3 million people a major say in who becomes the next President. A strong showing in Iowa can springboard a virtual unknown into prominence (George McGovern in 1972), even send you all the way to the White House (Jimmy Carter in 1976). But it can just as easily go horribly wrong in Iowa as well: after being an early frontrunner, Governor Howard Dean's disappointing third place and subsequent hysterical-sounding 'Dean Scream' to supporters here all but ended his campaign in 2004. It's often said that there are just three tickets out of Iowa: first, second and third. Come fourth or worse and history says you just won't make it. Since the changes made in the early 1970s, no candidate has gone on to win their party's Presidential nomination without finishing in the top three in Iowa's caucuses. Yet, as Howard Dean found out, even a top three place can look like a defeat if you were expected by the media pundits to perform better.

I wanted to know whether candidates like Richardson or maybe Illinois Senator Barack Obama can still do as McGovern tried to do and Carter did – win the most powerful political office on earth from relatively humble beginnings in a small state like Iowa – or if the billion-dollar campaign and compressed voting calendar has indeed ended that. Because McGovern and Carter were Democrats and because the Democrats were favoured to retake the White House in 2008, I decided to focus largely on them.

For an outsider with an interest in politics, seeing an American President – or even one of the twenty or so people currently running for the Presidency – is pretty exciting, but you soon realise that these Iowans are used to seeing Presidential candidates up close. For the two years before an election, would-be Commanders-in-Chief rent cars or buses and drive the length and breadth of Iowa's 99 counties, speaking to groups at churches, community centres, coffee shops and restaurants. They call this 'retail politics', the sort of door-to-door campaigning that involves lots of hand-shaking and speech-making. It's up to the individual candidate to attract local staff, volunteers and supporters to their campaign. Early on, it's often just the candidate and their campaign manager driving from town to town in Iowa to speak at meetings organised by party members, courting the support of small-town party members and calling on would-be donors. They make a joke about the Iowan who says, 'I don't know if I can vote for this guy, I only met him five or six times.'

⁂

Iowa City is a 2-hour drive due east of Des Moines along Route 80, through flat fields of corn and soy beans. Here, at the solid-looking early 20th century campus of the University of Iowa, Professor Peverill Squire explains that he's in the process of packing up his office and moving to another academic posting, so we meet in a book-lined conference room in the Department of Political Science instead. We decided he'd be a good person to start explaining this whole process, and he's happy to oblige. Peverill Squire is a leading expert on modern American politics and Iowa in particular, although his name suggests a character from a Mark Twain story (and there is an old-worldly quaintness about his looks and manner). He has rimless glasses, a faintly amused mouth, and the sort of slightly bulbous forehead that suggests a large brain.

Professor Squire explains that the Iowa caucuses are a throwback to the way elections were held in the very early history of the US:

> They are public events where you go with others of your same political party into a high school gym or the bay of a fire station and you discuss the candidate and their various merits and then you vote publicly and identify yourself with a particular candidate ... so it's a very unusual process.

It's also a very time-consuming process, he says, sometimes taking up to four or five hours on a cold January night to reach a final vote. Squire says Iowans have an unparalleled opportunity to see and meet the candidates: 'This is an extraordinary thing in a country of 300 million people, that 3 million people in Iowa have this unprecedented access to candidates. And it's something Iowans appreciate.'

There is a mostly friendly rivalry between Iowa and New Hampshire. Iowans are proud to say they are the first to vote, but in New Hampshire they point out that Iowa's caucus isn't as directly binding a vote as their own primary. It was former New Hampshire Governor John H. Sununu who famously claimed, 'Iowa picks corn; New Hampshire picks Presidents.' Iowa's delegates are elected at almost 1800 precinct caucuses and are then sent to county conventions, which in turn vote for district and state delegates. In this long and convoluted process, which takes several months, Iowa delegates can change their minds and vote for another candidate.

Iowa's significance dates back to 1972. That was the year a bright and ambitious young campaign manager named Gary Hart focused on building strong local support through grassroots campaigning in Iowa in Democrat Senator George McGovern's unlikely Presidential nomination campaign. It worked: the liberal, anti-Vietnam War McGovern was the surprise winner of the Democratic Party's endorsement.

Gary Hart later became a Senator himself, and twice ran for the Presidency. Hart again focused on grassroots campaigning in Iowa, and only narrowly missed out on the nomination in 1984. Sadly for Gary Hart's Presidential ambitions in 1988, he answered rumours that he was an adulterer by challenging the press to follow him and see what they could uncover – they did, and they dug up a photograph of him with a young blonde model named Donna Rice sitting on his lap while cruising on his boat (which, to the delight of headline writers, was named *Monkey Business*). But despite all that, Gary Hart is still credited by many Iowans with helping make their little state a very big deal come election time.

Back at the State Fair in Des Moines, Bill Richardson has finished his Soap Box speech and takes questions from the crowd on issues from illegal immigration to the war in Iraq. Then it's time to face the press. Sitting on a nearby bench in the beating sun, the Governor tells a dozen or so slightly heat-struck reporters and camera operators that he enjoys this sort of campaigning:

> Well I like to sweat, I like people to know I'm sweating, I like the physical side of campaigning. You know I broke the world record for hand-shaking at the New Mexico State Fair … [*We know*] and the way I'm going to win Iowa is by shaking hundreds and hundreds of thousands of hands.

I ask him what's the toughest part of this sort of campaigning:

> The toughest part is raising the money. We're competitive in that area but we're not like the mega-stars. I'm the hardest working candidate and I love this kind of campaigning, I know I'm sweating, I know I probably don't look so good, but I'm getting votes and I'm connecting with voters and that's what I like.

Bill Richardson is clearly getting into the spirit of Iowa-style campaigning:

> Electing Presidents should be about voters knowing their candidates and in Iowa this can happen. That's why Iowa should stay as the first caucus or primary: you've made Presidents out of underdogs and that's what I hope you make of me.

In the year 2000, as Governor of Vermont, Howard Dean gave an interview to Canadian Television that would come back to haunt him four years later as he ran for the White House. Dean attacked the role of Iowa, saying:

> If you look at the caucus system, they are dominated by special interests
> on both sides and both parties … I can't stand there listening to
> everybody else's opinion for eight hours about how to change the world.

Dean isn't alone in questioning the caucus process and the role Iowa plays – it represents just 1 per cent of the total US population, and is one of the least racially diverse states in America, at 94 per cent white, compared with about 67 per cent nationally. And usually, only around 200,000 Iowans take part in the Republican and Democratic caucus vote for the Presidential candidates. After his spectacular flame-out in Iowa in 2004, Howard Dean was elevated to the Chairmanship of the Democratic National Committee (DNC), a senior party administrative role.

When we meet in Iowa, Dean seems shorter, slighter and fitter than he appears on TV, but he has the same slightly crazed underbite that probably helped people think twice about putting him in charge of one and a half million GIs, Marines, Navy and Air Force personnel, let alone the world's largest nuclear arsenal.

I ask Governor Dean about the importance of Iowa. 'It's still first, it's still very, very important,' he says, 'and it requires, most importantly, an enormous amount of grassroots organisation, which is the real key.'

But what about criticisms that Iowans aren't really representative of America – why should these people have so much influence? 'That's why we changed the calendar around this year,' Dean says:

> We've also got New Hampshire, Nevada and South Carolina, so there's
> a strong geographic and ethnic mix very early in the campaign, with

significant voting from African-Americans, Hispanics, Asian Americans and Native Americans … so we've sought to balance that out and I'm very happy that we have.

But unfortunately for Howard Dean's plans to balance Iowa's influence and make the vote more representative by moving the South Carolina primary and the Nevada caucus to January, immediately following Iowa and New Hampshire, this rather scared the horses. Bigger states with many more votes at stake (such as New York, Florida and California) decided that they wanted a greater say in who the candidates for the Presidency would be, so they moved their polling dates forward as well. That led to a number of other states trying to leapfrog the larger states, posing more problems for New Hampshire and Iowa, whose state laws insist that they remain first. As a result, the 2008 schedule was thrown into confusion, with state party officials deciding that the Iowa caucus and New Hampshire primaries should be almost two weeks earlier, so that they would retain their 'first in the nation' status.

In the end, two important states – Florida and Michigan – went ahead with earlier primaries, but were told by the DNC they would be stripped of their delegates to the Democratic National Convention, effectively making their votes worthless. Ultimately, a compromise would see half the delegates seated at the convention, but it didn't change the result. With this slightly chaotic and fluid voting schedule leading to pundit predictions that the whole nomination process would be rushed into a mad month of voting, I asked Howard Dean if he thinks it's still possible for a candidate to do as Jimmy Carter did and start small in the early states, overcome a lack of money or name recognition and win:

Oh I do, I think this is a calendar that suits people who don't know anybody and don't have any money when they start but have a powerful message. They have to hang in there, go door to door and meet as many people [as possible] and look them in the eye … that's why we have four small states early.

Jody Powell spent a lot of time on the campaign trail in Iowa. These days he lives a couple of hours outside Washington DC – in rural Maryland, in a large timber house with stunning views over Chesapeake Bay. Powell is best remembered as President Jimmy Carter's White House spokesman, the man who talked to reporters about the historic Egypt–Israel peace deal at Camp David and the capture of the US hostages in Iran. Back in 1975, Jody Powell and former Georgia Governor James Earl Carter drove a lot of miles in rented cars campaigning around Iowa. Now in his mid-sixties, these days Powell looks more like a outdoorsman and hunter – which he is – than the sharp-suited spin doctor that he was.

In his powerful Georgian drawl, Jody Powell recalls grassroots campaigning in Iowa:

> We spent a lot of time in the small towns, getting to know people, and as President Carter is fond of recalling, sleeping on people's couches – actually as I recall he got the guest bedroom and I got the couch!

Jody Powell's expansive living room has just a few mementos from a life spent around politics and power. On a bookcase full of volumes by and about President Carter, there is also a man's shoe that has been bronzed. Powell explains that the shoe is a keepsake from the campaign in 1976. He turns it over to reveal the sole – it has been worn through by walking many miles with the candidate that year around states like Iowa, and by scuffing out thousands of cigarettes with the ball of his foot.

'It was, I think, a very rich and good experience for anyone who wants to lead this or any country,' Powell says of their Iowa campaign. 'It's very rare that in a Presidential campaign a candidate has the chance to make any significant, real or meaningful contact with any individual voter, but in a smaller state like Iowa it was possible in 1975 and '76. I'm not sure it is today.'

≈≈≈

Bill Richardson is on his feet again, still sweating, looking people in the eye and shaking more hands at the Iowa State Fair. As he moves through the crowds of families on their summer vacations, he's followed by a gaggle of cameras, blazing TV lights and radio microphones. He smiles widely and introduces himself to any fair-goer within reach. Some scurry away at the sight of some big sweaty guy surrounded by cameras, but he doesn't give up: 'Hey, come back, I want to shake hands with you!' Richardson shouts. Then it gets weird – the professionally grinning candidate, a minder or two, a dozen cameras and mics … but no actual people … eeerrrmm … now what? Ah, here's a woman on a stalled mobility scooter … 'Hi, I'm Bill Richardson, I'm running for President.'

The folks at the fair try to beat the intense heat in shorts and T-shirts with slogans like *PETA – People Eating Tasty Animals*. The uniform seems to be John Deere tractor caps for the men and sun visors for the women. Some look as if they've just come off the farm (blue overalls and checked shirts), others look like ageing Marlboro men (cowboy hats and fancy boots). After more than three hours at the fair, I notice a black man pushing a stroller and realise he's the first African-American I've seen all day.

Walking around the Iowa State Fair is a step back in time, like wandering onto an old set of *Bonanza*, except that it's populated with contestants from *The Biggest Loser*. And it's no wonder Iowans have all been supersized. There are no fewer than 30 items of deep-fried food on a stick available: corn-dogs, cotton candy, the pork chop on a stick, the chest pain-inducing fried potato lollypop (six slices of Russet potato, battered and deep-fried) – and someone even worked out a way to put fried eggs on a stick. According to the State Fair's impossibly perky spokesperson, Lori Chappell, it's just a matter of practicality. 'That way you can eat as you walk, 'cause you wouldn't want to miss a minute of the action by sitting down and eating something.' Indeed. But many Iowans don't seem to walk at all – the fairgrounds are thick with substantially overweight people in golf carts and on electric wheelchairs or scooters, one hand on the steering wheel and the other wrapped around something unhealthy on a stick. Some slow down only momentarily at the Presidential Soap Box to see the next man or woman who would be their Commander-in-Chief make their pitch; others switch off their motor and sit awhile.

Another small-state politician who had dreams of following in Jimmy Carter's footsteps was Iowa's own Tom Vilsack. The 56-year-old was the first Democrat to announce his intention to run for the White House in 2008. He is tall and softly spoken, with greying hair, friendly eyes and a slightly downcast face. We meet in his office in the tallest building in Iowa, the 45-storey '801 Grand' Building in downtown Des Moines. The popular two-term Governor says Howard Dean's changes to the electoral schedule made things very difficult for him:

> Now that the calendar is so condensed – these large states like
> California, New York and Florida moving up – it isn't enough to have
> the resources to do well in the early states. You now have to have the
> resources to set up a campaign structure in those large states and have
> enough for a media buy in those large states immediately after the
> small states caucus and primary ... it's tough, very tough.

In the end, three months after announcing his candidacy, and just under a year before the Iowa caucus vote, Tom Vilsack withdrew from the Presidential race following a poll which had him in fourth place in Iowa behind Hillary Clinton, Barack Obama and John Edwards – that place has now been taken by Bill Richardson. Vilsack decided that even a strong showing in his home state wasn't going to be enough to catapult him into serious contention in the primaries of major states like California or New York, which would follow just a month later, in February 2008; there was simply no longer enough time between the polls. So Tom Vilsack endorsed his old friend Hillary Clinton and became co-chairman of her campaign.

The town of Ames is only about 45 minutes to the north of Des Moines, but the number of identical corn fields in between makes it seem further. The Ames Straw Poll is run by the Iowa Republican Party for Republicans only, and designed to be a fundraiser where voters pay $35 each to cast a ballot for their chosen Presidential candidates. In reality, though, most Straw Poll voters have their tickets paid for by the campaigns, and are driven to Ames in free buses, many of them emblazoned with the candidate's name: *SAM BROWNBACK '08* and *MIKE HUCKABEE PRESIDENT*. The Ames Straw Poll has emerged as a key indicator of the campaigns' success in attracting volunteer support and organisational strength, and no candidate who skips the Straw Poll in Ames has ever gone on to win the Iowa caucus five months later.

But this year is a bit different. The best-known Republicans, former New York Mayor Rudy Giuliani and Arizona Senator John McCain, both decided not to take part after opinion polls showed they were likely to lose to cashed-up former Massachusetts Governor Mitt Romney. Romney, a practising Mormon, is betting on a strong showing in Iowa to challenge Giuliani, McCain and the still-to-declare candidate Fred Thompson in the larger states that follow. Mitt Romney has the square-jawed good looks of a 1950s B-grade movie star and a personal fortune in the hundreds of millions, thanks to some good years in venture capital in the 1980s. He is reported to have spent $5 million on advertising in the months leading up to the Straw Poll, and it paid off handsomely – although if you believe the other campaigns, most of the 4516 votes (32 per cent) he won in Ames were people on Romney's campaign payroll. There were dark mutterings and some talk of a legal challenge by supporters of the quixotic Texas Republican Ron Paul after a malfunction with ballot scanners held up the declaration of the vote by a couple of hours.

Even though John McCain didn't actively contest the Ames Straw Poll, he was on the ballot, and he won less than 1 per cent support. At this stage of the race his campaign is showing all the signs of being in serious trouble. Once the Republican frontrunner, he's now lagging behind Giuliani and Romney in opinion polls, several key staff members have been sacked and there's talk of cost-cutting as the campaign burns through $2 million a month.

During the war in Vietnam, John McCain was a Navy pilot. He was shot down and held as a prisoner of the North Vietnamese for over five years. After leaving the Navy he became a Senator (in 1986) and is running for the White House for the second time. At his previous attempt, in 2000, he got Bush-whacked in the ugliest way when people with links to 'the President's Brain', Karl Rove, created a push-poll that suggested – erroneously – to voters that McCain's adopted Bangladeshi-orphan daughter Bridget was his illegitimate black love child. Question: 'Would you be more or less likely to vote for Senator McCain if you knew he had a child to an unmarried black woman?' Desired reaction: 'Whoaa, honey! I just got a telephone call sayin' McCain has a bastard black kid! Must be true, it was one of them polling people! Boy, I gotta call up the girls and tell them!' Another leaflet from Bush supporters in South Carolina described McCain as 'the fag candidate'. The inconsistency of the two claims didn't seem to matter; McCain's early electoral advantage over George W. Bush was lost, and Bush won the Republican nomination and the Presidency.

It's blindingly hot again at the Iowa State Fair and Senator McCain looks a bit overdressed. He's ditched the jacket and tie, but wears dark blue suit pants, a light blue business shirt and the sort of white cap usually reserved for the golf course at a retirement resort in Florida – except that it reads 'Iowa Farm Bureau'. McCain is smaller, older and paler than you'd expect; at 70, he's starting to look his age. His opening line about the heat is just about as old as he is – 'It's hot here in Iowa, but it's still hotter today in Arizona, where I'm from … it's so hot there the trees chase the dogs!'

A few hundred people gather between the Red Cross tent and the soy bean stall to hear McCain speak. He promises to keep his remarks brief on account of the heat – but the fair's public address system keeps interrupting: 'What we need in Iraq … WOULD WILMA COOPER PLEASE REPORT TO THE ADMINISTRATION BUILDING … WILMA COOPER … what we need in Iraq is a … WILMA COOPER, TO THE ADMINISTRATION BUILDING.' McCain accuses the public address system of being a Democrat, drawing a laugh from the largely Republican crowd.

'I just paid a visit to the world's largest boar, Big Red, who weighs 1203 lb [544 kg],' McCain says, 'and I was very impressed – it reminded me of our need to eliminate pork-barrel spending in Washington.'

But there's no way that McCain or any Presidential candidate will eliminate pork-barrelling in Iowa these days. 'Pork barrelling' refers to government spending aimed at winning votes. Here, it comes in the form of agricultural subsidies … and a $50 million indoor rainforest 'tourist attraction'.

And that pandering to local interests is part of the problem with a small, unrepresentative state like Iowa voting first, according to Professor Tom Patterson from Harvard University:

When you start in a state like Iowa, it's about satisfying people in a
face-to-face context, but you're getting away from what the Presidency

is all about. The Presidency is not about retail politics; it's about national leadership. You go into Iowa, and in some ways it distorts your agenda … these candidates all start saying, 'We've got to have more ethanol.' Why? Because Iowa is a corn state and those farmers make a lot of money off ethanol.

In 2000, John McCain was one of the few candidates to tell Iowans something they didn't want to hear: that giving farmers subsidies to grow corn for ethanol was a waste of money. This time he's learnt his lesson; he's all for ethanol as a way to achieve 'energy independence from Middle Eastern oil' – and save the environment, to boot.

For John McCain and the rest of the would-be Presidents of the United States, no day at the Iowa State Fair is complete without a visit to the 'Big Boar'. This obscene animal is the single most popular attraction at the fair – politicians can only dream of this hog's crowd-pulling power. But in a nation where the World Series of Baseball only involves one team from outside the US (and that's from neighbouring Canada) you'd be forgiven for being sceptical of American claims of being 'the world's' anything.

'Big Red' is a Duroc hog from Westminster County, Iowa and was bred by farming brothers Mike and John Cormany. His keeper, Jerry, is trying to keep the heaving mound of pig flesh cool in the stifling heat of the late afternoon by squirting water from a pump into Big Red's fleshy mouth. At over half a ton, Big Red is aptly named. The massive beast looks more like a seriously lost hippopotamus than a pig. Jerry explains that a healthy hog should weigh about one-sixth what Big Red weighs. 'The rest is just pig fat!' he chuckles.

It's all Big Red can do to keep breathing in the heat and humidity of an Iowa summer afternoon. He lies on his side, drooling and panting, with electric fans whirling around his sawdust-filled stall. Turns out there is another pig who claims the title of the world's biggest, and he's also an American. 'Big Norm' weighed in at the New York State Fair at just on 1600 lb [727 kg], and was described as looking like a VW Beetle with a tail. Fair-goers eating corn dogs stop by Big Red's pen and invariably say, 'Gee he's fat!' The irony is lost on them.

'How do you get a pig this big?' I ask Jerry, wondering if the pig's on a special diet involving fair food on a stick.

'Oh, jus' lots of corn and soya beans.' Jerry says. But the glory of being the 'Big Boar' is pretty short-lived. A pig can only enter the competition once; after that it's a one-way ride to the abattoir.

'You like pepperoni on your pizza?' Jerry asks with a wide smile. 'That's all he's good for – pepperoni. There's too much fat for anything else.'

Apart from Big Red, the star attraction at the Iowa State Fair this year is singer Don McLean, who famously sang about the 1959 plane crash in this state that killed Buddy Holly, Richie Valens and 'The Big Bopper', J.P. Richardson. You don't get much more American than the singer of *American Pie* and I figured that as everyone seems to have an opinion on politics, I would ask for his. We spoke outside his trailer, parked behind the main stage where he had been doing a sound check in the sweltering heat of the late afternoon. What does Don McLean think of all these Presidential candidates passing through the fairground?

'It's important to realise that with all the baby-kissing and pie-tasting and the hand-shaking and the concern, these people are potentially very dangerous,' McLean says, unselfconsciously picking some hot dog from between his teeth with his fingernail. 'You never know what kind of person is going to take power – we've just figured that out in the last seven years. Our American electorate should be careful and choose a negotiator, not someone who is always ready to use the military.'

A group of fans gathers around to get old album covers and

T-shirts signed. A man asks McLean if he can make the dedication out to 'Steve'. McLean says 'No, I just sign my name.'

There are more Democratic candidates than Republicans at the Iowa State Fair this week because of the weekend Democratic candidate debate at nearby Drake University. Among them is Joe Biden, a 64-year-old Senator from the State of Delaware with even more expensive-looking teeth than Bill Richardson. He's a handsome man with a balding pate that can miraculously look like a full head of hair if combed just right and viewed from a certain angle. Like John McCain, Joe Biden has been down this road once before, briefly running for the Democratic Presidential nomination in 1988. That campaign ended badly, amid claims that Biden had plagiarised a speech from then British Labour leader Neil Kinnock. Biden defended the oversight by saying that he usually attributed the reference to Kinnock but just failed to do so once or twice. He has learned his lesson, and when he quotes poet Seamus Heaney at the end of his stump-speech today he gives full attribution. Joe Biden has built a very solid reputation as a Senator: he's twice been chairman of the powerful Senate Foreign Relations Committee, and his 2008 Presidential campaign has sought to highlight his experience dealing with global issues and his plan (the most conservative of any Democrat) for when to pull troops out of Iraq. It's going to take some more time, Joe says.

Like other candidates outside the 'top tier' – currently Clinton, Obama and Edwards – Joe Biden needs a strong showing in Iowa to have any chance of winning the White House, and like the other long shots, he's worried that the days of 'retail politics' in Iowa may be numbered. 'If we dumb down the consequences of Iowa, just forget it, folks. The big interests will own it because you gotta raise $100 million.'

Joe Biden seems to talk non-stop during his visit to the State Fair

– answering dozens of questions from the crowd after he makes his stump speech, spending another 15 minutes talking to reporters from the US, Britain, Japan and Australia, and chatting some more to fairgoers as he walks between golf cart displays in the Hall of Industry. Biden stops by the fairground's 'Crystal Studio' of the local News Radio station WHO-1040 for a 3-minute interview: they want to talk about how great the Iowa State Fair is, and he wants to talk about how great his plan for Iraq is. With all this talking, even if a lot of it is scripted and rehearsed, it's not surprising that candidates occasionally misspeak, and the media is always ready to pounce.

Outside the 'Crystal Studio' I point a microphone at Senator Biden and he's happy to oblige, even if it's just like batting practice for him. There's not a lot of point in any of these Presidential candidates talking to a reporter from Australia – there are no votes in it, and there is always the danger they'll say something dumb and it'll make its way onto CNN via YouTube. We walk for a few minutes through the fairground, camera rolling, Biden talking matter-of-factly about the crucial role Iowa will play in this campaign:

> Whoever wins these early states like Iowa is going to be the nominee.
> You can't do this kind of campaigning in California, you can't do this
> in New York. If those other states move up [earlier in the schedule]
> and dumb down the significance of Iowa you'll never see a Presidential
> candidate again – and do you think they'll ever answer your questions
> – give me a break!

Joe Biden has a remarkable life story. In 1972, just after he was first elected to the Senate, his wife Neilia and infant daughter Naomi were killed when their car was hit by a tractor-trailer as they were coming home from Christmas shopping with the tree. His two young sons, Beau and Hunter, were seriously injured in the collision and took many months to recover. Biden's extended family rallied around the junior Senator, and colleagues convinced him not to give up on his political career. Still, ever since then Biden has caught the Amtrak train to Washington DC from Delaware every day instead of driving. The first time you hear the story you think 'What a guy!', but unfortunately, when he and others repeat it, it can seem a little crass.

In person, Joe Biden is very friendly and unscripted, which is perhaps why he has also been known to suffer from 'foot-in-mouth disease'. In early 2007 Biden was trying to praise fellow Democratic Senator Barack Obama as being the first viable black Presidential candidate, and described him as 'articulate, bright and clean' – the unintended implication being that most black people, or at least previous black Presidential candidates Shirley Chisholm, Jesse Jackson, Carol Mosley Braun and Alan Keyes, were somehow 'inarticulate, stupid and unclean'. The media pounced. Biden apologised to African-Americans generally and Obama in particular, but the incident reminded several people in the media that Biden had made a number of other unfortunate racial remarks.

In 2006 in New Hampshire, he was commenting on the growth of the Indian-American population in his state of Delaware, and said: 'You cannot go into a 7-11 or a Dunkin' Donuts unless you have a slight Indian accent!' He's also boasted that his candidacy would appeal to people from the southern states because Delaware was a 'slave state'. Nobody has ever suggested that Biden is a racist; the concern is that he's gaffe-prone, that he lacks discipline and can't control what comes out of his mouth. The level of media scrutiny and the emergence of YouTube and the blogosphere are a key difference Biden tells me he sees between his Presidential campaigns of 1988 and 2008: 'You have to assume that no matter who you're talking to and what you're saying, there's a camera.'

Hillary Clinton knows the cameras are always on her. She arrives at the fairground just as Joe Biden is leaving, but unlike with Biden, there's no way the media can just walk up and start asking her questions. Hillary arrives in a mini-motorcade of dark green vans with tinted windows, with a police escort. Casually dressed Secret Service bodyguards in polo shirts and slacks form a cordon, as the former First Lady steps out of her vehicle wearing a bright yellow linen shirt that's hard to look at in the midsummer glare. The media is kept about 10 metres back by a yellow nylon rope held by campaign helpers – and which, by accident or design, matches the colour of Hillary's shirt. As the leading Democratic Presidential candidate in nationwide polls approaches, hand-picked supporters are allowed forward to greet her. Meanwhile, we're in the middle of a pack of about 40 reporters, photographers and TV camera operators being dragged back by the yellow rope like a herd of unbroken horses. The media grumbles at being corralled in this way, but it does make for the best possible pictures: just Hillary and regular people, not surrounded by a scrum of microphones and cameras.

As Hillary walks through the main street of the fair, the reporters get good at jogging backwards, and every wave or smile from the surprisingly diminutive candidate sets off a volley of camera flashes. Former Iowa Governor Tom Vilsack is by her side, smiling a fixed grin and playing the sort of silent second fiddle that Bill Clinton might be getting used to. As Iowans approach Senator Clinton for a few words, Vilsack hands them a voter registration form, encouraging them to turn out on caucus night. There are no real questions from supporters, just lots of 'Hi' and 'How are you?', and the candidate carefully ignores the cameras and the questions of hog-tied reporters. It's the sort of deliberate deafness that Presidents become very good at, often with the assistance of the *Marine One* Presidential helicopter whirring in the background. With no chopper, Hillary almost seems to be miming as she walks and waves and smiles at nobody in particular. The crowd gets thicker as Hillary's walk takes on a Pied Piper look, and the Secret Service guards with crewcuts, sunglasses and spirals of wire in their ears expertly clear a path to the Soap Box where, surrounded by hay bales and TV cameras, she gives a well-practised stump speech.

Like every touring rock act or stand-up comedian, Hillary works in a few references to Iowa's State Fair and all the wonderful food on a stick: 'I'm going to do my own investigation – I'm going to eat my way across the fair!' 'Whooooo-hoooo!' says the tightly packed throng. 'It's a pleasure to be back here in Iowa, especially on a wonderful summer day like this,' she says. But here the script gets it wrong; the crowd of maybe a thousand people is fanning themselves as the temperature climbs to well over 40ºC and there are groans of 'Oh no, it's too hot!' The candidate pushes on. 'It's so wonderful to be here. All the families that are here and everybody is having a good time and I'm grateful to say a few words to you.' (Hillary makes no mention of the Big Boar. As a Senator from New York, she probably knows about 1600 lb Norm but is too tactful to say anything.)

Then she gets to the point:

> I'm running for President because I think America can do better! [Cheer!] I'm absolutely positive that we can solve the problems that we face as a country. We can roll up our sleeves and we can start acting like Americans again!

When her speech is over, Hillary, unlike almost all the other candidates, takes no questions from the audience, gives no interviews to the media. She just smiles and waves as she makes her way back to the green van. And she didn't sweat.

The following day at the fair is just as hot and even more humid. Locals say if you drive a few miles out of town to the corn fields around Des Moines you can hear the ears of corn cracking as they grow. It's so hot it's a wonder the corn isn't popping. The main attraction at the

Presidential Soap Box today is the current Republican frontrunner, Rudy Giuliani. The former New York City Mayor who stood firm in the face of the 9/11 attacks is trying to prove he has what it takes to lead the nation. Mayor Giuliani arrives to speak to a crowd of several hundred, dabbing the perspiration from his balding head and upper lip with a folded handkerchief. He's wearing very expensive-looking brown leather shoes, beige pants hitched up to the height reserved for ageing men and a silk shirt that shows growing patches of sweat. Up close, Rudy Giuliani's speech impediment is more noticeable. A lateral lisp has him pronounce an 's' or soft 'c' as a 'th' – as in: 'Ath Mayor of New York Thity, I got thingth done.' With a microphone in his hand he also has the slightly neurotic New Yorker quality of Woody Allen, his free hand waving, grasping and pointing with every word so that it looks like a form of sign language. He warms up the Iowan crowd with a compliment: 'Everyone in Iowa, from the person in the thity, to the thuburbs, to the little town, everybody ith a political thientist – right?' (He laughs as much as the crowd at this.)

Despite conservatives' concerns that Giuliani is too 'liberal' on issues like abortion and gay marriage, today he's singing from the Republican small-government hymn sheet:

I believe very sthrongly in lowering taxeth. I believe you will do a
better job with your money if I hand it back to you than the people in
Washington will do … ['That's right!' someone shouts, 'Yeah, yeah!'
someone else agrees] … and I don't think the people in Washington do
a very good job with most things … I am the person in thith race who
has held the most executive offices under the most pressure and the
most difficulty and I've produced results for people. Tho I want to be
your President becauth I've handled responsibilities like that before.

He takes questions on Iraq, terrorism, immigration, healthcare, education and more, impressively rattling off his policy on whatever subject as if he's giving answers in a spelling bee: 'Iraq … what I would do in Iraq ith this …' 'Education … the thing to do about education in thith country …'

Before he became the hero of 9/11 and *Time Magazine*'s Man of the Year in 2001, Rudy Giuliani was a two-term New York mayor on his way out. In 2000 he campaigned for a US Senate seat against Hillary Clinton, but pulled out of a tough race after being diagnosed with prostate cancer. It also was during that campaign he made one of several infamous public appearances in women's clothing – at the Mayor's Inner Circle Press Roast. In a comedic video replayed millions of times since on YouTube, Giuliani, wearing a blonde wig, beauty mark and ball gown, flirts with Property tycoon Donald Trump, before Trump sprays perfume on Rudy's décolletage and nuzzles in between his fake breasts. You suspect that back in those light-hearted days of 2000 Rudy wasn't planning to run for the White House eight years later. Now, just 15 months from election day, the polls say he is the Republican Party's leading candidate for the Presidency.

2 ★ Grassroots

'I Fee-e-e-I good … I knew that I would now …
I fee-e-e-I good … I knew that I wo-o-o-uld now …'

The voice of James Brown floats over the baking hot concrete in the car park behind a warehouse in suburban Des Moines, Iowa. It's almost 10 o'clock on a Monday morning and already the temperature is back into the high 30s. The music is pumping out of speakers attached to a slick modern bus which is decked out in red, white and blue lettering that says: *John Edwards 08, Iowa Bus Tour 2007,* and *Fighting for One America.*

A crowd of around 200 middle-aged and 'senior American' supporters has gathered to see former North Carolina Senator John Edwards embark on a seven-day trip across Iowa. John Edwards ran a surprisingly strong campaign for the Democratic Party's Presidential nomination in 2004, and his sunny-side-up positive message was rewarded with the Vice Presidential nomination on the ticket below the rather patrician Massachusetts Senator John Kerry.

Kerry–Edwards fell 118,601 votes short in the state of Ohio from defeating President George W. Bush. However, some Democrats, including Robert F. Kennedy Jr, son of the late Bobby Kennedy, contend that the 2004 election result was rigged and that 80,000 votes in Ohio that were cast for Kerry were counted for Bush. Either way, until Hillary Clinton and Barack Obama declared their intention to run for the White House, John Edwards was considered the frontrunner for the Democratic Party's Presidential nomination in 2008.

The Edwards campaign in 2004 was built on an unexpectedly strong second place in the Iowa caucus, and he's been making frequent visits to the 'Hawkeye State' ever since. Given his better funded and higher profile opponents, John Edwards needs to do well here in 2008.

Half a dozen TV cameras have set up on a small platform or 'riser' at the back of the crowd, about 20 metres from the side of the Edwards bus. Other cameras and radio reporters move among the crowd, who are already using their *John Edwards 08* signs as fans.

'And I fe-e-e-e-l nice … sugar and spice …'

At least 20 or 30 people in the crowd seem to be activists of some kind. They stand around in pairs with matching T-shirts proclaiming 'END THE WAR' and 'DividedWeFall.org'. A woman in her forties wearing an apron that was last seen on reruns of *Leave It To Beaver* moves through the crowd handing out cookies. A member of Edwards' campaign team comes over to hand out press releases which helpfully suggest what any story you might write about this event should say, including quotes of what the candidate hasn't yet said. 'If you have any questions, y'all just holler!'

'So good … so good, I got you! Dum dum dum dum dum dum YEAH!!'

It's now well past 10 am – the time Edwards was due to speak. Everyone is looking expectantly at the temporary wooden stage erected alongside the bus. It's ringed with hay bales, presumably to give it a folksy Iowa appearance for the cameras. Is he in the bus? Is he somewhere else? It's hot. How much longer are we going to be kept waiting? Some die-hard candidate groupies have been here in the car park behind Edwards' Iowa campaign HQ for an hour already. They wisely brought fold-up chairs, but even so they are starting to wilt in the sun. A lobby group calling itself 'Sensible Iowans' is handing out what appear to be Frisbees with pie-charts on them. It's hard to read the pie-chart, though, when they're either skimming through the air or being used as fans, so what the Iowans are being sensible about remains a mystery.

The 'Godfather of Soul' failed to elicit so much as a shoulder shrug in time with the music, and now a bored-sounding down-tempo cover version of a Beatles classic does even less to lift the flagging crowd.

'You tell me that it's evolution … well you know … we all want to change the world …'

Another 20 minutes slowly pass and the exclusively white Iowan crowd has turned pink. You get the sense that somebody, somewhere out of sight, is frantically trying to stop the crowd from going home to their air conditioning. Ah ha! Bottles of chilled water are suddenly being distributed as if we're survivors of a natural disaster … well, a natural disaster other than Hurricane Katrina, that is.

Then the music fades down and someone is up on stage. 'Hi everyone … sorry to have you all waiting, I know it's hot … John's running a bit late … it's hard to run this kind of campaign, especially when you also have a family, so hang in there.' A collective empathetic nod

… oh, that's right, he has a family.

John Edwards is probably the best-looking Presidential candidate since Bobby Kennedy, and even has the same dazzling teeth and floppy fringe. Indeed Edwards' hair has become an issue in the campaign after it was revealed that he paid $400 for a haircut, and then a video appeared on YouTube showing Edwards preparing for a TV interview by repeatedly brushing, primping and fiddling with his hair, set to the tune of 'I Feel Pretty' from *My Fair Lady*. It's typical of modern American politics that a potential strength (good looks) can be turned into a negative (vanity).

It's now an hour after John Edwards was due to appear, and a reporter lurking up the back of the press pack quips, 'He's probably still doing his hair.' Suddenly a disembodied voice says, 'Ladies and gentlemen, will you please welcome the next President of the United States, JOHN EDWARDS!'

The boyish and tanned 54-year-old candidate appears from somewhere behind the campaign bus, waving and smiling. He's dressed in jeans, with a dark blue casual shirt rolled up a couple of turns to show a solid work ethic, and a yellow wristband indicating his support for the 'Live Strong' cancer charity of cyclist Lance Armstrong. Unfortunately it looks as if he's wearing the kind of yellow plastic bangle a teenage girl might spend all her babysitting money on.

There are 'whoo-hoos' and enthusiastic applause from his suddenly revitalised supporters. Edwards has with him his 9-year-old daughter, Emma Claire, and his 7-year-old son, Jack. They come from Central Casting as the all-American family, but just like Senator Joe Biden, there is tragedy in their story too: Edwards' eldest son, Wade, was killed in a car accident in 1996 at the age of 16, when his Jeep was blown off a North Carolina highway in a freak wind gust. The story goes that it was Wade's death that led Edwards to abandon his highly paid career as a trial lawyer and enter politics.

The candidate is introduced by a local politician whose first name is Ed and whose second name is lost as the PA system floats in and out of hearing range across the shimmering tarmac. Ed is here because he's endorsed John Edwards for the Presidency. In a state like Iowa, local councillors, Mayors, Senators and ultimately the Governor can all provide valuable support. Endorsements are also keenly sought from labour unions, farming groups, political organisations, business people and anyone who has been on TV enough to draw a crowd or attract more cameras. First Ed spends a few minutes explaining why he's for Edwards, including the issue that has become a key campaign theme: 'We need a candidate who is not only good on the issues but who has the capacity to win the election in November, and I have every confidence that John Edwards is the most electable Democratic candidate.' The unspoken but obvious point is that Edwards is the Democrats' top white male running for the Presidency, a job only ever filled by white men.

Senator Edwards takes the microphone from Ed and begins by telling his kids they can now go sit in the bus. 'Let me say, first, I apologise for being late, and thank you for being so patient ... Elizabeth ate something at breakfast this morning that didn't agree with her. She's doing fine, she's doing fine,' he assures the crowd. 'She'll be back with us in just a little bit.' The health of Elizabeth Edwards has become an issue. The day after John Kerry and John Edwards lost the 2004 Presidential election, Elizabeth revealed that she had breast cancer. She had what appeared to be a successful course of chemotherapy and radiotherapy, but then in March 2007, with her husband running for the Presidency, she announced that the cancer was back with metastases to the bone and possibly the lung. John and Elizabeth Edwards said that while the cancer was 'no longer curable, it is completely treatable', and vowed to continue their bid for the White House.

After his standard campaign speech refraining a class-war riff about 'Two Americas', Edwards signs a few autographs and speaks to well-wishers as a press gaggle forms around him. The second question from a Radio Iowa reporter is whether Elizabeth Edwards has food poisoning or if she's undergoing more chemotherapy. 'Oh no, no, I don't think that has anything to do with it,' Edwards says. 'She's doing great.' Young Jack Edwards appears at the window of the bus and snaps a photo of the dozen or so television cameras and as many press photographers, who return the favour by photographing him photographing them.

Next are questions on Iraq, the draft, Karl Rove's resignation and the Republican Straw Poll. The fundraiser vote in Ames was won by Mitt Romney, skipped by Giuliani and McCain, but it's the surprise second place of Mike Huckabee that's gaining the most interest. Edwards simply observes, 'It looks like Mitt Romney spent a lot of money.'

A reporter from the UK asks Edwards why he has spent so much time campaigning in Iowa. The answer:

This is grassroots campaigning at its best. The caucus-goers of Iowa – a huge percentage of them – will see every Presidential candidate up close. They'll be able to ask them questions, participate in town hall meetings. They won't just get sound bites on television; they'll get a serious look and a chance to evaluate every one of us, which is exactly the way these decisions should be made, so this is a great way to start the process.

Another reporter asks how much money Edwards has spent in Iowa:

Spending money in Iowa is not the thing that matters. What matters is when you stand in front of Iowa caucus-goers in their living rooms or at town hall meetings – do you have what it takes to be President? Are you a candidate that has a specific vision and ideas, and do you have the personal qualities that Iowans want to see in the next President of the United States?

At this point one of Edwards staff interrupts with, 'OK everybody, thanks very much, cameras and stills [TV cameras and stills photographers for newspapers and magazines], we'll be rolling out of here in a minute.' The question-and-answer session is over. On cue the sound systems kicks in again with something upbeat and optimistic from U2 and the rest is made-for-TV pictures: Edwards smiling from the steps of the bus, Edwards heading inside the bus, Edwards appearing again to wave from the window as the vehicle slowly pulls away from the hay bales. It's as contrived as a fashion shoot. A look at the press releases handed out an hour earlier reveals that most of what was just said – all except the bit about Elizabeth's illness – is already there in black and white. Ear-splitting air horns sound as the *John Edwards 08, Iowa Bus Tour 2007, Fighting for One America* bus disappears from view around the corner of the warehouse and down the street.

One of the many businesses in Iowa that profit from all the Presidential campaigns coming to the state is Carter Printing in downtown Des Moines. Manager Ron Hoyt is happy to guide us through the print shop. It's a bit hard to hear Ron over the combined racket of the state-of-the-art digital printing machines, room fans whirring at high speed and the local 'Classic Hits' radio station, which is turned way up loud to be heard over the din. Ron shows me some of their current jobs, including 900,000 Bill Richardson baseball cards with a photo of the portly candidate on a pitcher's mound. Ron says they're a bargain, at 'a little under a penny apiece'.

Churning off another printer are the last of 40,000 Hillary Clinton voter registration cards, designed to be filled out so the campaign can put you on file and make sure you vote on caucus night. All together, Ron tells me, they're doing work for 'six or seven' Democratic campaigns right now. Ron Hoyt says that like many Iowans, he's planning to vote in the caucus, but he doesn't want to say who he supports because it might lose him business.

Then it's back to the Iowa State Fair because, well, there isn't a whole lot more to do in Des Moines in mid-August. I've arranged via a string of emails to meet with an Iowa political scientist named Professor Dave Redlawsk, who's also in town to see some of the Presidential candidates up close.

On the fair's Soap Box today is Senator Chris Dodd – a respected Democrat from Connecticut. He's respected in part because nobody thought he would ever run for President (Tom Vilsack had said as much the other day). But in the heat of the early afternoon, Senator Dodd comes across as red-faced and angry, with a barking edge to his voice that is magnified by a distorting microphone that nobody thinks to turn down. He's a fit-looking 63-year-old with intelligent eyes, a helmet of snowy white hair and jet black eyebrows. But there's something about his soft jawline that suggests that he may not possess the sort of steely reserve required of the Commander-in-Chief of the US armed forces ... or at least not the sort of steely reserve required by casting agents looking for a Commander-in-Chief of the US armed forces in, say, a Harrison Ford movie ... these things matter. After 10 minutes of talking about the 'war on terror', the imperilled US Constitution (a copy of which he keeps in his pocket) and other such weighty things, Senator Dodd takes a few questions from the crowd of maybe a hundred onlookers.

It's easy to identify his communications manager – she's the only woman at the fair wearing a corporate skirt suit. She also has a clipboard, which presumably has a schedule which is always getting away from her. Can I have a few minutes with the candidate for a quick interview? Oh, ahm, where are you from? Australia? (No votes, but still the chance a slip-up can get on YouTube, CNN etc.) The communications manager, whose name is Taylor or Tyler, says she can't make any promises. With the questions from the rapidly dispersing crowd exhausted, and other press pretty thin on the ground, I decide to just wander up, point a microphone and camera at the candidate and start an interview before Taylor/Tyler can say otherwise.

I don't really have much I particularly want to ask Chris Dodd, but a fishing exercise can sometimes land you something interesting. It can be the most simple, even innocent-sounding question that gets the most revealing answer. Back in 1980, Democratic Senator Ted Kennedy was running for President against incumbent Jimmy Carter, and gave what was supposed to be a fairly soft interview with CBS newsman and personal friend Roger Mudd. Mudd simply asked, 'Why do you want to be President?'

Maybe in that instant a hundred thoughts flashed through Teddy's mind: his handsome elder brother Jack being sworn in as America's first Catholic President in 1961; his assassination in Dallas less than three years later; the blood and gore on Jackie's dress; his other brother Bobby running for the Presidency in 1968 only to be shot and killed himself after winning the California primary; Teddy's own scandal at Chappaquiddick in 1969, when he left a party with a young campaign worker named Mary-Jo Kopechne, drove his limo off a bridge into Poucha Pond and went back to the party to get help while she drowned. That scandal ruled out a run in 1972 and 1976. 'Why do you want to be President?' Mudd had asked. Teddy Kennedy's fumbling, waffling non-answer was the first stumble in a campaign that was beset by bad luck, bad timing and bad history. He lost the nomination to Carter, who lost the Presidency to Reagan.

'Senator Dodd, why do you want to be President?' I ask, channelling Mudd and mentally polishing my Pulitzer. Without missing a beat he says, 'Frankly, I don't like the way my country is headed. I know how to do this, and I think my country is ready for experienced leadership and proven credentials.' Damn.

I press on. 'You're running against some pretty big names, though. How are you going to beat them?'

He's ready for that one too. 'People in Iowa aren't impressed by names,' he says brightly. 'They want to know what you stand for, what you believe in and if you get elected, what you're going to do. The fact that you have a big name and a lot of money, that doesn't overly impress people in this state.'

Taylor/Tyler steps in and the interview is over. The Senator is now being talked to by an Iowan with a cause printed on their T-shirt. No Pulitzer today.

It's time to find Dave Redlawsk, the political scientist I'm due to interview. We find each other in the crowd of fair-goers with the help of our mobile phones, and a few minutes later we're sitting in a shady spot filming an interview for our documentary.

Dave's one of those quite rare academics who not only knows their stuff but can communicate it in the sort of pithy statements the media like. One of the frustrations of being a journalist is the number of super-bright people you speak to for a story whose heads are so full of the complexities of their area of expertise that they can't explain it to anyone without a PhD. That's maybe why you see more football players than professors on TV.

Professor Dave talks about the way in which the current crop of candidates campaigning around Iowa is challenging the traditional image of a US President like never before:

> This is really an interesting thing. We've reached a time where a woman [Hillary Clinton] can be a serious candidate … we have a black man [Barack Obama] running with a serious chance, we have a Hispanic man [Bill Richardson] running with a serious chance … and that's just three of the roughly twenty or so currently running. But that's unique in American politics … this has been the domain of white men since the beginning, and this does shake things up a little bit this year and make things interesting.

I ask where that leaves a white male candidate like John Edwards:

> This is probably frustrating to the Edwards campaign … on the Democratic side he really was the first to lay out specific issue positions

… and yet he can't break through the media hype about Clinton and Obama. So part of the strategy for Edwards is to become more passionate, even more angry on 'the stump', and he's been out there pushing the 'working people' theme, which is code in America for poor people. The problem for John Edwards is there aren't many votes in that.

Just as John Edwards is struggling to 'cut through' with voters and a press which seems captivated by the historic possibility of America electing its first female, black or Latino President, so is fellow Democratic Presidential candidate Dennis Kucinich – for different reasons. An internet poll of Democratic voters in mid-2007 asked them to select their candidate based on policies alone. The candidates' policies were listed, but not their names. As it turned out, Kucinich received more than 50 per cent support in the anonymous poll – far ahead of Obama, Hillary, Edwards and the rest. But, it would seem, there are a few things standing in the way of a President Dennis J. Kucinich: the Congressman from Ohio isn't only white and male, he's just 5-and-a-half feet tall, a vegan, and at 61 years old, he still has the kind of brushed flat hair and sheepish smile that suggests he's posing for his 5th grade school photo.

In the race for the Democratic Party's Presidential nomination in 2004, Dennis Kucinich attracted 1 or 2 per cent support in most primaries, but doggedly stayed in the race against Senator John Kerry as all his other rivals pulled out. Kucinich's support peaked in the Hawaii caucus on 24 February, where he won 31 per cent support. In the final vote, long after Senator Kerry had enough delegates to win the nomination, Kucinich technically came in second, with 4 per cent in the New Jersey primary behind Kerry's 92 per cent. Undaunted, he's running for the Presidency again in 2008.

I'm keen to test the thesis of our doco that a long shot can still break from the pack. After all, if a woman and a black man can set out to shatter the mould and are being taken seriously, why not a short steak dodger with a name that rhymes with 'spinach'? And, given the internet poll, if not, why not? So we joined the Congressman on the Presidential campaign trail in Iowa.

Dennis Kucinich doesn't have an expensive bus. He has a white charger – a Dodge Charger – and a 6-foot English damsel to match: his willowy 29-year-old red-headed wife Elizabeth. While Dennis Kucinich looks like the wimpy kid who got picked on a lot at school, Elizabeth Kucinich looks like the winsomely beautiful girl who inspired boys to write bad poetry. You sometimes get the feeling that he doesn't really care about getting elected President; he just wants to travel around America showing off his wife.

Behind the wheel of the white Charger as it speeds through southern Iowa this day in August is Kucinich 2008 campaign manager Mike Klein – a stocky ex-Marine with blonde hair and anxious eyes. As we trail behind in a less-muscular rental car, Mike's raspy voice on the mobile phone says they are going to make a 'comfort stop' at the next gas station. Kucinich stays in the front passenger seat, his eye height just above the windowsill, as Mike fuels up and Elizabeth glides into the store. People turn to stare at her, not because she's the wife of a Presidential candidate, but because in a state where most people are rather shorter, pinker and fatter, she's like a fairytale princess. With auburn hair almost down to her waist and a full-length dark green dress, she looks uncannily like actress Julianne Moore on stilts. I wonder if Kucinich stays in the car because he's afraid of being recognised, or maybe, having only 1 per cent support in Iowa right now, he's afraid of not being recognised … or maybe he just doesn't need to go to the toilet.

No fear of Dennis Kucinich going unrecognised at our next campaign stop: Fairfield, Iowa – the existential capital of America and home to the Maharishi's own university. Here they believe in the power of meditation, the spirit and 'yogic flying' – which looks to the unenlightened eye like a bunch of people bouncing around on their buttocks. They claim that for a brief moment they aren't bouncing – they're flying.

Dennis is due to speak to a crowd of a hundred or so gathered in a yoga hall above a restaurant named Gupta's Vegetarian Cuisine. Fairfield, Iowa looks rather like the deserted backlot set of a 1930s Mickey Rooney movie, but where the Carvel General Store should be there are cafés serving only organic food and New Age art galleries – it's *Andy Hardy Drops Too Much Acid and Becomes a Faded Hippie*.

A three-piece band – a guitar, a bongo and a lost-looking girl singer – plod through a rendition of 'Kum Ba Ya' and move on to several other songs, apparently sung to the same tune and tempo as 'Kum Ba Ya'.

'He's here, he's here!' someone shouts. The music stops, and everyone turns around. Someone else says, 'Start playing, start playing!' so, one at a time, the band starts another round of 'Kum Ba Ya'. But he's not here. It's starting to look as if all Presidential candidates turn up late. Did Elizabeth Kucinich eat a bad lentil pattie?

Deflated, the band stops playing again and an old wood-grained colour TV on the stage flickers to life with a slightly grainy VHS recording of Dennis Kucinich speaking about peace. The TV is on a stand which has been covered with some exotic-looking fabric (maybe someone's discarded kaftan), and it gives the whole scene the unsettling look of a cult leader issuing instructions (from a remote location) to drink the Kool-Aid and catch the next flying saucer to the planet Crackpot.

After a while longer, a woman who looks more than a little like Janis Joplin climbs onto the stage and nervously announces that Dennis will be here soon; he's just having his lunch. She then asks someone to find the pause button on the VCR, which, after a further short discussion, someone does. It turns out her name is Carol. She explains that she started the campaign for Dennis Kucinich in Iowa because nobody else was doing it and because Dennis is the American hero. After a while someone called Alan interrupts and says Dennis is going to be here any minute so we'd better have the band start up again ...

'Amazing grace, how sweet the sound ... IS MY MIC ON?
... that saved a soul like me ... WHERE'S MY SOUND MAN??
... I once was lost, but now I'm found ...'

The crowd starts clapping; at first, almost in time with the music, but then in a sort of syncopation which soon becomes about as random as heavy rain on a tin roof but not quite as soothing. This throws the musical trio off, and each one now decides to head in their own individual rhythmic direction.

'Hallay-looo-yuh, hallay-looo-yuh ... hallay-loo-yuh,
praise god ... Hare Krishna, Hare Krishna ...'

'He's here he's here!'
And this time he is.

The first thing that appears at the top of the stairs is Elizabeth Kucinich's long red hair, followed by her strikingly beautiful face, bare shoulders and black dress. Much further down, holding her hand like a 5-year-old crossing a busy road with his mum, is Presidential candidate Dennis Kucinich, wearing a black corduroy jacket, white shirt and beige slacks.

'Here they are – Dennis and Elizabeth Kucinich – our hero and heroine!' Someone has let Carol back near the microphone.

'Amazing grace, how sweet the sound ...'

Dennis parts the crowd, shaking hands and acknowledging the applause as he heads towards the stage.

'Hallay-loo-yuh Praise God!!!'

Kucinich thanks the audience and begins his speech in a deliberately low-key manner, with lots of pauses, some which seem more intentional than others. He outlines his doctrine of 'Strength Through Peace', which has become his campaign slogan.

Dennis Kucinich was the only Democrat who voted against the war in Iraq when it came before the US Congress – a fact that wins him some respect, if not many votes. Senators Clinton, Edwards, Biden and Dodd all voted for authorisation of the war; Barack Obama wasn't yet in the Senate, but says he opposed the war and would have voted against the invasion given the chance; and Mike Gravel (pronounced: gruh-VELL) had been out of the Senate for more than 20 years. The Democrats who voted for the war later recanted, to varying degrees, saying they were wrong or misled.

Kucinich takes questions from his supporters. One woman asks about his electability, to which he replies, with a smile, that if people vote for him he'll become electable. Another questioner rambles for a while about some perceived astrological significance of Kucinich's campaign, to which Dennis replies ambiguously, 'If it's in your heart, it's in the stars.'

Carol, the Janis Joplin lookalike, also asks a question that meanders through a series of observations about big corporations giving big money to everyone but Dennis, to which the candidate replies pointedly:

We have to realise what's happening in this country. Our
Presidential elections are becoming like auctions, and America
is getting sold right now. It's like an auction – candidates are
unfortunately finding themselves going to the highest bidder. That
may be a great way to run an auction, but it's a lousy way to run an
election and a country.

In a campaign dominated by tightly controlled 'messages', it's refreshing to hear a Presidential candidate speak so openly about the shortcomings of the political process. I can't help but wonder, though, if such honesty is a luxury only enjoyed by those with single-digit support – they have almost nothing to lose.

Kucinich steps down from the stage and heads for the door with Elizabeth and his Iowa campaign director, Marcos Rubenstein ... and a man with thick glasses, a grey ponytail and facial tic trailing behind. As Kucinich leaves the Yoga Centre a well-dressed woman in her fifties wearing a white linen shirt and white slacks hands the candidate a piece of paper. It's a cheque for $2300 – the maximum any individual is allowed by law to give to a Presidential campaign.

Standing outside on the lawn in an old-fashioned town square, we set up for an interview with Kucinich. A small crowd of supporters gathers around, including Carol, the guy with the tic and the drummer from the band. After some perfunctory introductions to the Kuciniches, I go straight for the Teddy Kennedy-stumper question: looking deeply into his eyes I ask, 'Why do you want to be President?' He answers, completely unfazed:

> It's so important for America to have a leader who is unbought and unbossed. Someone who understands that the world is in fact one, that we are interconnected and interdependent and that when a leader has that awareness, that leader – and this is me – has the potential to change this country and help this country change the world for the better.

I ask if he was one of those kids who dreamed of being President some day. He says:

> My parents never owned a home – my parents were renters. We moved around a lot – 21 homes, including a couple of cars, before I was 17 ... I think that my presence in American politics is a demonstration that yes it is possible for someone to be able to rise from humble beginnings.

Living in a car is certainly an interesting update on the 'born in a log cabin' of early American Presidents. He continues:

> When I was in the 10th grade, I wrote an autobiographical essay
> – where we were asked to write about where we saw ourselves in the
> future, and I predicted in that essay that I would have a career in
> national politics and that I would aim for the very top [the Presidency]
> … Now this was the dream of an American child who at one time lived
> in a car.

What does Kucinich say to those who maintain that it's just a pipe dream, that he can never be elected President?

> Look, I was 31 years old when I was elected the Mayor of Cleveland
> – the youngest person ever elected mayor of a major American city
> in the history of the United States, and I think that my life has been
> about creating outcomes that other people said were impossible.

Dennis Kucinich started his working life as a copyboy for a newspaper in Cleveland and has also worked as a talk radio presenter. Given these insights into the workings of the media, what does he think of the way he's covered (or dismissed) by the press?

'This campaign is going to attract more and more attention from the media as they become aware that this is really the big story of the 2008 election,' Kucinich says with a broad smile.

Suddenly, he's like all the other candidates, staying 'on message' and upbeat. 'Watch what happens,' he continues, smile fixed in place. 'If people start to cover this campaign they are going to see the political version of Sea Biscuit – that horse that came from nowhere and won the big race!'

With that, Kucinich is heading back across the lawn to his rented white Charger and onto Des Moines for the next day's Democratic candidate debate.

The candidate's self-belief is remarkable, if not delusional. Later, a critic of Kucinich in Cleveland would tell me, grudgingly, that he admires the fact that Kucinich has made his life and political career out of nothing. Kucinich, this Democrat powerbroker told me, came from a very disrupted and difficult childhood, and became a big city Mayor and a US Congressman and Presidential candidate despite all the evidence, the nay-sayers, and the odds – simply based on the seemingly unwavering certainty that he could.

The hippie drummer taps out an easy walking pace on his bongos as we all head to our cars. Wandering along behind Congressman Kucinich, Carol, the Janis Joplin lookalike, explains to the guy with the ponytail, thick glasses and facial tic that 'this is strictly a grassroots'. He thinks for a moment, looks down then says, 'Aren't we standing on grass roots? Grass roots are under the grass, right?'

As we walk over the grass to our own rental car, I wonder if these people in Fairfield, Iowa, who have abandoned so much that is conventional in their lives, are simply better able to overlook the fact that Dennis Kucinich doesn't look Presidential in the conventional sense – just as they are blind to the fact that kaftans went out in 1973. Perhaps they're just less superficial than I am. After all, surely we should be able to look past a quite trivial issue such as the height of the President, just as we should race or gender. And the kaftan *is* a very comfortable item of clothing.

3 You Watch, We Decide

'I-O-W-A Barack Obama all the way!'
'I-O-W-A Barack Obama all the way!'

Late August 2007: It's 5.45 am on a Sunday morning outside Drake University in Des Moines, Iowa. It's warm and steamy in the bluish pre-dawn light. The chanting is coming from crowds of a few hundred students and what appear to be their parents or grandparents, all wearing T-shirts and waving signs reading *BIDEN* or *HILLARY* or *HOPE – Barack Obama for President.*

It's a pep rally, with banners, cheers and songs, just as you'd see at any number of high school or college football matches on any given weekend around the US. But this one is purely political ... and at 5.45 on a Sunday morning.

'Here we go Hillary, here we go!' (Clap! Clap!)
'Here we go Hillary, here we go!' (Clap! Clap!)

We're here, yawning and rubbing sleep from our eyes after blearily drinking about a litre of watery motel room coffee, to see the contenders as they arrive for the first Presidential candidate debate to be held in this, the first state to vote.

The eight current Democratic Party candidates – Senators Hillary Clinton, Barack Obama and John Edwards, Governor Bill Richardson, Senators Joe Biden and Chris Dodd, Congressman Dennis Kucinich and Senator Mike Gravel – are all here at this odd hour because 8 o'clock on Sunday morning happens to be the time the political talk show *This Week with George Stephanopoulos* airs on America's ABC television – and George is hosting this debate.

'Two-zero-zero-eight – Who we gonna nominate?'
'Edwards!' (Clap! Clap!) 'Edwards!'

In the midst of the excited crowd, huge bunches of helium-filled red, white and blue balloons sway gently on their strings, suggesting that there must be a breeze, but the air remains still and stuffy. If you were inside, you'd open a window, but out here there's not much you can do but quietly sweat.

As the pep groups are all lined up along the grassy embankment, it's an interesting opportunity to compare the supporters of the candidates.

'Ready to lead – HILL-A-RY!'
'Ready to lead – HILL-A-RY!'

In the Hillary group there seem to be dozens of bookish-looking white college girls without makeup, there's a black woman in her thirties with straightened hair and gold earrings, and a white woman in her seventies with her ill-looking husband. Here and there a few matching middle-aged, mid-western couples and earnest younger guys who may well be here to impress the bookish-looking girls.

'O-BA-MA!'
'O-BA-MA!'

There are so many Obama kids out here this morning that they don't all fit by the side of the road, so they have a semitrailer as a portable stage as well. Everywhere signs read *HOPE* and *CHANGE*.

A black youth in his late teens bounces up and down on the spot like a Masai warrior, right hand punching the air. Next to him a young Asian college student is using a rolled-up *HOPE* sign as a megaphone.

'Oh-Oh-Oh-Obama!'
'Oh-Oh-Oh-Obama!'

The Joe Biden group includes a bunch of maybe 30 white people who look as if they might be from three generations of one or two large families (or maybe they're all just from the same part of Iowa). I count around 25 plastic *BIDEN '08* yard signs pegged into the ground on wire frames and at least 10 hand-held rally signs for every person. There is also a very homemade-looking scoreboard comparing *Ears of Experience* … 35 'ears' of corn representing Joe Biden's 35 years in the US Senate. Clinton and Edwards are given six 'ears', and Obama only scores two.

'Let's go, Joe!!'
'Let's go, Joe!!'

A bit further along, past the Biden-boosters, are the supporters of Senator Chris Dodd:

> *'D-O-D-D … Chris Dodd ready to lead!'*
> *'D-O-D-D … Chris Dodd ready to lead!'*

The relatively few Doddites are mostly middle-aged and almost entirely hidden behind their dozens of cardboard rally signs, many of them stapled onto wooden poles. They may be using the same *Ready to lead* line as the Hillary crowd, but at least their mascot is original – a man in a rabbit suit with the sign *Dodd White Hare* hanging around his neck. Chris Dodd's white hair seems to be all people have noticed about him so far.

> *'Give me a G!' ('G??')*
> *'O' ('O??')*
> *'Go John, go!'*
> *'Go …?'*

The John Edwards supporter group is bigger in size than all but Clinton's and Obama's, but looks less organised. About half don't have campaign shirts on, and they seem to be having trouble catching on to the chant being led by a chubby red-headed youth.

The *John Edwards 2008, Iowa Bus Tour 2007, Fighting for One America* bus rounds the corner, honking its horns, drowning out the cheer squad. It stops to drop off some more Edwards supporters, rolls slowly around the corner, then reappears and sounds its horns again.

But the mood of reverie is abruptly dampened when I look over the road to another sign being held by a middle-aged man. It shows a giant photo of a headless, dismembered foetus, presumably the result of the rare but controversial procedure known to its opponents as 'partial-birth abortion' and to the medical profession as 'intact dilation and extraction'.

Another similarly creepy placard is being held by an older woman. It proclaims abortion as *America's Holocaust*, and has pictures of bodies at Auschwitz above more foetuses.

A second large sleek bus drives by sounding its air horns. It has *Fair Tax* written along the side. It's a lobby group pushing the idea of a flat consumption tax instead of income tax. Even the 'Sensible Iowans' are here, in a non-sensible-looking red van which is shaped like a pie-chart on wheels … I still don't know what they claim to be sensible about, but I suspect they support the smaller pieces of the pie, not the bigger ones.

It's quite apparent that all this – the campaign cheer squads and their supporters, the issue pushers and the zealots – is being done for the benefit of the media. Whenever we turn our camera onto them they perform on cue, restarting their chanting, waving, dancing, and even holding their aborted foetus signs nice and still for close-ups.

We wander over to a small group of reporters and cameras waiting near the entrance to the university hall where the debate is about to be staged. There's a crowd control barrier holding us back from the entry point, and only the ABC America crew is allowed to get any nearer – the host network's prerogative. I chat to an amiable, middle-aged radio reporter named Ken who at this early hour has the sweet smell of a freshly powdered baby. Then he's on the phone filing a voice report for the next news bulletin:

> The stage is set for this morning's Democratic Presidential candidate debate … Frontrunner Hillary Clinton will be looking for another strong performance … Senators Edwards and Obama will be looking to do anything to knock her off her game.

Ken tells me he's usually a sports reporter, and it shows in his patter. Just like the pep rally over the road, you could very well imagine Ken at the local college football game:

> The stage is set for tonight's big match between the Iowa Hawkeyes and the Iowa State Cyclones … the Hawkeyes will be looking for another

strong performance … the Cyclones will be looking to do anything to knock them off their game.

Reporters can be fun to talk to and to get some 'good oil' from, or even just find out where the next campaign event is being held, but the really juicy gossip always comes from the stills photographers, TV camera operators and 'soundies'. Unencumbered by facts, they'll tell any number of highly slanderous stories about each of the candidates. All of them involve sexual perversions of some sort – my lawyer has instructed me to say no more on the subject.

One by one the candidates and their entourages emerge from dark SUVs at the end of a pathway – giving them a 25-metre walk to the door. Again, it's all stage-managed for the benefit of the cameras. (And here I have to confess to some stage-management of my own.) As Hillary Clinton strides towards us in a brown pants suit, I wave frantically from behind our camera. Senator Clinton obligingly looks up and waves back, looking straight into the camera lens and saying perkily, 'Hi-yee everybody! Hello!' It's a good shot.

As a former First Lady, Hillary Clinton has lifetime Secret Service protection. Barack Obama was given Secret Service protection in July 2007 at his campaign's request – it was the earliest in a campaign cycle that any candidate had been given such protection. There were reports that he'd received a number of death threats, although at the time the Obama campaign denied there had been anything specific. Other candidates are only deemed to be needing protection if they rise to a high level of prominence in opinion polls.

The Secret Service agents in Iowa this morning look just like the ones in the movies: dark suits, sunglasses (even though the sun isn't yet up) and that bit of curly wire connecting their ear to their collar. The agents mechanically scan the scene around them, and just being near them makes you feel strangely nervous and as if you are possibly guilty of something. It's like the moment you pass through a metal detector at the airport and half expect the alarm to sound. It's almost

40 years since a Presidential candidate, Senator Robert Kennedy, was shot and killed on the campaign trail, and its 35 years since another Democratic contender, Alabama Governor George Wallace, was shot and survived, but was left wheelchair-bound for life. Still, these Secret Service guys aren't taking any chances today. A bomb-sniffing Labrador is being led around the lush lawn in front of the university auditorium by a man with military bearing dressed in freshly pressed but casual beige slacks and a dark blue polo shirt.

The *John Edwards (etc. etc.)* bus comes back around the block, air horns blurting, just as the *Fair Tax* bus comes around the other way. They duel air horns good-naturedly for a short while before pulling over to the curb. Soon Senator Edwards appears, his $400 haircut looking immaculate, wearing an expensive-looking dark suit and light blue tie. He's flanked by his similarly smart-suited wife, Elizabeth. I can't help noticing that her greying blonde hair looks a little thin and frizzy – a reminder of her illness, whether it's a result of her earlier cancer treatment or not. They are walking up a long pathway from the bus with a small group of campaign aides, and pointedly following a different route from all the other candidates we see. (None of these things happens by chance; usually they happen after extensive polling – or at least lengthy discussion.) Behind them, a group of around 20 young supporters wearing *EDWARDS* T-shirts and holding *JOHN EDWARDS 2008* signs have now got their chanting act together:

> 'Two-zero-zero-eight, who we gonna nominate?
> Edwards! Edwards! Two-zero-zero-eight, who we gonna
> nominate? Edwards! Edwards!'

Camera operators, and 'soundies' with their microphones on long telescopic boom poles, jog backwards trying to stay ahead of this loyal band of followers. Senator Edwards is still wearing his incongruous-looking yellow cancer 'bangle', and seems serious and unsmiling in the middle of this cheering pack. Their team of male staffers points the way to the debate hall. One of them is holding what appears to be Elizabeth Edwards' handbag.

Senator Joe Biden steps out of another dark SUV, also wearing an expensive-looking dark suit, and walks confidently along the path to the debate hall. He's largely ignored by reporters, but is smiling widely as he greets a headset-wearing member of the TV floor crew like a long-lost friend, and waves to unseen (even non-existent) well-wishers.

The night before the debate I'd arranged to interview Mike Glover, who writes about politics in Iowa for Associated Press. AP is what they used to call a 'wire service', but these days it's referred to as a 'news agency'. Instead of having their own reporters in Iowa, newspapers from all over America and around the world can print AP articles or post them online as their own. Those Iowa stories are also closely read by other reporters from other newspapers, radio and TV, and will tend to inform their story selection – often they will also substitute for actual research. As a result, Mike Glover's coverage of politics in Iowa at this stage of the election cycle has significant influence.

Glover is a wiry man with a weatherbeaten face, grey hair, a slightly walrus-like moustache and the sort of glasses that magnify the eyes. You could imagine him in another life, working on a corn farm wearing blue overalls and an undershirt, talking matter-of-factly about the chance of rain today or grain prices.

We're speaking in what is today the Media File room at Drake University – the rest of the time it is just a lecture theatre full of tables and chairs. It has a direct video feed which will project the next day's debate onto a big pull-down screen, but at the moment it is just a brightly lit and empty room. I ask Mike Glover what the candidates might be hoping to achieve in the debate.

'We are more than a year and a quarter from the general election,' Glover says, 'but we're only a few months from when voting starts in these early-voting states. So the candidates are starting to engage and starting to mark out their differences from each other.'

But with so many candidates on the stage and just 90 minutes for the debate, I ask, how will he and other reporters decide who to write about and what to write?

> The media makes decisions on who to cover based on certain things: their ability to generate support – and support is measured by the amount of money they raise and the number of people they sign up – and their standing in the various polls. Those sorts of things influence who we decide to take seriously. There are eight candidates in this debate ... Realistically, you can't cover eight candidates, so you have to figure out which ones you're going to focus on.

A bit like the Secret Service – the media often doesn't worry too much about candidates until they get very popular or very unpopular. Maybe this is fair enough on both counts, unless of course you are the candidate without strong poll numbers or heavily armed protection.

Tom Vilsack, the former Iowa Governor and former Presidential candidate, had explained the difficult situation he had found himself in when we met in his office in Des Moines a few days earlier. Vilsack said that, as a candidate, if you have a lower profile and therefore lower poll numbers than your rivals, you get ignored by the press, and if the press ignores you, you can't raise money to put into advertising, which would in turn help raise your profile. 'You've got the media and the money looking at the early polls,' Vilsack said, 'so it makes it very difficult for someone who is at 1 per cent or 2 per cent to get better known.'

It's something of a Catch-22. 'It's tough,' Vilsack said ruefully.

One of the few chances a 'second tier' or long-shot candidate has to get press attention is in these sorts of debates – unless they still get ignored even though they're on the stage.

It's almost 8 am at Drake University and the Media File room is now teeming with reporters. Most of them are from the US, but there always seems to be at least one reporter from Japan, Finland and the BBC wherever you go on the campaign trail. A lot of the shop talk is about the latest laptop computers or which of the free pastries on the buffet are best. 'Try and get the cherry Danish before it's all gone,' one advises.

The volume comes up on the projector screen where the picture is being piped in from the actual debate venue, which is over the road. It occurs to me that we all could have stayed in our motel rooms to do this. No doubt some reporters have, but they will have had to pay for their pastries.

> This is a special edition of *This Week* – The Iowa Debate. This
> morning, the Democratic Presidential candidates … Live from
> Sheshlow Auditorium on the campus of Drake University, George
> Stephanopoulos …

George Stephanopoulos is a former Rhodes Scholar who was one of Bill Clinton's top advisers in his successful 1992 Presidential bid. He served in the Clinton White House as a senior policy and strategy adviser and was the public face of the administration in its early months, when he frequently handled the daily press briefings. After leaving the White House in Clinton's second term, Stephanopoulos began working as a political correspondent with ABC America, where he now hosts its flagship weekly politics program, *This Week*.

Stephanopoulos leads into the debate by running through the latest poll numbers in Iowa, which have Barack Obama ahead on

27 per cent, Hillary Clinton and John Edwards both on 26 per cent, Bill Richardson on 11 per cent, Joe Biden and Dennis Kucinich both on 2 per cent, Chris Dodd on 1 per cent and Mike Gravel registering no support, according to the survey. Senator Gravel smiles as the camera zooms in on his reaction, and the reporters in the Media File room laugh, as do the audience inside the debate hall. Stephanopoulos himself chuckles and says, 'It's not so bad, Senator Gravel, maybe it will go up after today!' Gravel says something but it's drowned out in the laughter.

George begins the questions. 'Senator Biden, last week you said Barack Obama is not ready to be President.' Biden nods and smiles expansively, expecting a question directed at him – but there's a switch. 'Senator Clinton, is he right?' The candidates, reporters and audience laugh again at the first-up curve-ball.

But Hillary Clinton's long history with Stephanopoulos is evident in the mildly scolding tone she takes in her answer. 'Well, George, you know, I was going to say, "Good morning, and as soon as I wake up I'll answer your question."'

Will it be the early morning wake-up call or even her years in the White House with her former subordinate George that will 'throw her off her game'? No, Hillary's soon back in her stride, saying she's campaigning on the basis of her experience, not anyone else's. Still, it becomes clear that both Obama and Edwards are out to try to take Clinton down a few pegs. They're almost like the anti-Clinton tag-team as they question her 'electability' and the fact that she voted to support the war in Iraq.

Additional questions in the debate come from David Yepsen, the Chief Political Correspondent for the local newspaper, *The Des Moines Register*. Yepsen frequently appears on political talk shows and is considered the 'Dean' of the Iowa press corps. We'd spoken to Yepsen on the set of another political talk show, *Iowa Press*, the previous Sunday – at the local PBS (Public Broadcasting Service) station, he sits sagely each week alongside AP's Mike Glover and others, quizzing candidates and party officials on the week's campaign developments. Wearing his TV makeup after the taping of the show, David Yepsen's dark lips, powdery face and widow's peak remind me a little of Grandpa Munster, the likeable vampire played on 1960s TV by the late Al Lewis. Yepsen's tone is thoughtful and measured, and his phrases have a naturally crafted feel to them.

Part of mounting a successful Presidential campaign in the TV age, Yepsen says, is to simply look and act Presidential. 'I think image is VERY important,' Yepsen tells me. 'I think you've got to look the part – thanks to television largely. Image is everything in politics today … And candidates have to know the rules, how to conduct themselves.' He continues, 'They almost have to be actors – and I don't think it's any coincidence that one of the most popular American politicians of the 20th century was in fact an actor [Ronald Reagan].'

I realise that with each of the Presidential candidates we've met so far, I've been running through a mental identikit of what they should look like and whether they fit the bill of being 'Presidential'. It's by no means a simple test – Hillary manages to look more Presidential than Chris Dodd even though there's never been a female President. And I confess to letting the weakness of a candidate's chin or their height, or the way they part their hair, affect my perceptions. It's something I found no shortage of opinions on.

Professor Tom Patterson is the Bradlee Professor of Government and the Press at the Kennedy School at Harvard University and the 'go-to guy' on anything to do with 'the Presidency and the media'. He says image is more than just physical appearance. If, as David Yepsen says, candidates are rather like actors, Tom Patterson believes that to an extent, the media fulfils the role of casting director. 'The media casts candidates … giving them a shorthand image. You can see that in just about every campaign,' he says. 'It's usually a negative image, and the American press tends to be a critical press, so they pick out some problem or flaw with the candidate and make that stand for a large part of their candidacy.'

An example of that, says Patterson, was Al Gore in 2000:

Gore had a tendency to exaggerate somewhat about the role he played and the media seized on that and showed Al Gore as not quite trustworthy and not quite truthful – that was a storyline that carried all the way through to the election. By the end of the campaign most Americans quite liked Gore but didn't think he was trustworthy.

Charles Bierbauer covered five Presidential campaigns for CNN, and was the network's senior White House correspondent for nine years during the Reagan and first-Bush administrations. He says:

The media likes stories – we want good stories, we want bad stories. We don't care which they are as long as they are good stories to tell. That may be a candidate that's on the rise, [it] may be a candidate that's stumbling and scrambling to keep a campaign going, it may be two candidates at a debate going at each other with a 'he-said-she-said' approach to things … sometimes that's more heat than light, more drama than substance.

Bierbauer is concerned about blurring the line between news and opinion:

[Often] there's not a lot to distinguish the reporting from the analysis … in the 24/7 news environment there's a lot of time filled with 'I think this is what's happening' rather than what's actually happening.

That's a trend that's been apparent for a while, according to Maxine Isaacs, who was Press Secretary for the 1984 Democratic Presidential candidate, former Vice President Walter Mondale. 'We basically felt that the press coverage was thorough and fair,' Isaacs says during our interview in her penthouse apartment in the Georgetown area of Washington DC. 'But there were a few reporters who stood out to us as biased – the reporters felt they had to put their own interpretation on what Mr Mondale had said rather than letting it stand on its own.'

The mistake the Mondale campaign made, Isaacs now says, was in making their candidate too accessible to the media:

> Mondale was the last of a certain kind of candidate. He wanted to give more access to reporters, so he sometimes did three press conferences a day because he believed there was a dialogue going on in the media that it was important the voters see. Reagan was doing the exact opposite; we felt the imbalance played very much to Mr Reagan's advantage and even contributed to his victory.

She echoes the thoughts of Bierbauer:

> In reality, the press don't really ask about issues, they ask about politics, so [Mondale] was being drawn in every day to whatever the press had agreed was the story of the day. So he was always reacting to breaking political news, and Reagan was on his message, optimistic, and he looked more Presidential.

Walter Mondale suffered one of the heaviest ever defeats in a Presidential election, winning just one state from Reagan. Mondale became a lesson to other campaigns: Presidential candidates need reporters to cover their events and write down their quotes – just try not to let them ask any questions, and if they do, give them only the pre-scripted talking points.

But Isaacs doesn't want to overstate the actual effect the media had on the outcome of the 1984 election: 'The press are a lot less influential in this process than they think they are – the idea that they can determine the outcome of an election, I don't buy that at all.'

By the end of 2007, still almost a year from the Presidential election, most candidates had been actively campaigning and fundraising for about 12 months. According to the compulsory quarterly financial reports filed with the Federal Electoral Commission, Democratic frontrunners Barack Obama and Hillary Clinton had each gathered in just over $100 million, John Edwards had raised close to $35 million, Bill Richardson $22 million, Chris Dodd around $16 million, Joe Biden about $11 million, Dennis Kucinich $4 million and Mike Gravel about $500,000.

Professor Tom Patterson says research showed that the media coverage was allocated along similar lines over this period:

> Hillary Clinton received about a third of the coverage, Barack Obama about a third … John Edwards gets a sixth of the early coverage and all the other candidates together get the other sixth of the early coverage.

He sees the same Catch-22 identified early on in the campaign by Tom Vilsack. 'If you look at the polls it's Obama and Clinton, and because they are at the top they get the coverage, and because they get the coverage they stay at the top.' Patterson says. 'It makes it very difficult for candidates like Governor Richardson, Senator Dodd and Senator Biden … to even break through … so the media are very significant in the early going in how they allocate their attention.'

But the same research also found that media coverage can be a mixed blessing for a candidate, and that a lot of Hillary Clinton's press had been negative. 'She was portrayed as calculating and insincere … the candidate with the most favourable coverage was Barack Obama – exciting, charismatic, young.' Yet Patterson sounds a warning: 'At some point, if it looks like he'll be the nominee, then the media will return to its usual negative mode.'

Among the Republicans, money has been a bit harder to come by this time around, reflecting the prevailing view that 2008 is likely be a Democratic Presidential year. Still, Rudy Giuliani was able to rake in close to $60 million in 2007, Mitt Romney earned about

$50 million and chipped in another $25 million out of his own very deep pockets, John McCain made about $40 million and spent just about every cent, and Mike Huckabee could only scrape together $9 million, despite being the big mover in the opinion polls in Iowa.

With the exception of Huckabee, the other candidates made money that was roughly proportionate to their poll numbers and the level of coverage they gained in the media. Governor Huckabee's down-home folksy charm won him a lot of press coverage after his second place in the Ames Straw Poll and his opinion-poll numbers took off in Iowa as a result, but his small campaign organisation struggled to turn that into serious dollars.

Tom Patterson says that Mike Huckabee's rise during 2007 was due in no small part to media pundits looking at the field of frontrunners – Giuliani, McCain and Romney – and deciding that there was an opportunity for a strong conservative voice to appeal to the Christian Right, even if he had failed to raise significant funds.

Pat Buchanan has been both Presidential candidate and conservative media commentator. He says the media certainly has something of a collective mind. 'I think Gene [Eugene] McCarthy got it correct when he said, "The media are like blackbirds sitting on a wire – when one flies off, they all fly off – and when one flies back, they all fly back."' But Buchanan says it goes beyond a herd instinct: 'There's a clear bias for particular candidates – it certainly helped John McCain, it helped Bill Clinton.'

As far as David Yepsen from *The Des Moines Register* is concerned, the media has a valid and important role in helping winnow the field of candidates. 'I think those of us in the media look at them and say, "You know, you're a nice guy, you've got an interesting message. But you're not going to be President of the United States."'

<hr>

Inside Sheshlow Auditorium at Drake University the Democratic debate is about to wrap up after 90 minutes of questions from Yepsen and Stephanopoulos. It occurs to me that America has turned its election into a talent quest. It's a two-year reality TV show – *Presidential Idol*. It helps that George Stephanopoulos bears an uncanny resemblance to Ryan Seacrest, the host of *American Idol*. It all makes sense: eight Democratic contestants up on stage in front of the cameras singing crowd pleasers like 'Let's Get Outta Iraq!' and that evergreen favourite, 'Healthcare for All'. Dennis Kucinich even took a stab at that old Broadway showstopper, 'Hooray for Gay Marriage!'

And they'll all keep right on going until the folks in Iowa start voting them off the show in January. Then they'll gradually get whittled down by the home viewers, until the grand finale in November 2008 when we'll have our winner. But there's always that moment, when you are down to the last two highly polished and professional performers, with their perfect pitch and their perfect hair, that you kind of miss the one who used to slide off-key or dance a bit like your dad.

We take our camera and sound gear next door to a small lyric theatre which is doubling this morning as the post-debate Spin Room. Yes, they actually call it that, freely conceding what you'll get inside is 'spin' from candidates and their supporters, not impartial analysis.

Being surrounded by well-known political types, dozens of reporters, cameras, lights and microphones creates the strange sensation of being not so much 'on' television but 'in' an actual TV set. I almost expect to see a 'news ticker' scrolling headlines across the floor somewhere down around our feet.

I have arranged to interview Senator Mike Gravel, the longest of long-shot candidates in the field. At 77, Mike Gravel is the oldest candidate in the race, making Republican John McCain look almost youthful at just 70. Because he's a former US Senator and filed all the necessary paperwork, Senator Gravel is being taken seriously – well, seriously enough to be allowed on stage. What Tom Patterson might call Gravel's 'shorthand' media image is as a bit of a curmudgeon – think Grandpa Simpson in a suit.

The Spin Room is filling up with campaign surrogates, each walking in with an assistant holding a sign above their head helpfully telling reporters who this is and who they're here to support: *Senator Charlie Seng – BIDEN* and *Governor Tom Vilsack – CLINTON*. The effect is like a mini Olympic opening ceremony full of one-person teams. It's getting very crowded and hot too, with high-wattage lights from cameras burning brightly. For reporters it's like feeding time at the zoo: wherever you look there's someone to give you a quote.

No sign of Mike Gravel, so I make my way over to Congressman Dennis Kucinich to see how he thinks the debate went. Kucinich is speaking to a small group of three or four reporters and cameras, with his wife Elizabeth by his side. He's standing under a sign which says *Kucinich – KUCINICH* and trying to spin a storyline he hopes journalists will pick up on – that Hillary Clinton now says she voted to support the war in Iraq in 2003 only because she was misled to by President Bush:

> Now something happened on that stage today and I hope the media didn't miss it. Essentially, Senator Clinton said that she was tricked by George Bush, and I think the media has a responsibility to probe this question – Was she tricked, was she lied to, was she deceived? Because a President of the United States needs to show the ability not to be deceived, not to be hustled or lied to.

Having been hand-fed a story, the press gaggle breaks up and I ask Kucinich whether he thinks he got a fair hearing in the debate. 'No, of course not. They spent so much time talking about the polls that they didn't talk about things the American people are concerned about … instead they got pulled into the horse race. Now, if they really want to cover a horse race they'd look at Sea Biscuit here – the horse that's going to close fast and win this race.' Again with the Sea Biscuit!

Kucinich goes on to repeat verbatim what he'd just said to the other reporters about Hillary Clinton and her Iraq vote – it's clearly the agreed post-debate message. Kucinich's campaign manager, Mike Klein, is also here and I ask him how he thinks his candidate is going to become Sea Biscuit and go from 2 per cent in Iowa to the White House. 'Gary Hart went from 3 per cent to 31 per cent in six weeks,' Klein says. 'There are examples of people making great moves.'

I point out that Gary Hart never got elected President. 'Yeah,' Klein laughs, 'But Gary Hart had a little problem with *Monkey Business* and Dennis doesn't have a problem with monkey business. I can assure you, with his lovely wife, he has no problems there!'

Senator Mike Gravel arrives, and I manage to recognise him even though he doesn't have a *Gravel – GRAVEL* sign above his head. He's a sturdy, good-looking man with big horsey teeth, white–grey hair and rimless glasses. I ask him how he thinks he went in the debate, and his answer is surprisingly candid: 'Pretty good. I tried to not come across quite so shrill and not as angry … you know.'

Hmm, Hillary or Obama wouldn't admit something like that. So far in this campaign, Gravel has developed a reputation for being outspoken and critical, not just of President Bush, but also of his Democratic rivals, using unusually blunt and colourful language. The Alaskan Senator came to national attention in the US in 1971 when he twice attempted a Senate filibuster to try to stop the draft for the Vietnam War: he took the floor and just kept on talking to prevent a Bill going to a vote. He also read sections of the leaked secret documents on planning for the Vietnam War (known as the Pentagon Papers) onto the Congressional record after their publication in the press was blocked by legal action by the US Justice Department.

As we speak 36 years later in Iowa during his run for the Presidency, I can well imagine Mike Gravel trying a Mr Smith-style filibuster; the guy is very likeable, but he sure can talk. I ask the Senator whether he's running in this campaign because he actually thinks he can be elected President or whether he just wants to get on stage and have his say. 'Both,' he says. 'You have to get on the stage and move the ball down by drawing the line, by pushing them.'

His animated answers have a scatter-gun quality. He never quite finishes a sentence before skipping ahead – from Iraq to Iran to big oil to campaign finance to airport security and the way politicians manipulate fear in the electorate – mangling metaphors at every turn:

> You're getting to get a feel for these people and so you can say, without losing respect for them, 'You're all wrong' – and so you can do that with a smile – and they are. This is politics as usual ... what you just heard [in the debate] you heard four years ago, you'll hear four years from now and four years after that. We didn't get into the difficulties we are in today just because of George Bush. No, we had the Clinton Administration and Bush One and Reagan – we are now paying the piper for our profligacy as a nation ... and so when I see Obama say we need 100,000 troops – for what? We should be getting out, not increasing American imperialism, and Joe's the same.

He makes some good points along the way, or almost makes them. 'And another thing. Stop and think ...' He's off again, this time going onto his pet project – direct democracy.

So what does Mike Gravel think of the way he's characterised by the media? 'I filibustered the end of the draft, I released the Pentagon Papers – I took the risk of going to jail. Back then I was marginalised by the media, which is what they're trying to do to me now.' Despite all the things I like about him, as we speak I find myself getting frustrated with Gravel's inability to finish a sentence – I'm already imagining all sorts of editing problems.

Wandering around the Spin Room, I feel a bit like I'm at a speed-dating event for political junkies. I sidle up to listen to Elizabeth Edwards talk about her husband being 'the most electable candidate'. I chat a bit to Governor Tom Vilsack about Hillary Clinton's performance, which, not surprisingly, he thinks was very strong. I try slipping in a question about whether Vilsack has any regrets sitting in the audience watching these people he knows so well seeking the job he also wanted, but the former candidate isn't biting. 'No, I'm very happy to be supportive of Senator Clinton,' he says, 'I think she is the best candidate I have ever seen and I have seen a lot in the last 20 years.' And with that he's guided by a Hillary staffer towards the next camera and another interview.

While Presidential candidates struggling in the polls and gaining little media – such as Mike Gravel, Dennis Kucinich and even Chris Dodd – will come down into this media feeding frenzy after a debate, you'll never see a top tier candidate like Clinton, Obama or Edwards in here. They tend to not give a lot of interviews, except on the eve of an important election, when suddenly they're everywhere – but even then it's an exchange based on shallow prompts and talking points, rather than a genuine discussion.

This morning there's one more person I want to ask about the way the media covers Presidential politics in the US – the Iowa screamer himself, Howard Dean, who is here as Chairman of the Democratic National Committee. 'I think it's pretty abysmal,' Dean says. 'It's the usual "gotcha" and "who-did-what-to-who" stuff.'

How does the 2004 Presidential candidate think the media can be improved? 'Bring back the fairness doctrine first of all and make sure the media isn't concentrated in the hands of a few large corporations.' The fairness doctrine Dean's referring to was introduced by the Federal Communications Commission (FCC) in 1949, and required owners of broadcast licences to cover issues in the public interest in a 'balanced and fair' manner. The requirement was scrapped in the 1980s.

Certainly, Howard Dean has reason to complain about the way the media covered his spectacular flame-out. To those who were at the now-infamous Iowa rally in 2004, he was simply raising his voice to be heard above the crowd. It was the TV microphones, which filtered out the background crowd noise, that made his scream sound rather deranged – yet the media reported it as if the scream was bizarre and incongruous to those at the rally.

Outside the Spin Room the sun is now getting high in the late morning sky. One of the anti-abortionists is waiting for a bus. I wonder what the other passengers will make of the big dead foetus sign – will its carrier have to buy it a ticket the way you do with a surfboard or bike? As we walk back to our hotel a few blocks from Drake University, we pass an old-style cinema where the sign that usually spells out which movie is showing in large black letters has been replaced by HILLARY FOR PREZ. It reminded me of Yepsen's comment that it was no coincidence that a former actor, Ronald Reagan, was one of the most popular Presidents of the 20th century and that another part-time actor, Tennessee Senator Fred Thompson, was seeking the Republican nomination in 2008.

Is the Presidency of the United States just a performance – an extended run, an eight-year role some actors get to play? Are politicians and actors essentially the same creatures?

***

Of all the stars in Hollywood, few, if any, have been as intimately involved in politics for as long as Shirley MacLaine. Long before the Oscar-winning actress ever peered into a crystal, spotted a flying saucer or discovered that in a past life her daughter was her mother, she was raising money to help get John F. Kennedy elected President – that was in 1960. She also performed with Rat Packer Frank Sinatra and a host of other stars, including Nat 'King' Cole, Jimmy Durante, Ella Fitzgerald and Mahalia Jackson at the Kennedy Presidential Gala in January 1961, on the eve of JFK's swearing-in. This time, perhaps incongruously, she's backing Dennis Kucinich.

OK, her agent says, Shirley will be happy to talk to you when she's in Malibu, but there are a few conditions. It turns out she requires a certain kind of diffused lighting rig, a video monitor connected to the camera so she can see what the camera is seeing – that is, herself – and a

#4 Pro-Mist camera filter that we soon learn is so soft-focus the Grand Canyon would look as smooth as a frozen lake through it. Finally, we are to provide a chauffeur-driven limousine to get her to and from the interview. But what the hell – it's Shirley MacLaine, right?

Shirley MacLaine is a lifelong Democrat and actively committed. She worked for Senator Robert Kennedy during his 1968 Presidential bid, and took a year off show business to be a campaign organiser for Senator George McGovern's 1972 White House run. There were even reports at the time that she may have served as an 'Under-Secretary-for-One-Thing-or-Another' in a McGovern Administration.

Still strikingly beautiful at 73, but with the slightly feline appearance that suggests one too many facelifts, Shirley MacLaine has been a little bit testy ever since arriving for today's interview. We are using a fill-in cameraman because Rebecca has had to organise a replacement for a lost passport back in LA. But our cameraman has managed to upset Miss MacLaine by fiddling with the beeper on his belt while she was trying to concentrate. 'Get out!' she commands him, leaving us, rather unusually, to do the interview alone, with an unmanned camera fixed on her face.

Trying to avoid another blow-up I ask, tentatively, why she took a year off show business in 1972 to campaign for George McGovern.

'I was so furious with Richard Nixon. He was not trustworthy; he was a liar,' she says firmly. 'My father was for Nixon. He used to go on at me for supporting McGovern because he was inexperienced and because he said he had a Novocain upper lip – somehow George's upper lip doesn't move,' MacLaine laughs.

I'm relieved that she suddenly appears to be in better humour. Does she think actors and politicians have much in common? 'Oh, I think politicians are desperate to communicate their truth with the audience, and that's also what an actor does, expressing truth through their character.' But she draws a distinction between the star quality of famous actors and the charisma of great politicians:

When you look at the experience of being with Bill Clinton, as opposed to being with a really fine actor, it's entirely different, because Bill Clinton works a room like no one you ever saw – an actor is usually shy around real people. A politician wants to shake every hand in the room, an actor wants to go home.

As well as *Law and Order* star Fred Thompson in the 2008 Presidential race, California's 'Governator', Arnold Schwarzenegger, and President Ronald Reagan in the 1980s, actor Clint Eastwood was elected Mayor of Carmel, California in the 1980s, 1930s movie song and dance man George Murphy became a US Senator in the 1960s, Charlton Heston was head of the influential National Rifle Association – heck, even Shirley Temple became a US Ambassador. And it's not exclusively a US phenomenon either; former Philippines President Joseph Estrada had been a action movie hero, and actress Eva Peron became virtual co-ruler of Argentina as First Lady.

But it occurs to me, at the risk of offending any of them, that none of the above list was necessarily renowned for being, well, a particularly *great* actor before they went into politics …

'You're right,' Shirley nods. 'Look at Ronald Reagan.' As well as his experience as an actor, MacLaine says Ronald Reagan relied heavily on being a big New Ager. 'One of the reasons he was so powerful in his communication skills is that he used to go to many psychics whom I know – and we know about Nancy and her astrology.'

But she says that while astrology and psychics may have had a big role in the Reagan White House, they helped end her own political aspirations. 'A bunch of the "money people" in California asked me to run for the Senate – and you know what I said?'

No, I admit, I don't.

'I said, "I'll run – it's time for a woman – but I want to make two pictures a year and have six weeks in Vegas." They said no, I said no.' Then she adds, with a deep laugh, 'Once I got into UFOs and high consciousness and past-life understanding they stopped asking me!'

More laughter! Perhaps now I could ask the question that had been on my mind for a while: how can someone who campaigned for the Kennedys now endorse Dennis Kucinich for President? To borrow a quote, Dennis Kucinich is 'no Jack Kennedy'.

'I've seen polls where over 50 per cent say they agree with everything Kucinich says but that he can't win,' MacLaine says. 'Well I say if you agree with what he's saying why don't you help him win and vote for him?' But then she adds, 'If you want to have an *elf* as President!' she laughs throatily, before adding seriously that Kucinich is a 'dear friend' and she's godmother to his daughter.

So even one of Kucinich's closest friends admits that his height is an issue. It seems I'm not alone in being put off by the simple fact that he doesn't look the part.

With the interview wrapped up and Shirley MacLaine in our limousine, the cameraman comes back in and says, 'I hope your audio is OK.'

'What do you mean? Why wouldn't it be?' I ask.

'When she ordered us all out, I'd disconnected the microphone,' he says, matter-of-factly.

'What?' I splutter. 'You did what??!!'

'I was adjusting the boom mic when she told me to leave, so I left. I told you.'

'You told me you had disconnected the microphone?' I ask incredulously. 'I think I might have remembered that, and said, "We need SOUND FOR AN INTERVIEW!"' We replay the tape and the audio is awful, useless for the film.

Image may be everything in show business and in politics, I think to myself ruefully, but sound is pretty important too.

Postscript: Two months after our interview, Miss MacLaine published her latest book, *Sage-ing While Age-ing*, in which she revealed that her 'dear friend' Dennis Kucinich had encountered a UFO above her house.

Kucinich was asked about it in the next Democratic candidate debate, on 30 October 2007:

NBC's Tim Russert: Shirley MacLaine writes in her new book that you sighted a UFO over her home in Washington State – that you found the encounter extremely moving, that it was a triangular craft, silent and hovering, that you felt a connection to your heart and heard directions in your mind. Now, did you see a UFO?

Kucinich: Uh, I did … It was an unidentified flying object, okay? It's like, it's unidentified … And also you have to keep in mind that President Jimmy Carter saw a UFO and that also, more people in this country have seen a UFO than approve of George W. Bush's Presidency.

The UFO sighting story gained Kucinich more media attention than he'd had at any other time during the campaign, but it was largely as the butt of jokes and probably ended any possible hope of him being taken seriously as a candidate. Old Sea Biscuit had been nobbled – and by a close friend.

But Kucinich was right – Carter did claim to have seen a UFO while he was Governor of Georgia in 1973. Although it is now generally believed that he misidentified the planet Venus, many UFO-logists cite it as proof that 'They are out there.' According to an Ipsos/AP poll taken at the time of Kucinich's debate comments, 14 per cent of Americans claimed to have seen a UFO, 34 per cent believed in the existence of UFOs and ghosts, and 31 per cent said they supported President Bush.

Just weeks before the Iowa Caucus, Kucinich was excluded from the final Iowa candidate debate despite his frequently having had higher national poll numbers than either Senator Biden or Senator Dodd, who were invited and did take part in the debate. Two months after the August Iowa debate, America's NBC Television had excluded Mike Gravel, saying he hadn't raised enough money to be considered a viable contender – NBC is owned by General Electric, one of the largest donors to Presidential campaigns, and a major manufacturer of military hardware, fridges and washer-dryers. In March 2008 Senator Gravel left the Democratic Party to seek the nomination of the minor Libertarian Party.

In June 2008 Tim Russert died of a heart attack, age 58.

4 Get Out the Vote

Iowa, January 2008: It's the day before the Iowa caucus – the first vote in the 11-month series of caucus and primary ballots which will culminate in the election of America's 44th President on Tuesday, 4 November 2008.

A record corn crop, in excess of 2.5 billion bushels, was harvested three months ago, meeting the growing demand for ethanol, and now the flat fields of Iowa are buried under more than a foot of snow. The temperature gauge on the rental car reads –15°C, 55°C lower than when we saw the Presidential candidates here at the Iowa State Fair back in August.

Senator John Edwards is speaking this morning to a group of 20 or so reporters, standing ankle deep in snow in the front yard of Bob Petrzelka's neat brick and weatherboard house in the town of Mt Pleasant, Iowa. The white paintwork is probably a few years past needing a touch-up, but there are two lush green Christmas wreaths with bright red ribbons that give the front porch a welcoming appearance.

The House Party is an important part of old-style retail politics in Iowa: a candidate turns up to speak to a few dozen locals, takes questions, explains his or her policies and tries to win over some votes. But there is enormous media interest in this quaint electioneering ritual, and there are often so many TV cameras that they can't fit very many real Iowans into these House Parties. The Edwards campaign staff has overcome the problem by telling the media to stay in the bus – they seem happy to oblige, working on their laptops, phoning in copy on their mobiles or catching up on some sleep.

The party is just about over, so the media is summoned for 'press availability' on the front lawn. Senator Edwards is dressed fairly casually – blue jeans, an open-neck business shirt and a heavy black overcoat. He looks tired and sounds a bit stuffed up; catching a cold is an occupational hazard for every candidate on the campaign trail because of all the hand-shaking, endless talking, long days and not enough sleep – not to mention the weather. Arkansas Governor Bill Clinton lost his voice altogether in the weeks leading up to his 1992 Presidential election win. It may be nothing with Edwards, though – everyone out here this morning has a runny nose and streaming eyes because of the intensely dry, cold air. Dense plumes of steam are coming out of the reporters' mouths like burps of fairy floss as they ask their questions.

Several dark blue plastic *John Edwards 2008* signs on wire hoops have been pushed into the snow – they look like a miniature slalom course. The beanie-clad media pack stomp their feet and thwack their gloved hands together while their toasty warm press bus chugs invitingly behind them. The sky is a brilliant clear blue, and there's the kind of fresh powder snow that makes a satisfying creaking noise like dry corn flour as it compacts under your feet.

But before anyone can get out of the cold and into the bus, John Edwards has something to say about his chances in the upcoming caucus. 'As long as I continue to show the energy and passion that I have to make this country what it's capable of being, we'll do well tomorrow night.'

Edwards will need plenty of energy; he is planning to campaign non-stop for the next 36 hours, without sleeping, until the caucus is over.

Opinion polls in the last few days have Senator Edwards finishing anywhere from first to third in the Iowa Democratic Party caucus tomorrow night. A win for Edwards in Iowa would be a major blow to both national frontrunner Hillary Clinton and second-placed Barack Obama. It would send a definite message to the Democratic Party from its voter base: let's not try to make history with the first female President or the first black President – let's just win back the White House. But former Iowa Governor Tom Vilsack warned me last summer that polls are notoriously unreliable in this state because many people who say they intend to caucus in fact don't. Vilsack also said that many voters don't make up their minds until the very last minute, and those who do ultimately go along to caucus may arrive at the meeting supporting one candidate, but leave having been convinced to vote for another.

Somewhere a freight train sounds a baleful horn and a dog barks right on cue to give the scene an appropriately downtrodden working-class American soundtrack. Bruce Springsteen sings about places like this, and Edwards is courting the blue-collar vote with a theme of reuniting the 'two Americas': the 'haves' and the 'have-nots'.

A few minutes after the candidate and the press bus leave, Elizabeth Edwards emerges from a fly-screened back door, thanking a supporter and proclaiming cheerily, 'And he's not done yet!' Now the Senator has gone, the few remaining press are free to invite themselves inside the house, where Mr Petrzelka explains why he hosted this House Party for Edwards:

I really started out open-minded about all of the candidates, but
frankly you can drown in the issues and the position papers, and to be
perfectly honest, it came down to the person that I thought I could
trust the most to create the world for the future of my kids … and
John Edwards was that person.

Bob Petrzelka is a white middle-aged Democratic Iowa caucus-goer.
He started out supporting Tom Vilsack's Presidential bid, and now
says that even though he favours Edwards, he's still interested in hearing what other Democratic candidates have to say:

> I went to see Bill Richardson last night, and I've seen others before,
> but I really like Edwards as a person, and in places like Iowa it comes
> down to your gut feeling about that person, and Senator Edwards
> gives you a good feeling in your gut.

A few dozen of Bob's neighbours are standing around his living room,
which still has the tree and trimmings up a week after Christmas. The
mostly middle-aged group is chatting, wishing each other happy New
Year and eating from a large box of sugar-coated pastries, excited at
the possibility that they may have just met America's next President.
A few disconnected phrases leap out of the din: 'Joe Biden', and 'My
mother would have a heart attack if he won!', and 'She's the Obama-
pusher.'

Also in the Petrzelkas' living room is Bill Leber, another middle-
aged white man. Bill's all the way from Columbus, Ohio – a drive
of more than 1000 kilometres. He says he's come to Iowa this
week to volunteer for John Edwards, and says today's House Party
is fairly typical of the campaigning in Iowa he's seen: 'It's really
at a one-on-one level here, and to have a national candidate in
your living room – it's not the kind of thing we see in the rest of the
states.' Electability is an important issue for Bill Leber, as is the Iraq
War:

The main thing for me is his [Edwards'] position on the war – of the candidates with a realistic opportunity, he has put the end to the Iraq War at the top of his list of priorities, and I think he'll fight to get it done.

Edwards isn't the only candidate campaigning in small-town Iowa today. At the Coralville Conference Center, just northwest of Iowa City, another Democratic Presidential hopeful, Barack Obama, is speaking this afternoon. How Coralville got its name is a mystery – there can't have been coral anywhere near here for several million years. How the conference centre got its name is all too apparent.

Senator Barack Hussein Obama is 46 years old – the same age Bill Clinton was when he was elected to the Presidency in 1992. Obama is the son of a white woman from Kansas and a black Kenyan father – his parents met when they were both learning Russian at the University of Hawaii. They married, had a son and separated all within three years, at a time when 'nice' white girls didn't tend to mingle with black men from Kenya – or indeed black men from anywhere. His story has become a part of his campaign; he, like America, is a mixing pot. Obama grew up in Honolulu and Jakarta, after his mother married an Indonesian man. Obama likes to say he has family of just about every colour. The young Barack returned to the US to study in the 1980s, and in 1990 he was the first black student elected to the position of editor of the prestigious *Harvard Law Review*. After graduation, Obama became a community organiser in Chicago, and was elected to the Illinois state legislature in 1996. He was seen within the party as a rising star, but it wasn't until the Democratic National Convention in July 2004, which nominated Senator John Kerry as the Democratic Presidential candidate to take on George W. Bush, that Obama came to wider attention.

Obama was selected to make the keynote address – this turned out to be four years before his Presidential run. Again there are echoes of Clinton: Bill Clinton made the keynote address in 1988, four years before his first Presidential run. But unlike Clinton, whose 32-minute convention speech in Atlanta was long-winded and uninspiring, Obama rose to the occasion in 2004 with a bravura speech called 'The Audacity of Hope'; it was immediately compared to some of the great pieces of American political rhetoric and became the title of his second book. The then 42-year-old was running for the Senate, hoping to become the only black person among 100 US Senators in Washington DC, and in that speech he called for an end to the deep divisions that had emerged in the US in recent years. He also warned that the media and politicians would continue to try to exploit those divisions:

> Now, even as we speak, there are those who are preparing to divide us – the spin masters, the negative ad peddlers who embrace the politics of 'Anything Goes'. Well I say to them tonight, there is not a *liberal* America and a *conservative* America – there is the *United States* of America. There is not a *black* America and a *white* America and a *Latino* America and *Asian* America – there's the *United States* of America.

Thousands of Democratic delegates at the Fleet Centre in Boston and millions more watching at home on TV knew they had seen something remarkable – possibly the beginning of a great political career. Obama's classical oratorical skills and easy presence stood in sharp contrast to John Kerry, the stiff, French-speaking son of the New England elite. Barack Obama was part Martin Luther King Jr, part John F. Kennedy, with just a little bit of Puff Daddy too. Within two years of being elected to the US Senate, Obama was running for the Presidency. There were questions about whether this 'freshman' first-term Senator had the experience to run for the highest office in the land – why not let Hillary run now, maybe be

Vice President and then stand in eight years?

Obama's response was to quote the Reverend Martin Luther King Jr. 'I'm running because of what Dr King called "the fierce urgency of now",' Obama told audiences all over the US in the long nominating campaign of 2007/08. 'I believe in such a thing as being too late – and that hour is almost upon us.'

A temporary stage has been erected in the Coralville Conference Center auditorium. Behind the rostrum where the Presidential candidate will soon speak are five rows of elevated bench seats with about 100 Iowans of various ages and ethnicities. They are holding signs saying *CHANGE WE CAN BELIEVE IN* and, simply, *HOPE*. They're all here as a backdrop for the TV cameras, but some of the 'senior Iowans' are struggling with the bright lights, squinting and shielding their eyes with *OBAMA* stickers.

Given that this state is 95 per cent white, they must have every black and Asian-American in Coralville up here this afternoon. Another five or six hundred Obama supporters are in front of the stage – all still wearing bubble coats and scarves, listening to a pair of preppy warm-up guys doing some shtick about how to caucus. 'Chris' and 'Dean' tell the crowd to arrive at their caucus site tomorrow night by 6.30 pm because the doors are locked at 7 o'clock sharp. Clearly the Obama campaign is trying to ensure that plenty of their young first-time caucus-goers actually show up and vote.

The music gets suddenly louder, and the crowd starts cheering – Barack Obama is making his way from an unseen door to the side of the stage, smiling widely, shaking hands two at a time, waving amid a barrage of camera flashes and hugging a few apparently better known supporters. Obama jogs up the few steps to the podium like a super keen gameshow host, clapping his hands then reaching into the breast pocket of his dark suit for a handful of palm cards.

'Look at this crowd! I know it's cold outside, but I'm FIRED UP!' The crowd whoo-hoos its approval.

Senator Obama begins with a string of thank yous to key supporters and campaign organisers, but his language is surprisingly hip – asking the crowd to 'Give it up' for this Congressman, that Senator and all the volunteers. 'That's what I'm talking about!' the candidate nods as he lays out the palm cards on the rostrum like a croupier and refers to them for more names to thank.

Pacing back and forth across the stage like a stand-up comic mid-anecdote, Obama asks the crowd how many of them plan to vote at the caucus tomorrow – about 90 per cent of the five or six hundred people's hands go up. Then he asks how many will be going to caucus for the first time – about a quarter of the hands go up again.

'Look at that! You know there's been a lot of discussion among the pundits lately because they don't think you'll show up. They say, "A lot of them are students – they never show up." Well are you going to prove them wrong?' The crowd lets out a loud cheer, and Obama plays to them: 'I can't hear you! Are you going to show up?'

'YAAAAAAAAAAIRS!!!!!' they scream in unison.

Obama asks the crowd if there are any caucus-goers who aren't yet sure who they'll vote for, and a few scattered hands go up. Obama says that's OK, it's his job to convince them to caucus for him. He jokes, 'A lightbulb will go off over your head, a beam of light will shine down on you – you will have an epiphany and you will say, "I have to vote for Barack!"'

The crowd laughs, and the candidate beams, before turning serious:

> Iowa, you have this unique privilege, this unique possibility of impacting who is going to be the next leader of the free world. More than anybody on the planet you have an effect on that. Exercise it – it will only take a few hours.

The failure of Governor Howard Dean to turn his vocal young supporters into caucus-goers in Iowa in 2004 is still fresh in everyone's memory. Like Obama, Howard Dean had been in front of his rivals in many of the opinion polls before the caucus, but ended up coming in a distant third. A similarly underwhelming performance in Iowa could badly damage perceptions of Obama's electability.

There's no escaping the imminent Iowa caucus. Back in Des Moines, the hottest ticket in town tonight is for *Caucus! – The Musical*, by local composer Robert John Ford – actually, being Des Moines, it may be the *only* ticket in town tonight. As the name suggests, *Caucus! – The Musical* is a musical about the Iowa caucus, or, more particularly, what it's like to be an Iowan getting lots and lots of attention during the Presidential election cycle.

It includes the show-stopping 'Anything for a Vote' which pokes fun at past White House contenders:

> I remember back in '84
> I went to open up my door
> And there stood Walter Mondale in my yard
> He'd been there since the break of dawn,
> That's when he mowed and raked my lawn!

The musical was largely written in 2003 and was strangely prescient, in that it contains an African-American candidate, a female candidate, a candidate who was scrutinised for his past marriages and a candidate who wore his religion on his sleeve – Obama, Clinton, Giuliani and Huckabee? It even features a fictional Presidential candidate who gives a Howard Dean-like scream then says, 'I'm screwed, aren't I?'

The line between fiction and reality is further blurred by this evening's extra added attraction – Hillary and Bill Clinton are showing up in the same Iowa Historical Museum building that houses the *Caucus!* theatre.

In the lobby among the tightly packed crowd waiting for the

Clintons to arrive is retired General Wesley Clark, the former Supreme Allied Commander of NATO and a 2004 Presidential candidate who skipped the Iowa caucus – a decision which he later admitted cost him any chance of winning the Democratic nomination. Former Secretary of State Madeleine Albright is here too, seated by the stage where the Clintons will soon speak. The legally blind African-American Lieutenant Governor of New York, David Patterson, is also here – just two months later he will suddenly become the Governor of his state following revelations that Governor Eliot Spitzer had a habit of paying high-priced prostitutes for sex. And over there it's Mitt Romney's doppelganger – the actor Ted Danson, who has endorsed Hillary Clinton's candidacy and made several appearances on the campaign trail.

Interestingly, when the MC introduces them all to the crowd, Ted Danson gets a much louder cheer than the former Secretary of State, the former NATO commander or the soon-to-be Governor of New York.

After another 10 minutes or so the MC is back to ask the crowd to welcome Governor Tom Vilsack and his wife Christie, Chelsea Clinton, President Bill Clinton, 'and the next President of the United States – HILLARY CLINTON!' The crowd threatens to raise the roof, sending all the VU-meters on the media's recording equipment dangerously into the red. Bachman-Turner Overdrive's *Takin' Care of Business* kicks in loudly over the PA system as Senator Clinton emerges from the crush.

President, Senator and 27-year-old Chelsea Clinton wave happily, while Governor Tom Vilsack claps along behind them. Bill Clinton welcomes everyone and says, 'Happy New Year – I hope it's going to be an even happier New Year tomorrow night!'

President Clinton, looking older and much slimmer since his 2004 heart bypass surgery, explains that he's going to make a two and a half-minute introductory speech so that Hillary can start speaking right in time for the 10 pm newscasts to cross live:

To be a great President you need someone who has the strength, compassion and common sense … And they have to be tough enough to get elected … and implement the promises made to you and the people of America in this election … and do that without getting carried away about being President – which is easy to do: after all, they play that song [*Hail to the Chief*] every time you walk into a room!

The crowd laughs in appreciation, Hillary chuckles as if she hasn't heard these lines countless times before. President Clinton jokes some more about how great it is to be President: 'You never wait in traffic, you live in America's best public housing, your airplane is so cool.'
Finally Bill Clinton says:

I think it would be a great thing if we had our first woman President, I think about my working grandmother, who raised me 'til I was four, my working mother, who was sometimes discriminated against because of her gender, our daughter, who we raised to think she can do whatever she wants to do … I think it would be great. But most importantly, I think she would be a great President.

The Clintons hug and the crowd cheers and starts chanting 'HILL-A-RY, HILL-A-RY!'
'The process of picking a President starts in Iowa tomorrow night,' Hillary says. 'And we'll know tomorrow night what Iowans have decided, and I hope as you go into the caucuses you will be thinking about the most important question of them all – who can be the best President for America in *this* time?'

***

With voting not compulsory in American elections, weather can be a major factor in the turnout: too hot, too cold or too wet and more people tend to stay at home. Iowa caucus day, 3 January 2008, dawns cold but clear – no repeat of the ice storms which brought much of the mid-west to a frigid standstill just before Christmas, blocking roads and freezing flags mid-wave.

For our documentary film, we wanted to follow an Iowan to the caucus – and who better than someone who's keenly observed the process: the writer and composer of *Caucus! – The Musical*, Robert John Ford? Ford is a native son of Fort Dodge, Iowa who left for the bright lights of California in his twenties but is now back in his home state, where his musical has become something of a hit. Like so many Iowans we've met, Robert Ford takes the state's political role very seriously, but he's also able to laugh at it all. 'Coming from Iowa, we can acknowledge that there is some silliness to this process.' But, he says, one of the serious points his musical production raises is the notion of 'electability':

> People are trying to analyse who it is that has the best chance of being elected – not necessarily because of what they stand for, but who has the most money and momentum … and really it comes down to the media and others telling us who is electable and we believe it.

Ford admits that he too has bought into the idea of 'electability'. Like many Democrats we've met, he says that based on policies alone he would vote for Dennis Kucinich, but he has been planning to vote for Hillary Clinton because she's more electable. Yet now, with just hours to go until the caucus, Ford says he's realised he was more excited by Bill Clinton than by Hillary at the Historical Society last night, and he's questioning whether Hillary will be his first choice after all:

> I've always been impressed with Barack Obama, but I think I've decided I will not be caucusing for him tonight … primarily because I question whether he has the experience to lead the country at this point. I think the person who has re-emerged in my mind is John

Edwards – I voted for him in the caucuses four years ago and just within the past 24 hours I've started looking at him again.

But he says he's still not sure who he'll vote for; he'll just go where his heart leads him at the time.

Its 6.30 pm on caucus night, and the doors at the Central Campus High School on Grand Avenue in Des Moines are now open. Dozens of Iowans aged from 17 to their eighties are queuing up at tables to get their names marked off rolls of registered Democratic voters. At venues all around the state, hundreds of thousands of other Democrats and Republicans are doing the same.

As the crowd at Central Campus High swells, caucus organisers become concerned about the size of the venue – the school cafeteria. No one can recall a crowd as large as this, and there's a sense that something unique is happening here tonight.

Robert Ford heads inside and over to the Edwards group, where he introduces himself to one of their 'Caucus Captains'. She tells him about Senator Edwards' policy positions on healthcare and the war in Iraq. Ford asks the middle-aged woman some specifics about when a 'President Edwards' would bring the troops home and she's a little unsure: 'Ahhhh … as President,' she says unconvincingly, 'ahhhh … I think it's within 6 to 9 months he would bring them home … I believe.' He asks how that compares with the other candidates and she's even less sure. She offers him a printed form which apparently spells it out: 'I think it's there. I would have to look at that again.'

Outside the main caucus room, people are still lining up to get in. Between rows of school lockers, Tiffany Jackson, a 21-year-old black woman from Des Moines, explains that this is her first Iowa caucus, and she's here tonight to vote for Obama. 'I really felt drawn to him when I saw him on TV and I thought I would come out for the first time and give it a try.'

Also here tonight is Deborah Tezak, who has just switched

from being a registered member of the Republican Party to become a Democrat in order to caucus for Senator Joe Biden. [You have to indicate your preferred party before you can register to vote in the Iowa Caucus.] A well-dressed middle-aged woman with blonde hair and dark eyeliner, she says this is the first time she's gone to caucus too:

> I've followed him and felt strongly about Senator Biden. I've met most of the candidates, and his experience and depth of knowledge in foreign policy ... I think we need change, but I'd like change in someone with experience.

While the Republican Party caucus is a straightforward 'go in and vote' process, the Democratic Party caucus is much more involved. If a candidate doesn't achieve 15 per cent support at a particular caucus site they are regarded as unviable and eliminated from the voting. The supporters of unviable Democratic candidates can then either go home or change their support to another candidate – it's a physical form of preferential voting. Deborah Tezak says she isn't interested in the top tier Democrats: 'I'll vote for Biden, Richardson or Dodd because of their experience, or I'll go back to being a Republican.' She laughs.

The corridors are filling up with more and more caucus-goers and the cafeteria is now packed with hundreds of Iowans, some in candidate T-shirts, others in overcoats or bulky jackets. Many talk excitedly, greeting friends and neighbours; others nervously sip coffee from styrofoam cups.

The crowd of maybe four or five hundred is already roughly divided into groups supporting the various Democratic candidates. Hillary's group is told to move up the front near the caucus organising official with the microphone; Richardson supporters over to the left; the big group of Obama supporters in the middle of the room; Edwards supporters off to the right; the small but vocal bunch for Kucinich up the back; and the similarly modest groups for Biden and Dodd over near the door. It looks as if nobody is here to support Senator Mike Gravel.

The room erupts into calls of 'Biden people over here!' and 'Hey Cathy, c'mon, there's room over with us!' Friends and neighbours shout across the room in a happy, spirited way and you can see some groups swell and others suddenly dwindle as people drift from one candidate to another.

A woman in a red T-shirt hollers out for all of the Obama supporters to raise their hands and she starts counting them: '1, 2, 3 – hands up! – 4, 5, 6 … 18 … 19 …'

The Kucinich group do a rough head count of their own and realise they won't have the 15 per cent of caucus-goers to make it through to the second round of voting, so they start debating among themselves. One older man says, 'I say we go over to Obama'; another says, 'Remember what the Congressman said yesterday.' Dennis Kucinich had told his Iowa supporters yesterday that if they didn't have enough support to be viable they should give their support to Obama over the other contenders. 'Nah – can't do it,' says a tall man in a baseball cap.

A woman in a black suit jacket and a blonde bob comes over to the Kucinich group and tells them they should give their vote to Bill Richardson: 'If you're with a third tier person, and we're with a third tier person, why don't we all get together and make a one tier person?' Some of the 12 Kucinich supporters are already heading over to the Obama group. Another middle-aged woman in a red coat is an emissary from Biden's group; they also want the Kucinich people to move across.

Meanwhile, Robert Ford looks as if he has almost decided. He's standing with the John Edwards group, which seems to be growing as supporters of the less-popular candidates realise that they won't make it through to the second vote. But when the head counter tries to name him '16' he says, 'Not yet, I'm waiting.'

The Richardson group realise that they aren't going to get the 45 votes they figure they'll need to be viable, and suddenly a black man with a shaved head and quilted green vest appears, guiding them over to the Obama supporters with a broad smile and a traffic cop's practised hand gestures.

The room keeps erupting into cheers as individuals move into new groups. Sometimes there are sudden mass defections – it's like watching months of shifting opinions polls compressed into a few minutes.

Another organiser asks Robert Ford if he's with Edwards, and finally he says, 'Yes, OK, count me in.' He explains that he was waiting to make sure Hillary had enough votes without him to be viable before he gave his vote to Edwards. A woman in a black jumper and a cap tells Robert she thinks this is such a primitive form of voting, and Robert replies, 'It is primitive, but you gotta love it.' They are joined by another woman wearing a *Caucus! – The Musical* T-shirt, and Robert asks whether she's seen it. Yes, and she loved it. 'Good, because I wrote it,' he says with genuine modesty.

The predominantly female gathering of Hillary supporters up the front is now looking sombre. They can see the imposing size of the Obama group – and it's getting bigger.

The haggling continues. The shaved-headed Obama organiser's voice booms out – 'Three more! Three more!' The head count is underway again; '56 … 57 … 70, 71 …'

There are excited cheers from the Edwards group. The organiser who was a little unsure about the policy detail when she spoke to Robert earlier now announces that they have 72 votes and there are more to come.

The caucus Precinct Captain announces that the viability figure is 71.

'Clinton has 106 … Obama 245 … Edwards 75 … just for the record, Dodd is 12, Biden in 18, uncommitted is 4 and Kucinich is 5 …'

'What about Richardson?' someone asks.

'Richardson is 26,' the Captain says.

Now caucus-goers are told that supporters of the 'unviable

candidates' – Dodd, Biden, Richardson and Kucinich – have 15 minutes to join other groups, be counted as 'uncommitted' or go home.

'Come on over to Edwards, folks,' an older man calls out, and the Edwards supporters cheer and clap in encouragement. There is more cajoling as the Obama, Clinton and Edwards organisers all implore the supporters of the unviable candidates to come across.

'Obama! Obama!' starts the chant. 'Edwards! Edwards!' comes the reply from across the room. The calls form a new rhythm: 'O-BA-MA! EDWARDS! O-BA-MA! EDWARDS! O-BA-MA!' Hillary's supporters enter the contest: 'HILL-A-RY! EDWARDS! O-BA-MA! HILL-A-RY! EDWARDS! O-BA-MA!'

The Obama organiser is aggressively picking out Richardson and Biden supporters, saying, 'Come on, we got to get up front and get you counted!' He starts the Obama group clapping and cheering each new recruit.

Robert Ford is speaking to an older heavy-set man who asks him why he's supporting Edwards. Robert explains that it's partially because his father – who is over 90 – saw Edwards and liked him. The heavy-set man says he was supporting Hillary because his mother, who died last year, loved Hillary. But he says he went back to Obama's 2004 Convention speech, and, 'God, he won me then.'

An Edwards organiser sees Robert talking to an Obama supporter and fears he's been poached. They call out to him anxiously – 'It's OK,' Robert says. 'I'm just chatting.'

A youngish male reporter in a corduroy jacket and floppy fringe comes up to the heavy-set man and asks why he's supporting Obama – 'He's so inspirational …' the man begins, but then the Precinct Captain is back at the microphone, and the final count is on. This is the vote that, along with that of almost 1800 caucus precincts across Iowa tonight, will be beamed around the world as the result of more than 12 months of Presidential campaigning in the state.

The room falls silent.

'For Obama we have 276.' The news is greeted by a loud cheer and applause.

'For Clinton we have 109.' A few 'Whooooo-hooo!'

'For John Edwards we have 80.' A more vocal cheer.

And at the end of the process, from this venue, Obama gets five delegates, Hillary gets two, and so does Edwards. The rest get none. Those delegates will now go to the Iowa State Democratic Convention in March, which will in turn elect delegates to the Democratic Party Nominating Convention to be held in Denver, Colorado in August – that's where the Presidential nominee will formally, finally, be voted for … nobody said this was simple!

Robert Ford gives his name and phone number to the Edwards organisers as an 'alternate delegate' and may be called on if either of the two Edwards delegates can't make it to the State Convention.

The result at the Central Campus High School in Des Moines turns out to be pretty typical of how Iowans voted all over the state. The stunning victory for Senator Barack Obama in this predominantly white state proved he could win across racial lines and abruptly ended the belief that Hillary Clinton's nomination was inevitable. When all the votes in Iowa were tallied, Obama triumphed with almost 37 per cent, and John Edwards, with 30.1 per cent, had very narrowly forced Hillary (29.80 per cent) into a disappointing third place. Hillary Clinton's caucus night speech was upbeat; she didn't scream when she spoke to supporters, but you suspect she may have wanted to. Edwards too was sounding confident, although the pundits said he really needed a win in Iowa, not second place, to have a chance at beating either Clinton or Obama to the nomination. Bill Richardson finished fourth, with 2.1 per cent of the vote; Joe Biden gained just under 1 per cent, and Dodd, Kucinich and Gravel all finished with 0 per cent.

Turnout was huge: around 230,000 Democrats went to vote at caucus venues around Iowa. This was almost double the previous record number of votes, set in 2004. Professor Arthur Sanders from Drake University says the sheer number of Iowans who came out to caucus was astonishing: 'Given the size and who they voted for ... it says the country wants something different than what they have now – everybody was asking for change.'

Across on the other side of Des Moines, a few hundred supporters of Senator Joe Biden are gathering in a smallish room at a conference centre. The stage is decked out with four American flags and a large but cheap-looking vinyl *BIDEN President 2008* sign. The PA system is playing something philosophical with a honky-tonk piano by Randy Newman – it must be from the CD marked 'If we lose'.

The crowd gets livelier as the beer and wine gets passed around, and the chant goes up, 'Joe! Joe! Joe!' when they see that the candidate and his photogenic family have arrived.

On stage Senator Biden thanks all the supporters and volunteers who have helped his campaign over the past year in Iowa:

> We decided to do this for the right reasons, folks: the reason to do
> this is because we really believe in this country. I feel no regret. I hope
> we have been able to keep this campaign on the issues we should be
> talking about. The security of America is at risk.

Biden is testament to the fact that so many elements, including timing, have to come together to build a successful Presidential campaign. He stood on his unquestionable experience in an election where voters were looking instead for change. 'I congratulate Barack on such a significant win – he deserves great credit.'

And then Biden confirms that his own Presidential bid is over: 'I will be returning to the Senate as Chairman of the Foreign Relations Committee,' he says, and the crowd bursts into applause. He says he's happy tonight that he has his family with him and they are all healthy, and everyone knows what he's talking about.

'You know,' Biden concludes, again quoting Irish poet Seamus Heaney (from the poem 'Doubletake'), 'history forbids us to "hope on this side of the grave, but then, once in a lifetime" – now – that "longed for tide of justice rises up and hope and history rhyme".'

Tina Turner's 'Simply the Best' kicks in over the sound system – presumably from the CD marked 'Win or lose'.

Joe Biden is smiling widely as he turns around and gives his grand-daughter a big hug, then embraces his now 37-year-old son Hunter.

Postscript: Senator Chris Dodd and his 'White Hare' also ended their Presidential run after the vote in Iowa; he later endorsed Barack Obama. Bill Richardson vowed he would fight on after his fourth-place finish. Kucinich and Gravel also pledged to stay in the race. The Republican Party caucuses saw only 125,000 voters turn out. Former Arkansas Governor Mike Huckabee won strongly, ahead of the big-spending former Massachusetts Governor Mitt Romney. Next came former Senator-turned-actor Fred Thompson, Senator John McCain, Congressman Ron Paul and former New York Mayor Rudy Giuliani, lagging far behind. The TV pundits were already asking, 'Can Huckabee turn his big win in Iowa into a serious national campaign for the Presidency? Has Rudy blundered in all but skipping Iowa in the last couple of months? Can Romney regroup and use his considerable resources to outspend and outlast the likes of Huckabee and Thompson? And what about John McCain – can he come back in New Hampshire?' The answers to at least some of those questions were just five days away.

5 Hard Yards in the Granite State

New Hampshire, January 2008: There are only about 1.2 million people in the state of New Hampshire, but every one of them will probably tell you they have a bigger influence over who becomes President of the United States than the folks in Iowa or anyplace else. I'm not going to argue; the Granite state's motto – *Live Free or Die* – looks a little intimidating under the *Welcome! Bienvenue! to New Hampshire* sign on Route 3.

When they say New Hampshire is 'independent-minded', they aren't kidding. It was New Hampshire that first declared itself an independent nation free of the yoke of England, on 5 January 1776, and even today more voters identify themselves as 'independent' than as either Republican or Democratic. They are also the only state not to charge a general sales tax or income tax – how the state manages to stay afloat financially is a mystery.

New Hampshire is voting unusually early this Presidential election year. It was compelled to change its primary date (because of a state law that insists that New Hampshire's ballot is at least seven days before anyone else's) after the rush of big states decided to make their primaries earlier. Florida and Michigan wanted a greater say in who would be the Presidential nominees, and so defied a party ruling banning them from voting in January. It didn't work out too well – the DNC ruled that Michigan and Florida would lose half their delegates. So New Hampshire's primary is now on 8 January – almost a month earlier than back in 2000. In that year, and again in 2004, there were eight days between the votes in Iowa and New Hampshire; this year there are just five. It's the smallest gap ever. The concern is, with more than half of the states in America now voting before 'Super Tuesday', which is 5 February, that the nomination for both parties could be wrapped up in just four weeks, when in past years that process has taken more than five months.

The size of Barack Obama's win in Iowa stunned his opponents and confounded the many pundits who said America's mid-western heartland wasn't ready for a black President. Now, just a few days later, a win for Obama in New Hampshire could amount to a second-round knockout of his rivals.

Jim Spencer has been involved with 'Getting Out The Vote' – GOTV – in every Presidential campaign since 1980. In 2004 he took over John Kerry's Iowa GOTV in December and turned a 26 per cent deficit to Howard Dean into an upset win for Kerry in January. Spencer runs his company, which specialises in direct-mail campaigning, out of a modest old house on a suburban Boston street with industrial bay views; probably, you suspect, so that he can continue to chainsmoke at his desk.

As a veteran in the field of GOTV, Spencer is clearly impressed with the number of new voters Obama was able to mobilise in Iowa.

Usually, he says, if they haven't been to caucus before they aren't likely to be going this time:

> What Barack Obama did this year is so incredible. Those friggin' talking heads on TV, they say all kinds of crap – they don't really know – but it was an incredible, incredible thing he did. It took massive organisation.

There hasn't been time to conduct much meaningful post-Iowa polling to see what kind of 'bounce' in support Obama has gained from the first-up win – generally success tends to breed success in these votes but there is evidence from at least one poll (from John Zogby, one of the best-known and most accurate election pollsters in the US) that Obama is rising fast and threatening to snatch this state, a state in which Hillary has long enjoyed a healthy lead. That Zogby poll has Obama surging to a 13 per cent lead over Clinton in New Hampshire. But success can also breed inflated expectations: if Obama doesn't do very well here, he could be seen as a flash in the pan.

Denis Kanin knows what it's like to take on a Clinton and win in New Hampshire, yet somehow lose the expectations game. He also knows that in this sort of campaigning, anything can happen. In 1992, Kanin was running the Presidential campaign for Paul Tsongas – a Greek-American former Massachusetts Senator and cancer survivor whose thyroidal eyes and hangdog face seemed to suggest that he was faintly amused by, yet possibly a little disappointed with, the silliness of big-time politics. 'By the time we got to New Hampshire, we had two main opponents: Bill Clinton and Bob Kerrey, the Senator from Nebraska,' Kanin says.

Governor Clinton of Arkansas was in big trouble. He was facing claims that he was a draft-dodger and the Gennifer Flowers affair had just become the first of several sex scandals that six years later would all but derail his Presidency. The Iowa caucus had been won by that state's 'favourite son', Senator Tom Harkin, whose overwhelming local support had largely nullified the significance of the first-to-vote contest, but Paul Tsongas managed to come a distant second – ahead of both Clinton and Kerrey, which gave his campaign a boost heading into New Hampshire.

Paul Tsongas was doing well in opinion polls, leading both Clinton and Kerrey, but then a freak accident interrupted his campaign at a crucial stage. 'Paul went into a factory,' Kanin explains, 'and he got a piece of wood in his eye – a splinter – and came down with conjunctivitis.'

The injury took Tsongas out of the Presidential campaign during the final days before the 18 February primary. 'You don't really want a guy with an eye that's all puffed up out on the campaign trail,' Kanin says. 'Meanwhile, Clinton was campaigning 24 hours a day.'

Tsongas appeared in one debate before the New Hampshire vote, his swollen eye fairly effectively concealed behind a pair of heavy-framed spectacles. 'People kept asking, "Why are you wearing glasses all of a sudden?",' Kanin says, 'and in the debate I think the glasses threw him off a little bit.'

Kanin admits that having a candidate who had survived cancer meant that any health problem in the campaign could be an unwelcome reminder to voters. 'It was in our mind that it might be seen as an issue – it wasn't, it had nothing to do with it, but perception is everything.'

The gap between the candidates in New Hampshire closed, and Clinton was able to finish a closer-than-expected second, with almost 25 per cent to Tsongas' 33 per cent. Clinton's campaign dubbed the Arkansas Governor 'the Comeback Kid', and a month later, on Super Tuesday, he swept the southern primary states, effectively wrapping up the Presidential nomination.

Tsongas dropped out of the race and endorsed Clinton. Just a few years after his Presidential run, his non-Hodgkins Lymphoma returned. Paul Tsongas died of pneumonia and liver failure at the age of 55 on 18 January 1997, two days before Bill Clinton was sworn in for his second term as President of the United States.

※

Driving through the town of Nashua, New Hampshire on this clear, cold Sunday morning in the second week of 2008, it's easy to see there's an election in just 48 hours – the freshly snow-ploughed streets are lined with large plastic yard signs: *Hillary* – *Obama* – *RUDY* – *McCain* – and a surprising number backing the fringe Libertarian Ron Paul, who is seen as the Republicans' answer to Dennis Kucinich. About half the surviving Presidential candidates from both parties are passing through town today or tomorrow.

We're heading to a Hillary event at a local school gymnasium. At a roundabout up the road, a burly grey-haired man in a Hillary T-shirt over thermal underwear is holding two homemade-looking banners on sticks with coloured-in pictures of a smiling Hillary. He and a middle-aged woman are arguing with local police, who have ordered a tow-truck to move cars that are partially blocking the road to the school – the cop says Senator Clinton's bus won't be able to get past.

We decide to go the rest of the way up the road to the school on foot, despite being unfamiliar with walking on icy asphalt. Suddenly, the *Hillary New Hampshire* campaign bus roars by with *Time to Pick a President* written along its side – a reference to that old line of Governor Sununu's about Iowa picking corn and New Hampshire picking the President. Four large, dark SUVs with tinted windows and flashing police lights on the back luggage shelf follow the bus – one of them is likely to contain Senator Clinton, but for security reasons you aren't supposed to know which one. A second and third chartered bus full of the travelling press brings up the rear of the motorcade.

Outside the school gym at Nashua High School North, just as Hillary is arriving, California couple Joey Hughes and Judy Miller are leaving – there's no more room, they say, and they've decided to go and see Obama instead. The white-bearded Hughes says they've come to New Hampshire from Mill Valley near San Francisco because 'there's no way that you can get so close to candidates' in their home state. 'This morning we went to an event and we saw Gravel, Richardson and the Republican from South California, Duncan Hunter, so in one place you can go and see all that.'

It turns out they aren't letting any more media into the gymnasium either, so along with a few hundred others we're ushered into a second gym off to the side of the main hall where Hillary is now starting to speak. Her straining voice is being piped in through the PA as we all stand around an empty basketball court not quite knowing what to focus our eyes on. It's a bit like old-style radio – we all stare intently at the speaker on the wall. Word comes from Hillary's campaign staff that she'll pay us a visit later, but it seems silly to have come all the way from Australia to see the candidates only to be sent into an adjoining room, so we decide to sneak in the back way.

It's astonishing that for all the security surrounding Presidential candidates like Clinton, and the endless forms you have to fill out to get formal media accreditation and Secret Service clearance for every single campaign appearance, you can often just walk into the press area if you have something that looks vaguely like a press pass, a camera and microphone. This is a little surprising given how much a shotgun microphone can look like, well, a shotgun. A similar thought had occurred to me back at the Iowa State Fair in August as I sat on the grass about a metre from the very expensively shod feet of Rudy Giuliani. It was quite unsettling at the time, and I started to look around suspiciously, wondering if there were any potential assassins or backpack bombers in the crowd. Then I started to worry that by looking around suspiciously and even thinking about such things I might get dragged away by some men in dark sunglasses. Or maybe

I'd been programmed by some other guys in dark sunglasses to kill the candidate! … Maybe I shouldn't have watched *The Manchurian Candidate* on the flight over.

Inside the hangar-like gymnasium, Hillary seems to be in a feisty mood. She's striding around the stage in front of an enormous American flag – it must be 10 metres high – and seeming to punctuate every syllable with a karate chop of the hand. She's trying to debunk the notion that Obama is the 'change' candidate in this race, and reinforce the idea that *she's* the one who is ready to lead. 'We want a President who can go to work on the first day,' she tells the excited crowd, 'and face the problems that we will inherit from the failed Presidency of George Bush.'

If that's not making the point clear enough, sprinkled in among the *Hillary* signs in the audience are one-word placards reading *READY*. The event is going much longer than expected. Hillary takes more questions than usual, and gives long answers, pulling out all the stops – trying to convince everyone in the room, and everyone who will see the clips of her on tonight's news, that she is the one with the solutions to America's problems.

As promised, Hillary makes her way over to the basketball court to greet the people who didn't make it inside the main gym. After portable security barriers are erected and the Secret Service have scanned the room and checked the exits, Hillary Clinton appears. She's saying 'Hi' and 'Thank you' a lot and people crowd to get near her. Some want autographs for their cardboard *Hillary* signs; others are taking snaps with their mobile phone cameras, bending awkwardly, trying to get themselves and Senator Clinton in the same shot.

A man next to our camera tells Hillary to 'hang tough' after her loss in Iowa, and she replies with feeling, 'We have to, there's a lot at stake.' A girl of about five or six asks if the candidate can sign her $5 note, and Hillary says, 'Oh, I can't sign money, that's against the law, but I can sign another bit of paper, darling.'

There is something schoolmarmish about the way she says it, but the girl seems happy with the arrangement. As Hillary walks away the girl's father says, 'Awesome, huh?'

'Yeah!' the little girl agrees enthusiastically.

Later, shuffling out of the school, it's a bit like leaving a cinema – you hear snatches of different critiques of what people just saw: 'She's great,' one woman says, and, 'Yeah, I liked her,' another woman agrees, but a man who may have been her husband says, 'She was a little angry.'

Heading back to the car we come across the burly grey-haired guy with the two *Hillary* banners – still standing in the snow in the middle of the roundabout.

His name is Edward Kimmel, and he tells us he's a lawyer from Tacoma Park, Maryland and he's been standing out here in the snow for about three hours. Mr Kimmel says he looks back fondly on 'the Clinton years' and would like to see a return to that era of relative prosperity. 'When George W. Bush came in, the issue was what to do with a trillion-dollar surplus – the government was in better shape than it ever has been … and I want that back.'

A passing pickup honks its horn encouragingly at Mr Kimmel and he waves his banners back at it with equal gusto. Despite having campaigned for both of the Clintons over the years, and worked as what he calls a 'tiny little guy' in the 3600-person Clinton Administration in the 1990s, Edward Kimmel says he also likes the look of Obama: 'I really like him – I sent Obama money for his Senate campaign and if he gets the nomination I'll make some Obama signs, but I would rather have Hillary.'

The other Democrat needing a win in New Hampshire is Senator John Edwards. His campaign itinerary for the day before the primary illustrates the crazy-busy schedule these Presidential hopefuls and their spouses endure:

7 January 2008:

02.00 am:	'Graniteroots' (Grassroots in the Granite State) event, John and Elizabeth Edwards, campaign office, Berlin, NH.
04.00 am:	'Graniteroots' event, John and Elizabeth Edwards, Miller's Café, Littleton, NH.
06.35 am:	Breakfast with John and Elizabeth at the Daddypops Tumble Inn Diner, Claremont, NH.
10.45 am:	Senator Edwards, Town Hall meeting, Lakeport, NH.
11.30 am:	Elizabeth Edwards, House Party, Nashua, NH.
13.45 pm:	House Party with John and Elizabeth Edwards, Bedford, NH.
15.55 pm:	Senator Edwards event, Hampton, NH.
16.00 pm:	House Party with Elizabeth Edwards, Exeter, NH.
19.15 pm:	Rally with John and Elizabeth in Dover, NH.
21.20 pm:	'Graniteroots' event with John and Elizabeth Edwards, Somersworth, NH.
22.15 pm:	'Graniteroots' with John and Elizabeth Edwards, Rochester, NH.
23.25 pm:	House Party with John and Elizabeth Edwards, Durham, NH.

We caught up with Elizabeth Edwards in the middle of this non-stop, no-sleep 36-hour campaign sweep. She's at a House Party at the home of the Haskell family in Nashua, New Hampshire, imploring the 30 or so people present to do everything they can to drum up support for her husband: 'You're going to see people in your neighbourhoods … you all have phones, so I want you to use them.'

Everyone in the house, including Mrs Edwards, is standing or sitting in their socks so they don't traipse frozen mud over the carpets. She points to the group of reporters by the stairs leading to the Haskells' basement and says, 'John is in this for the long haul – but it sure makes it easier not to have these press people on his case if he has a great showing here [New Hampshire]!'

Elizabeth Edwards clearly has a deep understanding of policy issues and is said to be one of her husband's closest political advisers. A former lawyer and sometime substitute teacher, she's very comfortable speaking to large and small groups alike and taking plenty of questions from voters and the press. Mrs Edwards has incredible energy – it's hard to believe she is living with incurable breast cancer.

Also at the Haskells' house today to lend his support and celebrity to the Edwards campaign is *Desperate Housewives* star James Denton. Unlike some TV actors, who only seem to have turned up on the campaign trail since the Hollywood writers' strike put most productions on indefinite hold in late 2007, Denton has been speaking at Edwards events in New Hampshire and Iowa for months. He's not alone among familiar faces from TV, the movies and the music industry appearing on behalf of candidates during the campaign. Among others, actor Sean Penn has been hosting fundraisers and campaigning for Dennis Kucinich and ageing tough-guy Chuck Norris has been stumping for Republican Mike Huckabee.

At the Haskells' house party, Denton talks about the writers' strike and the fact that John Edwards is the only Presidential candidate to have joined their picket line in Hollywood. 'In this campaign I was so delighted to find someone who was brilliant and had guts,' Denton says, 'and someone who will take on the lobbyists and entrenched interests in Washington – and it just so happens her husband is running for President!' Everyone laughs at the compliment to Elizabeth Edwards, and the comment underscores the fact that she is possibly the most popular of the candidate-spouses, and her 'ordinariness' helps humanise Senator Edwards – an otherwise potentially too perfect Central Casting candidate.

I remember something Professor Dave Redlawsk had said on a blistering hot day back at the Iowa State Fair last year when I was wondering if it was possible for a Presidential candidate like Edwards or Mitt Romney to be too good-looking:

Americans like to think they could sit down and have a beer with the candidate. We want Presidents with gravitas, we want Presidents who can look and play the role, who can be taken seriously, but we don't want them too much above ourselves … There's a real contradiction: we want them to be better than us, but we don't want them to be *too* much better than us.

But as popular as the likes of James Denton might be with the soccer mom set, Oprah Winfrey's endorsement of Barack Obama and her ability to introduce him to her millions of daily viewers has arguably made her the most significant celebrity to give an endorsement since Sinatra's Rat Pack, including Shirley MacLaine, in 1960.

In December 2007, Oprah appeared at a rally for Obama in at the Verizon Arena in Manchester, New Hampshire, drawing 6000 screaming fans – it was more like a Beatles concert than a political rally, and it was the largest of its kind that anyone could remember. Oprah told the fired-up crowd:

> People ask me, 'Why are you doing this?' I feel now is the time for me to use my voice and say, 'If we're going to choose, we only get one choice for President – and that choice ought to be Barack Obama.'

She then sat on stage with Senator Obama's wife Michelle as Barack Obama delivered a speech outlining his plans for change in America; for ending the war in Iraq and 'fixing' healthcare. According to Obama, overhauling a healthcare system with almost 50 million people uninsured and many more under-insured is very personal to him:

> My mother died of ovarian cancer at 53. In those last months she wasn't thinking about getting well, she was reading insurance forms because the insurance company was saying maybe it was a pre-existing condition and we don't have to reimburse you. I was furious when I saw that happen.

Like the death of Joe Biden's wife and daughter, the death of John and Elizabeth Edwards' son and Elizabeth Edwards' battle with breast cancer, the death of Barack Obama's mom comes up in speeches and debates as a formative event that has helped shape his candidacy – it's important to have a reason they want to be President that is about more than just a power trip. Healthcare has become a key issue, with all Democrats supporting various forms of health insurance for most if not all, and Republicans condemning 'socialised medicine' while acknowledging that something needs to be done to fix the current system.

⚐⚐⚐

It's the afternoon before the New Hampshire primary. There is a bandstand right in the middle of the intersection of Front and Water streets in the old town of Exeter. The quaint rotunda has red and green Christmas stockings hung around the railings and fake ivy twisted candy-cane style up the columns. Inside, a man in his sixties, wearing a natty driving cap and tweed jacket, along with five male friends of various ages, walk around in a small circle holding *McCAIN* signs as if they're on a picket line. They've been rehearsing a pro-McCain spiel for any camera that comes along, and we get the full treatment. 'OK guys, I'll start off,' the man in the cap says. 'I'm John and I'm from Illinois and I live with John McCain and I want to know that … [they all join in] McCAIN WINS! – We believe that – McCAIN WINS! – good for America if – McCAIN WINS! – Roger that – McCAIN WINS!'

Hang on – did that old guy in the cap just say he lives with John McCain? Does Mrs McCain know about this?

No time to investigate further; the candidate is going to start speaking at the Town Hall just down Front Street in a few minutes, and I have a pressing issue to address. Like all travellers, especially those who spend a lot of time outside in temperatures around –10ºC, finding public toilets, or 'restrooms', becomes quite a preoccupation on the campaign trail; so does finding a decent coffee anywhere in the continental US. Sadly, the 5-gallon buckets of brown water with whipped cream and cinnamon on top that pass for a coffee hereabouts also hasten the need for the next restroom. It's a vicious cycle, and right now I'm in fairly urgent need of a 'rest'. Fortunately there's a coffee shop over the road from the Nashua Town Hall – unfortunately, it has a coffee-related pun name like 'Java-Nice-Day!' In my experience, nothing good ever comes from an establishment with a pun name.

However, the coffee shop not only has a restroom, it also has free WiFi (wireless networking), which is handy for checking emails and finding out what's happening in the rest of the world. So I go inside, place my order, take a seat and log on. It turns out a lot of the news is coming from here in Exeter, New Hampshire anyway – all of it falls into the innocuous 'this candidate says this and that about Iraq/the economy/healthcare' category. Every table seems to be occupied by a reporter with a laptop and mobile phone working overtime to file more copy or sound-bites. The last time Exeter made this much news was in September 1965, when a number of locals, including two policemen, claimed to have seen a UFO just outside town. It's a wonder Kucinich isn't campaigning here.

As I sit in the overheated café refilling my bladder from a vat of coffee you could high-dive into, potential First Lady Cindy McCain walks in with a bunch of men wearing very pricey-looking overcoats. I haven't made a detailed study of overcoat prices, but you somehow instinctively know when you are looking at one that costs more than you take home in a year. It appears they're here for the same reason I am – Mrs McCain needs a 'rest'. It's little wonder diners in the US advertise themselves as having 'the cleanest bathrooms in [insert town name here]' rather than boasting about their coffee.

At 53, Cindy McCain somehow manages to look both a lot older and a lot younger than she is. It's a strange effect. She's a natural beauty with unnaturally blonde hair and unnaturally smooth young skin. Cindy McCain is a former Rodeo Queen and cheerleader; she also has a masters in Special Education and is a philanthropist – she's the daughter of Jim Hensley, founder of the $300-million-a-year Hensley & Co. Arizona beer distribution empire. Hensley helped bankroll McCain's early political career. Cindy McCain is on the record as saying she'd like to be a more 'traditional' style of First Lady – one who does not sit in on Cabinet meetings. Right now she just wants to sit in on a loo, but there's a queue. Public toilets present one of the purer forms of egalitarianism: 'I don't care if you got $500 million and are married to the man who may be the next President of the United States – wait your damn turn, lady.'

A big crowd is gathering on the footpath outside the Exeter Town Hall to hear John McCain speak. It's only about 5.30 pm, but already it's quite dark. TV lights are trained on the front steps of the brownstone building, which looks as if it belongs to the neo-classical school of mid-19th century American architecture – all white columns and arched windows. There are fairy lights in the bare winter trees along Front Street, and thick snow piled along the roadside, giving the scene a festive air. You almost expect Santa to turn up, not a Presidential candidate. But John McCain is far from jolly in this campaign; he's made a point of telling some 'hard truths' about government only being able to do so much to help people, and the US needing to 'stay the course' in Iraq. He's pledged to continue his straight talk even if it costs him votes – but of course the real aim is to win votes by saying he's prepared to lose votes. This political reverse psychology worked a treat in New Hampshire back in 2000 when 'straight talking' John McCain beat George W. Bush in the primary, but that win only provoked a counterpunch that left McCain on the canvas in South Carolina.

Tonight the hand-painted red and blue signs proclaim *Mac is Back* – and so is the belief that he can be a serious contender in the Republican race. McCain has managed to regroup from the dark days of last summer when the candidate was carrying his own bags in economy class after the campaign money all but ran out.

We set up on the riser at the back of the crowd and hook up our wireless audio unit to the 'splitter box' which provides a sound feed from the microphone on stage to our camera, wherever we may move it. Some of the other TV and radio reporters are frowning as they twiddle with switches turning the audio from mono to stereo then from a 'line feed' to a 'mic feed'. There's a problem with the sound: it's badly distorted and buzzing intermittently. Everything through the microphone McCain is about to speak into comes out like a sci-fi movie robot voice. The reporter from National Public Radio suggests to the sound technician that he might like to try and fix it in a real hurry or the candidate is going to be on the news tonight sounding like an extra from *Plan Nine from Outer Space*. Maybe it's an Exeter UFO thing. The technician frowns and twiddles with the same switches we all tried, frowns some more, then disappears. He isn't seen again.

Meanwhile, Senator John McCain has been introduced by a former party chairwoman who says, 'John McCain has the courage – BRRUUUUUZZZZ – and most importantly, the experience – FFTHHHHHHHHHTTT – to not only manage, but lead our great country in difficult times – BRUUUUUUUUZZZZZ-FFFFTHUTTT!!'

Just in time, we realise that the interference is only in the left channel of the two-channel sound feed, so we shut it off. Problem solved.

John McCain appears, dressed in a dark blue blazer, grey trousers and a red sweater over a light blue shirt. This is the 100th Town Hall meeting he's addressed in New Hampshire this election campaign. McCain has the round-shouldered nuggetty hunch of a bulldog as he moves stiffly around the stage, and he comes out swinging, too, criticising better financed rivals such as Rudy Giuliani for not engaging in retail politics:

We've gone to the Town Hall meetings, we've gone to the diners and restaurants and stores and we've done what the people of New Hampshire expect you to do, and that's to see them face to face and talk to them and let them talk to you and give you their ideas and thoughts and dreams and aspirations … and we're going to prove, my friends, that you cannot buy an election in the state of New Hampshire!

The crowd of several hundred gives McCain a rousing cheer. He continues:

You know, the state's motto is 'Live Free or Die' … well we're up against an enemy in Al Qaeda whose motto may well be 'Live my way or die' … and, my friends, I will get Osama bin Laden if I have to follow him to the gates of hell, and I will do it and I will bring him to justice!

Somewhere nearby a police siren starts up – a few people laugh, apparently thinking, 'Wow, that was quick work bringing in Osama!'

McCain talks some more about the need to keep taking the fight to Al Qaeda in Iraq so that terror isn't revisited on the US, and pledges to see the war through to victory. The success of the Iraq troop 'surge' has coincided with a surge in support for McCain, and he remains the most vocal supporter of the Bush Administration's policy in Iraq under General David Petraeus.

As McCain leaves the stage on the steps of Exeter Town Hall, the sound system blares out Chuck Berry's hit *Johnny Be Goode*: 'Go-go, go Johnny go!' Far from running from the issue of age, it seems McCain is happy to be seen as something of a throwback to the Cold War Eisenhower era of the 1950s.

The next morning finds us back in Nashua. It's New Hampshire primary day and it's unseasonably warm and sunny – well above zero. The piled-up snow is starting to turn to mush, but the warmer weather is good news for voter turnout: it means there should be high numbers, particularly among older voters, who tend to stay inside when it's cold.

The Nashua Presidential campaign office for Senator John Edwards is just an ordinary shop front in a run-down retail district – the kind of place you might expect to find a laundromat or second-hand clothing store. The office is buzzing with campaign workers and volunteers, some on the phone making calls to potential Edwards voters, others standing around waiting to be assigned a street to doorknock. A few more are hovering around a desk with boxes of donuts and someone's homemade chocolate log cake.

The walls are covered with maps of the electoral precincts in Nashua, and the place feels as if a military operation is underway. Groups of two or three campaign volunteers are being sent out with signs and leaflets, plus clipboards with lists of addresses to visit to encourage people to go and vote. If needed, the Edwards volunteers can phone back to the campaign office and arrange lifts to the polling place – some volunteers are spending the day driving around the neighbourhood like pizza deliverers. And today they're trying to deliver as many votes as they can.

A guy named Matt seems to be the ranking officer in the Edwards Army here in Nashua. He wears a baseball cap and has a beard, and looks like a youngish film director – which may be deliberate, or may just represent two weeks without the time to shave. Matt twirls a pen in his fingers in a dexterous but nervous way and calls out instructions to the volunteers: 'I want to switch Eric and Cathy up … and get the Morats and – sorry, what's your name?' It's Pat. 'OK the Morats and Pat up to 19 and 20 and let's get something else for Eric and Cathy,' he says, stabbing at one of the area maps with his pen.

In the back of the room, dozens of phone calls are taking place at once: 'Hi, I'm calling for John Edwards – have you voted today? Do you need a ride to vote? Does Senator Edwards still have your support?' 'Hi, I'm calling for John Edwards ...'

Matt gives a new volunteer – a woman in her fifties wearing a blue parka – the 60-second rundown on election day campaigning: 'So, basically you go straight down Main Street ... we're asking people – especially if they're undecided – to vote for John Edwards today.' She nods, and Matt continues. 'We're delivering a positive, persuasive message about John Edwards. We have this script about what the momentum and success in this state means, but you're welcome to talk about what brought you, personally, out today. Talk to as many people as you can.' With that, she's given a clipboard with her list of addresses and she heads out the door into the bright sunshine, dropping her pen on the way.

Mary Perry is a nurse from nearby Exeter. She was driving home from night shift at the local hospital and decided to drop into the Edwards Nashua office to see if she could help out. 'I said, "Put me to work, 'cos I'm exhausted", [but] I think he's the only guy who can beat McCain.' Mary says healthcare is an important issue – neither of her adult children can afford it. Just like Robert Ford in Iowa, she says she would have supported Dennis Kucinich ahead of Edwards – she agrees most with his politics – but doesn't think Kucinich can win.

Harry Standel is a strongly built man in his sixties from Milford, New Hampshire. He's sitting at a desk working his way through a list of voters who have indicated to earlier callers that they are leaning toward John Edwards. He's using his own mobile phone to make the calls, and is laughing heartily as he hangs up from a conversation with one potential voter: 'He says he's a Republican and he already has health insurance!'

At the glass-topped desk at the front of the office, almost hidden behind donut boxes, another volunteer, Angela DeLauro, seems to be getting a lot of answering machines – there's every chance the registered Democratic voters of New Hampshire are screening their calls today, given that most have been getting several calls a day from the various campaigns for the past few months.

Finally Angela gets someone to pick up, but they say they've switched their support from Edwards to Bill Richardson. In almost a whisper, amid the noisy chatter of the crowded campaign office, Angela politely asks what it was about Richardson they were attracted to. They say they like his healthcare policy. Determined to win this vote back, Angela says John Edwards is the only candidate in favour of free, universal healthcare, and was the first to come up with a healthcare policy. They talk about healthcare and the war in Iraq for another five minutes or so; Angela explains that Edwards is the only candidate committed to a timeline for withdrawing American troops from Iraq. They talk some more and Angela changes tack, suggesting that Bill Richardson is likely to end his campaign after today and that while he's a good candidate he won't be a viable contender, whereas Edwards, she says, is the only one who is electable – 'Right now in the polls the only Democrat who beats McCain, Giuliani, Romney and Huckabee is John Edwards.' The voter says they'll think it over and maybe they will reconsider voting for Edwards instead of Richardson. Angela hangs up with a loud 'Phew!' but raises her eyebrows; she's not sure her marathon phone call made much of a difference.

The John Edwards New Hampshire primary election night party is to be held in an old mill building in Manchester. The significance is lost on nobody – the former trial lawyer and multimillionaire has talked up his working-class roots often, by speaking about his father Wallace working in a textile mill in North Carolina. John Edwards himself swept floors there during the summertime. The Tower Mills building down on Bedford Street, near the Merrimack River, is just a big empty space these days; its milling days are over. New Hampshire's mills used to turn a sizeable proportion of the cotton grown in the south into textiles which were exported around the world, but that era is long gone. The remnants of the old industry remain – you'll find the headquarters of Velcro over on Brown Avenue – but mostly the mills are being converted into function centres, performance spaces or apartments, or just knocked down.

As the polls close, hundreds of Edwards supporters gather in the low-ceilinged space where the massive looms used to grind away. A lot of them have union sloppy-joes on, and there are more beer drinkers than wine sippers here tonight. As the first results start to appear on the plasma TVs hung on the bare brick walls, Edwards' campaign manager, former Congressman David Bonior, takes the stage to thank the crowd: 'The effort that was put out by each and every one of you, the door-knocking, the phone-calling, the envelope-stuffing – was absolutely amazing. Just in the last two weeks, a quarter of a million phone calls [were] made.'

More speeches follow, including another one from James Denton from *Desperate Housewives*. But despite the back-slapping and the thankyous, the numbers on the dozen or more TVs around the room aren't encouraging: at the moment, Edwards is coming a distant third, with Clinton leading Obama. The music gets cranked up, the beer is flowing and someone has started handing out small American flags on sticks. Soon the crowd is cheering, swaying and waving in time with U2's 'In the Name of Love'.

More results flash up on the TV screens, and it becomes clear that it's a two-horse race between Clinton and Obama, and Edwards just isn't in the running tonight. The crowd gets angry at the TV networks because they are only showing graphics with the numbers for Hillary and Obama on the Democratic side, whereas they have numbers for the top three Republicans. 'They're pushing us out of the race!' As the final results are posted, Hillary Clinton has defied the opinion polls and recovered from her setback in Iowa to win New Hampshire with 39 per cent of the vote. Obama has 36.4 per cent, Edwards 16.9 and Bill Richardson 4.6.

Elizabeth Edwards appears to a huge cheer, and talks about how as President, John Edwards will look after workers and make sure the world is a better place for their children. 'The goal is still in sight,' she says, 'and that goal is to make our next President John Edwards!' Another ear-shattering cheer as her husband appears from backstage, smiling and shaking hands. John Mellencamp's 'This Is Our Country' plays the Senator onto the podium: 'The dream is still alive, some day it will come true, and this country belongs to folks like me and you …'

'Last week I congratulated Senator Obama when he won Iowa and I came second – one state down,' Edwards says. 'Tonight I congratulate Senator Clinton – two states down, but 48 to go.' The crowd starts chanting, 'EDWARDS! EDWARDS! EDWARDS! EDWARDS!' Senator Edwards beams. 'Ninety-nine per cent of Americans have not yet voted, and those 99 per cent deserve to have their voices heard.'

John Edwards knows that candidates who have been written off by the pundits can still come back into contention. Case in point; Republican John McCain.

Back in Nashua, McCain's celebrating a 5.5 per cent win in New Hampshire over his nearest rival, Mitt Romney. Those 100 Town Hall meetings have paid off. Mac *is* back, after his fourth place showing in Iowa. The McCain party is at the swish Crowne Plaza Hotel, but by the time we get there, at 12.30 am, it seems well and truly over. As Edwards noted, there's still a long way to go and candidates are going to need their rest.

Postscript: On 30 January 2008, following a disappointing third place finish in his home state of South Carolina, Senator John Edwards announced that he was leaving the contest for the Democratic Party's Presidential nomination – after almost five years of non-stop campaigning over two Presidential elections, and raising $52 million for his 2008 bid. On 14 May 2008 he endorsed Senator Obama with a reprieve of his own campaign theme: 'There is one man who knows in his heart that it is time to create one America, not two … and that man is Barack Obama.'

On New Hampshire primary night Governor Bill Richardson vowed to continue the race for the Democratic Party's Presidential nomination, but two days later he announced that he was dropping out. He had managed to raise about $22 million in campaign funds and had come fourth in both Iowa and New Hampshire. On 21 March 2008 Governor Richardson endorsed Barack Obama for President, describing him as 'an extraordinary American' who 'will make a great and historic President'. The Clintons were stunned, and reportedly felt betrayed that someone who had long been a political ally would endorse Hillary's rival.

On 25 January 2008 Congressman Dennis Kucinich abandoned his Presidential campaign after being excluded from yet another candidate debate in Nevada and facing a well-financed challenge to his preselection back in Cleveland. Kucinich had raised just over $4.5 million for his Presidential campaign, including contributions of $2300 from Larry Flynt, founder of Hustler magazine, and actor Woody Harrelson, who played Flynt in the film The People vs. Larry Flynt. Actor Michael Douglas gave Kucinich $2300, as did Sean Penn and his wife Robin Wright-Penn, and singer Willie Nelson chipped in $2100. On 4 March 2008 the diminutive vegan Kucinich survived a challenge from four other Democrats, including the owner of a local steak restaurant, and retained preselection to seek re-election to the Tenth Congressional district of Ohio in the US Congress in November 2008.

George McGovern's Dog

We fly into Sioux Falls, South Dakota and drive west for about an hour, across flat, snow-covered prairies, to the town of Mitchell. We are here to meet Senator George McGovern – the man who, perhaps more than anyone else, determined the way the Democratic Party chooses its Presidential candidate, and who, as a candidate for the White House himself, campaigned on a promise to end the war in Vietnam.

The downtown area of Mitchell seems full of boarded-up shops and shabby cocktail bars with darkened 1950s neon signs that are either switched off or broken. Mitchell is also the unlikely home of the McGovern Centre and Library at the Dakota Wesleyan University. It's a unique museum in that the star of the exhibit, 1972 Democratic Presidential nominee Senator George McGovern, is there himself some days, among the interactive audiovisual displays and faded campaign posters and buttons. That's when McGovern's not working for the UN on food programs, writing books on global politics, out on the campaign trail supporting Democratic candidates or, as he'll do the next day, heading someplace like Puerto Rico to escape the eyeball-hurting −20°C cold of winter in South Dakota.

The campus of Dakota Wesleyan is, it turns out, a fitting place for the McGovern Centre; it was here that he studied, and later taught history, after distinguished service in World War II and a brief career as a Methodist Minister.

At 85, George McGovern doesn't look all that different from how he looked at 49, when he ran for the White House against President Richard M. Nixon – that's one advantage of going bald early. McGovern looks fit and tanned and has teeth that may once have been as expensive as those of any of today's candidates. I look closely at his top lip, and I'll be damned, Shirley MacLaine's dad was right, it is a little stiff, as if he's taken a shot of Novocain that hasn't quite worn off.

Senator McGovern arrives for our interview in his clubby, old-fashioned office wearing a suit jacket, a striped blue business shirt and a red tie over denim jeans and white tennis shoes. McGovern's big black Newfoundland dog is with him. The dog follows him around the library and into his office, never more than a metre or so from his side, her large head bumping gently against his leg. The Senator says the dog's name is Ursa, which he explains is Russian for 'bear'. At 14, Ursa is old for a 'Newfie' and nearly blind: her deep cow-eyes are becoming milky from cataracts.

As Rebecca sets up the camera, lights and lapel microphones for our interview, she remarks on what a gentle nature Ursa has for such a large animal. McGovern agrees, saying that Newfoundlands are generally lovely dogs – in fact the only 'Newfie' he knew that wasn't nice belonged to his friend, the late Senator Robert F. Kennedy. 'He'd try to bite people … Bobby had 11 children and I think that dog was harassed from morning to night by all those little kids. They were trying to ride him … it spoiled his disposition.' It was Robert Kennedy who said, 'George McGovern is the most decent man in the US Senate.' That was just two months before Kennedy was killed.

McGovern sips coffee bought from the university cafeteria and feeds his dog bits of a muffin. Clearly he stays slim by giving most of his breakfast to Ursa. I ask him how the Presidential candidate selection process came to be the way it is now, with each state electing delegates who in turn vote for the nominee at the party's National Convention. It hasn't always been this way. Not so long ago, the primary elections had little impact on who the delegates would vote in as nominee; it was all done behind closed doors.

McGovern explains. The current nominating system has its origins back in 1968, when the incumbent Democratic President, Lyndon Baines Johnson, was seeking re-election. This was at the height of the Vietnam War. Unusually, he faced a challenge for the Presidential nomination from within his own party: from anti-war candidate Senator Eugene McCarthy, and later from Senator Bobby Kennedy:

> The so-called establishment of the Democratic Party was still backing
> Lyndon Johnson and the war. And yet McCarthy and Kennedy had
> a strong following across the country. I don't think they had enough
> strength to win the nomination, but they had enough that they wanted
> to be heard at the Democratic National Convention – they wanted to
> have something to say about the platform.

Gene McCarthy finished just 7 per cent behind President Johnson in the New Hampshire primary in March 1968. LBJ was shaken, and made a televised address to the nation:

> With America's sons in the fields far away, with America's future under
> challenge here at home, with our hopes and the world's hopes for peace
> in the balance every day, I do not believe I should devote an hour or a

day of my time to any personal partisan causes or to any duties other than the awesome duties of this office – the Presidency of your country. Accordingly, I shall not seek, nor will I accept, the nomination of my party for another term as your President.

But even with Lyndon Johnson giving up on re-election in 1968, the President and the old guard of the Democratic Party weren't giving up on deciding who their nominee would be – they wanted Vice President Hubert H. Humphrey, who was still a supporter of the Vietnam War effort, even though Humphrey was not standing in the primary elections against Robert Kennedy and Eugene McCarthy.

In June 1968 Robert Kennedy won the Democratic primary in California and became a serious chance to win the party's Presidential nomination. After making his victory speech at the Los Angeles Ambassador Hotel, Kennedy was shot in the head by a 24-year-old Palestinian named Sirhan Sirhan as he made his way out through the hotel kitchen. Bobby Kennedy died the next day at The Good Samaritan Hospital.

The Democrats held their National Convention at the International Amphitheatre in Chicago just two and a half months later. America was still coming to terms with a second Kennedy assassination, and the earlier assassination of Civil Rights leader Dr Martin Luther King Jr, which added racial violence to a nation already wracked by massive anti-war protests.

In the weeks leading up to the conference, Bobby Kennedy's delegates decided to back 'decent' George McGovern for the Presidential nomination, even though it was clear that pro-war Hubert Humphrey would win.

George McGovern describes the scene in Chicago in late August 1968 as things turned ugly:

> There were thousands of people outside the convention halls who had come from all over the country ... who had worked hard for Gene

McCarthy and Robert Kennedy and me ... but they were excluded from the convention because the delegates had already been picked – and without very much democracy: they were largely picked by the powers that be who identified with the war.

Under the old rules that existed then, practically all the delegates to the national convention were picked in back rooms by Governors, by political leaders in the state, without much input from the Kennedy and McCarthy insurgents.

The frustrations of the anti-war demonstrators outside the amphitheatre, including high-profile 'Yippies' Abbie Hoffman and Jerry Rubin, boiled over:

> I was watching most of it from across the street in the fourth floor of the hotel I was staying at. I saw the clashes in the street between the young anti-war protesters and the Chicago police and in a way I kind of felt sorry for both of them; these policemen were young people too and they felt they were doing their duty, trying to preserve order. They resented these equally young people who were out in the streets shouting slogans and waving banners and pushing and shoving.

The demonstrations and violence intensified over the next few days. So too did the police response ordered by party boss, Chicago Mayor Richard Daley. Tear gas was deployed and there were numerous beatings. Barricades and barbed wire greeted delegates as they tried to enter the convention hall.

When Senator Abe Ribicoff nominated George McGovern for President at the convention in 1968 he said, 'With George McGovern as President of the United States we wouldn't have Gestapo tactics in the streets of Chicago.' Mayor Daley, who was supporting Humphrey, was seen to angrily shake his fist at Senator Ribicoff and utter a string of expletives.

Despite it all, the party bosses had made sure that pro-war Vice President Humphrey had the delegate votes to defeat both McGovern and McCarthy. Hubert Humphrey would be the nominee – and would go on to lose a close election to former Vice President Nixon in November.

Bob Shrum is perhaps the best known Democratic strategist and speechwriter of the last 40 years. He ran Al Gore's ill-fated 2000 Presidential campaign and was also brought in to preside over John Kerry's unsuccessful 2004 White House bid. I spoke to him in early 2008 about 1968 and the way the nominating system was changed:

> In 1968 there was a widespread perception that the political bosses had ignored the primary voters and gone off and nominated Hubert Humphrey. The irony of that is that if Robert Kennedy had not been killed, Mayor Daley and a number of the political bosses would have moved towards him ... and you might have had an anti-war nominee – in fact I think he would have been nominated.
>
> Big events in history have big consequences ... certainly 1968 was a year where there was a profound sense of anger.

Shrum said that had Bobby Kennedy lived and been nominated, the party would never have changed the nominating system to the way it is today. So the anti-war and reform movements at the Democratic Convention of 1968 did have one significant victory – a commission was established to change the way the delegates were chosen and, as a result, the way the nominee was chosen. Senator McGovern, it was decided, would preside as its chairman:

> There weren't very many women at that convention, there weren't very many young people, or black people, or brown people or yellow people ... it was largely white middle-class middle-aged males ... I'm not against people like that – I was a white middle-class middle-aged

male myself – but they shouldn't dominate everything and that was the problem at that '68 convention.

Our interview with Senator George McGovern is a year and a day after the death of his wife Eleanor. As Rebecca changes the camera tape, he takes a sip of his cooling coffee and tells us how Eleanor had slipped and fallen on the ice in front of their house just over the street from the library. McGovern was out of town speaking at a political convention, and Eleanor had to crawl up their steps in the dark and into their house with a badly broken leg. She couldn't reach up to the phone but managed to drag a blanket off the bed and lie on the floor. Ursa, he says, wrapped herself around Eleanor to keep her warm and stayed right there curled up on the floor with her for 24 hours until McGovern came home. 'Good girl, Ursa,' he says and lightly pats her head.

We're rolling tape again. Ursa lumbers back behind McGovern's chair, circles, then settles.

The commission's reforms meant that the days of exclusively white male party elders gathering in smoke-filled rooms to choose the candidate from among themselves were over. Now, so the idea went, a group of democratically elected and demographically representative people from around the country would decide the nominee. But while the delegates elected in the primary and caucus votes would dominate, there would still be a sizeable group of party officials and office-holders who would be entitled to back the candidate of their choice – these are the so-called Super Delegates, who were to prove decisive in the close-run 2008 nominating contest between Obama and Clinton.

I wanted to know whether while redesigning the process for selecting his party's Presidential candidate, George McGovern was – as some have claimed – mindful of the fact that he wanted to run for the Presidency again in 1972.

'We didn't go in there to draft rules that would help nominate

George McGovern four years hence,' he says. 'That may have been one of the by-products of it – that it made it easier for a reform candidate to win – but that wasn't our purpose.' I believe him, but I'm also aware that I am speaking to a man whose greatest political asset was his aura of integrity and believability.

Heading into the 1972 primary contest to see who would take on Republican President Richard M. Nixon, McGovern was up against a wide field of Democrat hopefuls, including Gene McCarthy again, Henry 'Scoop' Jackson, and the 1968 Vice Presidential nominee and establishment favourite Edmund Muskie. It was widely expected that Hubert Humphrey would run, this time being forced to contest the primaries. It was also believed that if Senator Edward Kennedy entered the race, the nomination would probably be his. But early on, it was Senator Muskie who emerged as the favourite of the party – and the voters.

In mid-1971, as the campaigning for the primary season got underway, most polls gave George McGovern only about 5 per cent support and he wasn't given much hope of winning the nomination, much less the Presidency. But he had a straightforward plan. The key, McGovern says, was in a grassroots campaign:

> We'd go door to door, farm to farm, factory to factory, business place
> to business place, recruiting people at churches, at the universities,
> the Labor Halls … we got them mobilised in a way that had never
> happened before.

It worked. In the Iowa Caucus vote of 1972 McGovern finished a surprise second:

> I didn't win in Iowa – Ed Muskie did, and he was favoured to win the

nomination – but I came in much stronger than anyone suspected, so people in the press wrote stories like 'George McGovern in an amazingly strong second place showing'. It was almost as though it was better to be second than first!

Perception was everything, and the perception was that the Muskie campaign was under-performing and the candidate was under pressure.

As the New Hampshire primary approached in March 1972, the influential local paper *The Manchester Union Leader* printed a letter which claimed that Muskie had laughed at offensive remarks about French Canadians. The so-called Canuck letter had the potential to lose Muskie votes among New Englanders of French-Canadian descent. The *Union Leader* also printed a series of stories suggesting that Muskie's wife Jane was a drinker who used foul language on the campaign trail. Muskie decided to confront the paper in front of their editorial offices on a Saturday morning just 10 days before the primary election, addressing his remarks to the assembled press pack from the back of a flatbed truck.

What happened next has gone down in the history of Presidential campaign politics, and would have a distinct echo in the 2008 primary season. Senator Muskie was standing out in the open with snow falling heavily onto his bare head and shoulders. He angrily condemned the paper's owner, William Loeb, for these attacks on him and his family:

> By attacking me, by attacking my wife, he has proved himself to be a gutless coward. And maybe I said all I should on it … it's fortunate on this platform beside me. A good woman …

At this point Muskie's voice broke and several reporters observed the candidate shedding tears. McGovern says:

You know Ed was about 6 foot 4 and 250 pounds, a big athletic guy with a shock of thick hair that I always envied, and he had a big burly overcoat on because it was snowing and he looked huge, and I think that perhaps [there was] a tear or two. He always said it was snow melting, but wouldn't you cry if your wife was being assailed by somebody and you couldn't do anything about it?

The story became that Muskie had cracked under the pressure, the implication being that he wasn't emotionally strong or controlled enough to be President of the United States:

With tears streaming down his face and his voice choked with emotion, Sen. Edmund Muskie (D-Maine) stood in the snow outside the *Manchester Union Leader* this morning and accused its publisher of making vicious attacks on him and his wife, Jane. (David Broder, *The Washington Post*, 27 February 1972)

Fifteen years later, Broder wrote a column in the *Washington Post* in which he admitted to having doubts about the accuracy of his report, saying the question of whether Muskie really shed tears still 'nags' him.

Either way, McGovern doesn't think the reports of tears cost Muskie votes in the primary or the Presidential nomination. He says it was just a convenient narrative for the press to run with:

I think what happened was that the press, who had been widely predicting a Muskie win, had to come up with something to save their own predictive skins. After Ed broke down because of this newspaper publisher who was attacking his wife – and Ed was tired, as we all were at that stage; he may have shed a tear or two or it may have been snow melting on his face, as he said – we found in the next few days he actually went *up* in the polls.

Bob Shrum recalls, 'Muskie didn't convey a sense of mission to people

… McGovern was out there and he was saying, "If you want to end the war vote for me" … He had a sense of mission.'

Ed Muskie's campaign soon faltered, amid more signs of a candidate under pressure and his failure to meet the high expectations of supporters and the media. Muskie withdrew from the race in April, midway through the primary season. George McGovern won 11 state primaries in 1972 and enough delegates to defeat Hubert Humphrey for the Democratic Party presidential nomination. And McGovern's grassroots primary and caucus campaign became the template for other candidates to follow, from Jimmy Carter to Barack Obama.

But Harvard's Professor Tom Patterson told me he's not convinced that McGovern's reforms changed the process of selecting candidates for the better: it required candidates to go directly to the voters for their support, and Patterson says the unintended consequence of empowering the voters was to further empower the press:

> As they began to go to the voters and make their case, then the media
> as an intermediary stepped in. And the media's role has been an
> important part of nominating politics ever since that change, which
> began in 1972.

Tom Patterson believes the senior members of the parties would still prefer things to be the way they were before McGovern's reforms and be able to pick their own candidate:

> But that's a genie you can't put back into the bottle in American
> politics … I think American voters are accustomed to having a role in
> the nominating process and they're going to demand it, and the parties
> realise that.

Heading into the Democratic Party National Convention in Miami in July 1972, George McGovern's top advisers were confident that

Ted Kennedy would accept an invitation to be his Vice Presidential running mate. But Teddy again said no – as did other potential Vice Presidential candidates, including Senator Hubert Humphrey, Senator Walter Mondale and Georgia Governor Jimmy Carter (who had headed the 'Anybody-But-McGovern' movement). According to Jody Powell, Governor Carter's Press Secretary, 'the Democratic nominating process in 1972 was bitter and divisive ... and there was not a great deal of sentiment from any of the sides to say, "Let's all come together."'

George McGovern may have won the support of 1729 delegates from around the country – more than three times the number of delegate votes for his nearest rival – but he hadn't convinced senior members of his own party that his policies should be the Democrat's policies, or that he could beat Nixon.

'Governor Carter represented much more the centrist wing of his party,' Jody Powell says, 'and George McGovern – who I always thought was more moderate and centrist than he came across at that particular time – was seen as representing more one end [the left or 'liberal' end] of the spectrum.'

Bob Shrum agrees that McGovern wasn't nearly as extreme in his views as some believed:

There were a lot of people who were utterly resistant to him – who thought he was too radical. But I think back, and his radicalism consisted of – let's end the war in Vietnam, let's protect a woman's right to choose, and let's reform the tax system and lower rates and close loopholes – which Reagan did in 1986.

The nominating convention, which was supposed to be McGovern's crowning moment, descended into farce. Ballots for the Vice Presidential nominee included votes for anti-war demonstrator Jerry Rubin, high-profile reporter Roger Mudd ... and even Chairman Mao Zedong of China received one vote. Lengthy debates, speeches and political jockeying were all part of the general chaos played out in front of a live TV audience. So much for putting the mayhem of the 1968 Chicago convention behind them.

Among the many Vice Presidential nominees was Senator Mike Gravel of Alaska, who came third, with 266 votes. But finally, at 1.51 am on 14 July 1972, the Vice Presidential nomination fell to Thomas F. Eagleton, a little-known anti-Vietnam War Senator from Missouri. But it was so late at night that just about everybody watching the democratic mayhem on TV had gone to sleep and missed it.

So the Democratic Party's team of McGovern–Eagleton would take on Nixon–Agnew for the White House. But there was a problem: because Tom Eagleton was so far down the list of potential Vice Presidential candidates, he hadn't gone through the customary vetting process.

A few days later, in an otherwise positive profile piece, the *St Louis Post–Dispatch* reported that Eagleton 'has been troubled with gastric disturbances, which have led to occasional hospitalisations. The stomach troubles have contributed to rumours that he had a drinking problem.'

The national press pounced, repeating the 'rumours' about Eagleton's hospital admissions, and reporters began following anonymous tip-offs about his psychiatric history as well.

On 25 July 1972 Eagleton and McGovern called a joint media conference in Custer, South Dakota, and the Vice Presidential candidate disclosed that he had voluntarily hospitalised himself three times between 1960 and 1966 for 'nervous exhaustion and fatigue'. Reporters pressed the issue and Eagleton admitted that while in hospital, he'd twice received electro-shock therapy for depression.

At the time McGovern said, 'I think Tom Eagleton is fully fit in mind, body and spirit to be the Vice President of the United States and, if necessary, to take on the Presidency at a moment's notice.' Eagleton also offered to take a psychiatric examination, if all the other candidates running in 1972, including President Nixon, did the same.

In the days that followed, George McGovern stated that he was '1000 per cent' behind Eagleton. But the 'Eagleton Affair', as it had become known, continued to dominate the headlines, and just 18 days after the Miami convention, Tom Eagleton was dumped from the Democrats' Presidential ticket and replaced by Sargent Shriver. McGovern's perceived indecisiveness in the face of this 'crisis' had planted a seed of doubt in the minds of American voters.

Patrick J. Buchanan has a fairly unique perspective on the election of 1972, and on presidential politics in general. He was an adviser and speechwriter in Richard Nixon's Republican White House (1969–74). He also served in the Reagan White House (1981–89) and then ran for the Presidency himself three times – 1992, 1996 and 2000. In between he has been one of the most outspoken conservative political commentators in the US.

These days Pat Buchanan lives in a large white house in Arlington, Virginia, very close to the headquarters of the CIA. We speak in his dark wood-panelled living room, which is filled with books. The shelves also carry a collection of miniature busts – Confederate Civil War Generals, Stalin, Lenin, even a small Richard Nixon carved out of wood. There is a large painting of Buchanan himself campaigning in Iowa hung over the fireplace.

In 1972 it was Pat Buchanan who went through reams of newspaper clippings to find anything they could use against their Democratic Presidential rival, George McGovern:

I did the research on Senator McGovern at the behest of the President [Nixon] ... we had what was known as the '9.15 group' [the time they met each morning in the office of Chief White House Counsel Charles 'Tex' Colson], which later became known as the 'attack group'.

Buchanan explains that their objective in the campaign was to shift the focus away from President Nixon and onto the challenger:

> What did we want people thinking going into the voting booth in 1972? Did we want them thinking what a swell guy Richard Nixon is? No, a lot of people didn't think he was a swell guy. What you wanted them thinking was, 'We cannot have George McGovern in the White House.'

Buchanan uncovered quotes where McGovern had likened Nixon to Hitler and fed those quotes to amenable members of the press, who in turn demanded that McGovern apologise. They also arranged for political allies such as Republican Senator Bob Dole, who would later make two unsuccessful White House bids of his own, to make speeches attacking McGovern for wanting to make cuts to the military and close bases.

The 'attack group' managed to portray McGovern as being in favour of abortion on demand, the legalisation of hard drugs and a get out of jail free 'amnesty' for draft-dodgers.

'It was devastating,' McGovern says, shaking his head:

> I didn't realise at the time how effective they were. They picked out three things and pounded them day and night on TV radio and direct mail. 'He's for drugs, he's for abortion, he's for amnesty for soldiers' ... They called me the 'Triple A' candidate – Acid, Abortion and Amnesty ... I didn't think people would pay any attention to it but that was a miscalculation.

George McGovern, who had earned the Distinguished Flying Cross as the heroic pilot of a B-24 Liberator bomber in World War II, was now seen by many Americans as a free-love radical peacenik. McGovern's actual positions were more conservative and nuanced; he felt abortion should remain a state issue, that drug possession should be a misdemeanour, not a criminal offence, and that if you took the moral stand to refuse to serve in the military you should be prepared to go to prison while the war continued.

In 1972 the conservative columnist Robert Novak reported that the damaging description of McGovern as being in favour of 'Acid, Amnesty and Abortion' actually came from an 'unnamed Democratic Senator'; this person's identity would remain a mystery for decades.

After his death in 2007, it was reported that Tom Eagleton was in fact that unnamed Democrat Senator. Months before he was nominated for the Vice Presidency, he had come up with the line that was used to such devastating effect against his former running mate. 'That's what Bob Novak said. He said it was the first time he heard it [the phrase],' McGovern says. 'I don't know. I never discussed it with Tom Eagleton or any Senator, so I don't know where it came from.'

McGovern failed to effectively respond to the distortion of his policies and the attack on his character in much the same way fellow Democratic Senator and Presidential candidate John Kerry didn't respond to the 'Swift Boat' claims made in the 2004 campaign that he'd exaggerated his heroism. He says:

> Here you had John Kerry, twice injured in Vietnam, decorated for his leadership as a Lieutenant, and a wonderful war record. And he's attacked for his patriotism by two guys who were draft-dodgers – Bush and Cheney never had a day in combat – the nerve of that! A couple of draft-dodgers! But John Kerry made the same mistake I did in not jumping down their throats on those charges.

McGovern sighs: 'Maybe I put too much faith in the common sense of voters … I think I've had the tendency to do that sometimes in my career.'

McGovern–Shriver won just 39 per cent of the vote in November 1972 and carried only one state – Massachusetts – along with the District of Columbia. For the liberal wing of the Democratic Party and the anti-Vietnam War movement, it was a disaster. President Richard Nixon was triumphant.

Pat Buchanan's eyes twinkle at the memory. 'It was a very successful campaign. Unfortunately, a lot of my friends went to prison!' he chuckles. 'I guess it was because the things some of the boys were doing were a little overly enthusiastic about our cause.'

Those 'overly enthusiastic things' in the campaign against McGovern included the break-in at the offices of the Democratic National Committee in the Watergate Building in Washington DC on 17 June 1972 and the subsequent White House cover-up, and a plot to fire-bomb the Brookings Institution, a left-leaning thinktank.

Bob Shrum started 1972 working for Ed Muskie, but finished the year on George McGovern's campaign. 'It was painful to lose 49 states,' Shrum says, 'but getting to the White House wasn't worth the price of going to jail – so I would rather have been on the McGovern side than the Nixon side.'

Several senior members of the White House staff, including Nixon's two top aides, Bob Haldeman and John Ehrlichman, and Chief of Staff 'Tex' Colson, were indicted, convicted and sent to jail over the Watergate affair; Pat Buchanan was not. President Nixon himself resigned from office in August 1974 to avoid impeachment, and was pardoned less than a month later by his successor, President Gerald R. Ford.

As we sit in his lounge room all these years later, I ask Buchanan if he thinks George McGovern would have been such a bad President. He responds:

> McGovern is a good man personally; I've come to know him. But George McGovern was a very, very liberal candidate – the most left-wing candidate ever nominated in American politics for a major party. And this was a battle for the White House – for the control of the most powerful office on earth and it was a cause for all of us.

McGovern laughs wryly:

> Pat Buchanan and I have talked about this in the years since '72, and
> we've become more or less friends – not intimate friends, but I think
> we have a mutual respect for the other person as an individual – and
> Pat's gotten more mature, and maybe I have too.

McGovern says he felt vindicated when the Nixon Administration
was brought down, in part, by the excesses of their campaign against
him:

> I'd been warning against the bad conduct of the Nixon
> Administration: I warned against the implications of the Watergate
> break-in, I warned against everything they had done that I thought
> was illegal and improper. And so I drew some satisfaction out of
> the impeachment and resignation of President Nixon.

McGovern wasn't the only target of the Nixon White House. Some
months after the 'Muskie cry speech' it was revealed that the so-
called Canuck letter that helped to so unsettle Ed Muskie was a
forgery that came from the Committee to Re-Elect The President
– CREEP – a private organisation with deep links to the Nixon
White House which was later found to have been involved in a wide
range of anti-Democrat campaign dirty tricks, including the fabri-
cation of a number of potentially damaging letters.

Reflecting on the events of that time, the disappointment in
McGovern's voice is still profound. 'It's too bad that we lost in '72, it
really is. That could have been a turning point in American history.'
His regret is sincere and devoid of bitterness. Yet while McGovern's
passivity in the face of defeat may have helped him live a more
fulfilling life since, I wonder if something about that personality
trait may have in fact contributed to his loss.

Thirty-six years later, McGovern's 1972 Texas campaign co-ordinator, Hillary Rodham Clinton, was at a coffee shop in Plymouth, New Hampshire, running for the Presidency herself, when a supporter asked her how she was coping with the daily pressures of the campaign.

Sitting at a table, with microphone in hand, Hillary Clinton replied quietly, 'It's not easy, it's not easy, and I couldn't do it if I didn't passionately believe that it was the right thing to do.' She looked up, took a deep breath and paused before continuing in a weary tone, 'You know I've had so many opportunities from this country ...'

She shook her head before resting it in her left hand. Voice quivering slightly and eyes welling with tears, she said, 'I just don't want to see us fall backwards ... You know, this is very personal for me; it's not just political, it's not just public. I see what's happening and we have to reverse it.'

The press immediately compared Clinton's New Hampshire tears (or well-up) to Muskie's New Hampshire tears (or melting snow). She's cracking up, they said, she's cynically playing the 'gender card' to soften her image.

But McGovern believes that as with Muskie, the show of emotion probably helped Clinton win in New Hampshire, and he telephoned her to tell her so. 'She'd been working for months to win the nomination and then it falls through out there in Iowa,' McGovern says. 'It showed she's a human being – not a crass, hard, aggressive person without feelings. She's just like the rest of us and things disappoint her. I didn't think it hurt her a bit and I told her that.'

Utica, New York is almost 400 km northwest of New York City on Interstate 90. They used to call this part of the northeast of the US the 'manufacturing belt' or the 'steel belt'; now it's generally known as the 'rust belt'. Once this town of about 60,000 people was known as the 'Radio Capital of the World', thanks to the big General Electric plant, but it's gone now and so are most of the other big factories. When the work dried up, lots of people left – in the late 1980s there were bumper stickers saying, 'Would the last person to leave Utica turn out the lights?' Utica is the kind of place people come from, not go to – unless, like John Zogby, you never left.

Zogby, the founder of Zogby International, the polling company, was born and raised in Utica, and these days he employs many of the men and women he grew up with – Zogby International is among the biggest employers in town. The company has gained a reputation for being one of the most accurate predictors of elections in America … with a few notable exceptions, the 2008 New Hampshire primary among them – what happened to Obama's 13 per cent lead?

The office of Zogby International on Broad Street in Utica is in a converted factory building. The large one-time machine rooms suit the open-plan office – there are dozens of work stations with computers, telephones and headsets, and Zogby pollsters are calling people in places like South Carolina and Florida who will be voting in primaries in the next few weeks. There is an unusual variety of employees working the phones, from college kids to men and women who look well past retirement age, all asking distant, unseen voters questions like: 'Which of the following best sums up your political ideology – Libertarian …'

John Zogby himself is a shortish, solidly built man in his late fifties with curly greying hair and a light-olive complexion which shows his Lebanese-American background. His office feels like a large study in a suburban home – ill-matching furniture, a bit out of date and chipped, and shelves lined with hundreds of books about politics, politicians, and the war – all with pages marked with post-its. Zogby is wearing a brown jacket with no tie and he's seated in a black leather wingback chair that's almost taller than he is. His desk is cluttered with books, papers, diaries, a Blackberry, pens, a letter-opener, framed photos, a baseball, a banker's lamp, a PC, a pewter camel, a Batman figurine and several coffee mugs – one with a brass bell in it. It looks like the office of both a student and a professor.

We set the camera rolling and I ask Zogby what just happened in Iowa and New Hampshire – in particular why most of the polls, including his, got the Democrats' result in New Hampshire so wrong. It's become the big news story in the few days since Hillary's upset win, but Zogby isn't prepared to concede that they got it entirely wrong. 'We got Obama right, we got Edwards right, we got Richardson right – all we didn't get was Hillary Clinton.' The unseen variable in New Hampshire, John Zogby says, was the number of older women who turned out to vote for Hillary.

His secretary comes in to remind him that he has a radio interview to do. Zogby asks if Monica can get him another cup of coffee – then points out, 'for the record', that he usually gets his own coffee.

The phone interview is with Dennis Miller – the *Saturday Night Live* stand-up comedian turned conservative radio talkshow host. Zogby explains with a smile that Miller is going to be 'a real a—hole'.

As he's waiting on the phone, Zogby admits that there's no question they missed something in New Hampshire, but that political pundits in the media have blamed the pollsters for their own premature predictions. 'I think that the pundits were reprehensible this time: Hillary was inevitable in Iowa – URRRRNNNKKK!!!!' Zogby says, simulating a 'wrong' buzzer in a game show. 'Barack Obama was the reincarnation of Jack Kennedy … no,' he says, shaking his head. 'They're going to have to work for this one,' he predicts.

The voters in New Hampshire, Zogby believes, looked at the polls after Iowa, and heard the predictions that Obama had it wrapped up, and then decided that the race wasn't over just because the media commentators said it was.

He's on the air – 'Hey Dennis, how are you?' – Miller's first question takes about a minute and has Zogby chuckling politely, wondering when he'll get to speak.

Zogby then explains to Miller that their polling showed Hillary suddenly regaining her lead in New Hampshire the night before the primary, but it happened between 4 pm and 9 pm, after their polling for the rest of the day had showed Obama still in front. They didn't know what to do with the aberrant last-minute data, so they discounted it. But in retrospect, Zogby believes Hillary's tears may have made the difference, swinging back voters, particularly older females. 'Those tears, or almost-tears, were enough to suggest that this may be the only shot in our lifetime for a woman to become President of the United States,' Zogby tells Miller's audience.

When we spoke to Republican pollster and strategist Dr Whit Ayers a few days later, just outside Washington DC, he generally agreed with Zogby's assessment:

> It looked like if Barack Obama won the New Hampshire primary after having won the Iowa caucuses, he would be unstoppable. And there were apparently a number of women who felt Hillary deserved more of a chance, so they gave her that chance.

There are plenty of Democrats weighing up what sort of history they'd like to make first. Back in Mitchell, South Dakota, George McGovern explains why he endorsed Hillary's Presidential campaign:

> I'd like to see Hillary break the gender barrier that has kept any woman from ever becoming President, and then eight years from now I'd like to see Barack Obama break the racial barrier that has prevented a black person from ever reaching the White House. I hope I live that long, I'd like to see that.

We leave his office with his dog Ursa in tow and head into the McGovern Museum for a personal tour through the exhibition based on the Senator's life. As George McGovern points out various pictures and displays, he expresses confidence that whoever wins the Democratic Party nomination will become America's next President. And surprisingly, for someone supporting Clinton's campaign, McGovern has high praise for Obama:

> I admire Barack Obama very much. I think he has the makings of another Abraham Lincoln – and not just because he comes from Springfield [Illinois], as Lincoln did, but because he has some of the same capacity to tap deep moral and spiritual principles and to make them politically acceptable.

Not surprisingly, when I ask Pat Buchanan his view of Obama, it's somewhat different. Like many conservative commentators, Buchanan is prone to exaggerate Obama's admissions of having experimented with drugs during college, and to downplay his résumé:

> Look, we've got a 14 trillion dollar economy, we are involved in a number of wars [he starts chuckling], and we have a community organiser from south Chicago who is one step away from the Presidency of the United States [more laughter], with a bad drug problem in his past!

And at this Pat Buchanan laughs so hard that tears appear in his eyes – at least that's what I saw.

Postscript: The results in the Caucus in Iowa and the Primary in New Hampshire set the pattern for the 2008 Democratic nominating contest

– Barack Obama pulling ahead, only to see Hillary Clinton fight back. The race continued past the predicted end on Super Tuesday, with Obama winning more pledged delegates thanks to a run of 11 state victories in February.

In May, Senator McGovern made a phone call from South Dakota to Bill Clinton, who was campaigning for his wife in West Virginia, telling the former President that he was switching his support to Barack Obama and calling on Hillary Clinton to drop out of the race. McGovern told President Clinton he didn't want a repeat of 1972, when the race continued all the way to the convention and damaged the party's chances in the Presidential poll.

After McGovern's change of endorsement, a number of other senior Democratic Party figures – many of them with 'Super delegate' voting status at the Convention – announced that they too were changing their allegiance to Obama.

Follow the Money

It's a cold winter night in Wellesley, Massachusetts, just beyond suburban Boston. We're near the US$40,000-a-year (and that's just the fees) Wellesley College for girls, which for generations has been attended by the well-bred daughters of the rich and influential and the very bright girls from less advantaged backgrounds, including a certain Hillary Rodham, now Clinton.

We have been (kind of) invited to a cocktail party being held for the Governor of the neighbouring state of New Hampshire, John Lynch. The host this evening is an early-forties venture capitalist and his elegant Asian-American wife. Their house deserves a better title than 'house' – it isn't as gauche as a 'mansion' although that's probably what a real estate agent would call it. The exterior is largely obscured by the dark of this winter's evening and the tall snow-laden trees in the front garden, but the scale of the windows and front door alone says this is the dwelling of seriously well-to-do people.

We're here on something of a blind date with 'friends of friends' who had heard that a couple of Australian journalists were in town making a film and writing a book about American politics. They thought we might like to see another side of retail politics: the hands-on reality of raising the millions of dollars a year that every politician, not just Presidential candidates, needs to fund their election campaigns. I feel suddenly self-conscious – in this imposing residence in Wellesley, our travellers' wardrobe of blue jeans, black jumpers and now-damp parkas make us look more like the gardeners than the guests, but we are warmly welcomed by our hostess just the same. She takes our jackets, which have served us well in the bitter cold of Iowa and South Dakota, and piles them on a bed in the front room on top of cashmere and fur overcoats which would never be seen in Des Moines.

There are 30 to 40 people gathered in a large open-plan dining and lounge area, which is tastefully furnished in a classical style but with discreet hi-tech touches. A silver console on the lamp table next to the deep, richly upholstered sofa suggests you can probably open the garage door, water the back lawn and buy and sell entire companies at the press of a button.

Our 'friends of friends' aren't here yet, so we position ourselves near the kitchen door to get first dibs on the canapés as they arrive on silver trays carried by what seem to be about 50 waiters. These are no party pies and footy franks – they are nouvelle cuisine works of art, each so delicately arranged that I can't help but reduce them to mush as I clumsily pick them off the tray. As Rebecca and I down fistfuls of mini lobster crepes, Beluga blinis and sashimi-god-knows-what, we chat to a lawyer named Barry who tells us he's from New Hampshire and thought he'd drive down to Boston tonight and meet the Governor of his home state.

Because this is a 'social gathering' in a private house we were politely told it wouldn't be appropriate for us to pull out our camera and start filming, but we soon find that the 'off the record' background we get from Barry and others is invaluable. Barry often goes to these sorts of cocktail parties for politicians and typically pitches in a few hundred dollars as a campaign contribution.

I wanted to know how major campaigns for the Presidency or the Governorship of a state can raise tens, even hundreds of millions of dollars when the law says any individual can only give a maximum of $2300 to a candidate.

'Bundlers,' Barry says.

Bundlers are people who go around collecting up to $2300 from a whole lot of individuals. Maybe those individuals host fundraisers, he says, gesturing around the room; more often they go from door to door in major corporations, asking lots of individuals to make contributions. Barry explains that often those 'bundles' are just a way for the companies themselves and their wealthy owners to get around campaign finance limits.

For instance, Barry says, if you work for a big New York law firm and the head of that firm wants to support a particular candidate, and maybe they also want to get some business out of that candidate, they will let it be known to their staff that this is the candidate they should support. So, when the 'bundler' comes around seeking contributions, everyone in the law firm knows they should write a personal cheque for the maximum $2300. 'Do the math,' Barry says, 'a hundred lawyers – that's almost a quarter of a million dollars right there.'

'Not coincidentally,' Barry goes on, 'come the end of the year and time for the annual bonus from the law firm, everyone who gave to the preferred candidate will have an extra $2300 in their pay cheque … and then some.'

Barry says if that candidate is elected, the law firm that bundled together the quarter of a million dollars can expect to get extra business and more – maybe the heads of the firm will find themselves on the shortlist for Attorney General or an Ambassadorship, or just be on the guest list for these sorts of cocktail parties – but at the White House.

Bundlers have only really been needed since a ban on so-called soft money contributions came into effect with the McCain–Feingold Bill in 2002. That ended the era of wealthy individuals making as many large contributions to political parties as they wanted. Senator John McCain's co-sponsoring of that Campaign Finance Reform Bill with Democrat Senator Russ Feingold is just one of the reasons McCain has been unpopular with some members of his own party. The law was challenged by groups as diverse as the National Rifle Association and the AFL-CIO (the largest federation of unions in the US) and the case went all the way to the US Supreme Court. The court ultimately determined that the Bill, which also banned soft-money contributions in the form of issue advertisements which effectively supported particular candidates, was *not* unconstitutional, but it also ruled that the ban on minors making campaign contributions *was* unconstitutional.

Our friends-of-friends, Rick and Alicia, arrive, and we immediately have that warm reassuring feeling that these are 'our kind of people'. We introduce them to Barry and get to know each other over generous glasses of Californian pinot noir served in the kind of oversized stemware I've only ever seen in expensive restaurants. Soon Rick and Barry are talking about which college they went to and people they may both know, and swapping business cards.

Governor John Lynch and his wife Susan have arrived and are being methodically introduced to each of the party guests: 'Governor and Mrs Lynch, I'd like you to meet Mark Farber, he's a business associate of my husband.' 'Glad to know you, Mark.' From nowhere an official photographer appears and snaps the Governor, Mrs Lynch and Mark – chances are, within a week the picture will be framed on Mark's office wall.

The Governor is small and wiry, with the sort of tense beaky features and prominent Adam's apple the political cartoonists in New

Hampshire must love. Rebecca and I are introduced to Governor Lynch and I detect a slight wince when it's explained that we are journalists. 'Oh, how interesting,' he says, in a way that suggests he is not at all interested. Before anything more is said he's shaking my hand again like an old friend and smiling as the camera flash goes off, and he's being introduced to someone else. I wasn't offered a copy of the photo.

The formalities over, the host clears his throat and welcomes everyone to his home. He introduces New Hampshire's First Lady, who talks about her husband's achievements since his election in 2004. John Lynch must be doing something right – he's one of the most popular governors in the country, winning re-election in 2006 with over 73 per cent of the vote and holding similar approval ratings in opinion polls now.

Governor Lynch talks about what he's done to rebuild New Hampshire's economy: the state's tax system is attractive for companies as well as individuals, and tells the business and legal elite of Massachusetts that they can do business in his state, just a short drive up Interstate 93.

It's a quirk of New Hampshire politics that their governors face re-election every two years, not four, so for John Lynch it's a never-ending campaign – as soon as you win one election you're looking ahead to the next. That's why on a night like this, with cashed-up business people in the room he has to ask them for money. To an outsider it's a little unsettling to see the leader of a state telling people he needs their support – not their vote, but their money. It feels tacky, yet most of the party-goers have already written out a cheque.

Events like this cocktail party in Wellesley are just one of the ways politicians in the US today raise the money they need to pay for all the direct mail, TV and radio ads involved in a modern campaign.

Fundraising has become a huge part of the job, and it's something former Senator and Presidential candidate George McGovern says is damaging government at all levels:

> The average Senator in the United States now spends two days out of every week, once they're elected, raising money for the next election. Two days out of every week! And most of them hate it – it takes them away from their work, and they have less time for the problems of their state.

And those Senators are elected for six years, not two, like Governor Lynch. Not only does McGovern think that raising money distracts a candidate and adds to their level of fatigue on the campaign trail; the money also comes with strings attached:

> Absolutely you have to worry about big money in politics. I don't care how saintly a candidate is, when you're scooping up money by the millions, [building] huge campaign war chests, you're indebting yourself to people who didn't give you that money because they like the way you part your hair! They think that there is something in it for them other than just good government.

Former Senator and Presidential candidate Mike Gravel agrees – and manages a dig at a rival in the process. 'Obama raised $195,000 from UBS bank. The head of the bank raised the money – that's a foreign-owned bank. Isn't that interesting?'

It's not just Obama raking in money from Wall Street. According to compulsory declarations made to the Federal Electoral Commission, the agency charged with monitoring the candidates' campaign finances, as well as running elections, in the first three months of 2007, Obama topped the list of money-makers with $479,209 from employees of New York investment banks. Rudy Giuliani came a close second with $473,442, Hillary Clinton did OK too, with $447,625, and John

Edwards successfully put the hat around for $193.250. Typically these 'bundles' of money are channelled through a Political Action Committee – PAC – which has been set up to support a particular candidate.

I ask Mike Gravel what all of that money buys. 'It buys influence,' Gravel says simply. 'It buys influence.'

Tim Hagan is a Commissioner of Cuyahoga County, Ohio. The position of Commissioner is part of a system of government dating back to England in the 1700s, when the King would appoint three Commissioners to run each 'county'. Cuyahoga, centred on Cleveland, is the biggest county in the state, with a population of about 1.3 million people. Hagan was one of the first party officials to endorse his friend Ted Kennedy in Kennedy's failed 1980 White House bid. Since then he has had a chequered political career himself – he served on the Cuyahoga County Commission through much of the 1980s and 1990s, and ran (unsuccessfully) for Mayor of Cleveland in 1989 and Governor of Ohio in 2002. But Tim Hagan remains one of the party elders whose endorsement can be crucial to any candidate's chances of winning votes in Cleveland and, more broadly, the potentially decisive swing state of Ohio, which determined the 2004 Presidential election.

Most of the Democratic Presidential aspirants have been around to Hagan's office in the past few months trying to woo his support. 'Bill Richardson came by and said, "I've been told I have to kiss your ass",' Hagan laughs. It didn't work, though; Hagan says he's backing Barack Obama. But according to the Commissioner, no amount of local support or endorsements can win you an election if you don't have money – and lots of it. 'Every election is more expensive than the last one,' he says, holding his hands in front of his face as if in prayer, 'and money is the mother's milk of politics and also a corrupting influence on the political process in this country.'

'Money is corrupting on both sides – Democrat and Republican,' he continues. 'They willingly accept the kind of cash that is put into these campaigns and cannot deny there is an influence – just the access to the candidate helps shape the public policy discussion.' The massive amounts of money given by lobbyists for the current healthcare system, which excludes more than 40 million Americans, is an example of that, Hagan says.

George McGovern says plenty of powerful interests are very happy with the current arrangement. 'A lot of people want it done the way it is now; they find this present system just fine. When they go to a fundraiser and write a cheque they think that's great.'

There has been a push towards public financing of elections in the US in recent years. The Fair Elections Now Act seeks to extend to the Senate a taxpayer-funded system which has been trialled at local and state levels. Some public financing is also available to Presidential candidates, but it comes in the form of limited 'matching funds' to top up your coffers, and there are restrictions on how much money you spend and where you spend it.

'In the old days,' Pat Buchanan laughs, 'Nixon's finance guy could call up businessmen and say, "You're down for $50,000" .... that was in the pre-Watergate days.'

The 1972 Watergate scandal, which was in part about donations to the Republican Party that financed the dirty tricks campaign against McGovern, saw the start of the movement towards campaign finance reform and public financing. But while many candidates pay lip service to the idea of public funding, the potentially bigger pots of private money are hard to resist.

'Think of the hypocrisy,' Senator Mike Gravel says of his Presidential rivals. 'Everybody is *for* public financing – they could do that right now and up until the November election, but do you see anybody doing that? Heck no!' Senator Obama drew criticism after winning the Democratic nomination in June 2008 by announcing that he was opting out of what he called the 'broken system' of public financing, despite having previously voiced his support for it in principle.

And according to George McGovern, the big donors don't want

public financing either:

> They fear it will diminish their influence – which it does … There are
> lots of people that I have known in politics, and they expect you to
> toe the line when they've given you these huge sums of money – so I
> personally think we should scrap this present system of raising money
> and it should all be public funds.

There seem to be plenty of ordinary voters who are concerned about
the way US Presidential campaigns are financed too. Harry Standel,
the John Edwards supporter from Milford, New Hampshire whom
we met the day of the primary in Nashua, said it's his top issue of
concern:

> So long as large corporations are allowed to effectively elect our
> representatives – including the President – they are beholden to those
> corporations and not the people: they are the people who get the face-
> time and the issues that are before us are not addressed.

Speaking in the sonorous voice that seems to belong to a sportscaster
rather than the construction firm president that he is, Standel had
said that corporate influence has permeated all levels of public policy
in America: 'The fact that we don't have an energy policy at this point
– Exxon-Mobile made $46 billion last year, the largest profit of any
corporation in the history of the US – is just unconscionable.'

John Edwards made a virtue of the fact that he hadn't accepted any
contributions from lobbyists in his 2008 White House bid, although
his critics point out that he has no such qualms about taking lots of
money from Wall Street financiers and trial lawyers. And that money
is essential to any modern American political campaign, none more
so than Presidential campaigns. In 2007 the 19 candidates seeking
to become the 44th President of the United States raised more than
half a billion dollars between them before a single vote was cast, and

they spent it just as fast. On average, about 40 per cent was spent on administrative costs – things like staff salaries, travel expenses, rents on campaign offices, transport and hire of equipment ($1.8 million alone was spent on food). The next biggest ticket item – at almost 30 per cent of total campaign expenditure, valuing $228 million – was spent on media, of which the vast majority (about 75 per cent) went on television advertising.

'Money speaks in American politics in a way it does in very few systems,' Professor Tom Patterson from Harvard told me, 'and it's not the general amount of money, but where it is coming from and who gets it.' Furthermore, he says the money has become something of an entry fee for would-be Presidents. 'We don't necessarily select the candidate who is most qualified,' he says, 'we narrow our question of those qualified to those who can raise enough money to compete effectively.'

Bob Shrum agrees it's a big problem: 'If I could change the system in one way – and it won't happen – there would be complete public funding and a level playing field. But it's not going to occur.' He says there are too many powerful interests with too much to lose from reducing the cost of elections. 'The Republican Party is ideologically opposed to it,' Shrum says, 'and there are a lot of Democrats opposed to it, and the television stations wouldn't like it at all.'

In Presidential elections, the public financing is capped at $45 million per candidate. In 2008, six of the top candidates in the nominating process opted out of public financing, believing they could raise more money on their own. That left the public money to the second and third tier candidates who would have struggled to raise that much. Senator John Edwards initially said he would opt out of the public financing system too, but opted back in when he found he couldn't keep up with the fundraising of Democrat frontrunners Hillary Clinton and Barack Obama.

'Money does count in a close race,' Patterson says, 'and if you're a candidate and you have the same assets [that is, personal abilities] as two other candidates, but they have twice as much money – usually the process will reward the moneyed candidates.'

⁂

The Center for Responsive Politics is a non-partisan research organisation dedicated to following the money in American politics. On their website (www.opensecrets.org) you can look up who has given what money to which candidates. Sheila Krumholz has been with the organisation for almost 20 years; she started as a researcher, and is now Executive Director and spokesperson. We speak at the Center's DC offices on 14th Street, in a meeting room with large sheets of butcher's paper on the walls – 'Who Gives What' and 'Who Gets What' are scrawled on them in thick marker pen.

'People who give money to Presidential candidates are often looking for a seat at the table,' she says. 'What all donors want is access.' And that's a concern, Krumholz says, when the donors are lobbyists who not only buy a seat at the table but have been invited into Congressional offices, handed the pen and asked to draft the legislation they want. Washington lobbyists have become like an ersatz public service. They provide a continuity of high-level knowledge in particular areas that outlives the terms of most Senators, members of Congress and Presidents. But they are also acting for the interests of particular industries and groups, not the American people as a whole.

'They have incredible power, incredible influence, and they gain that not just by their expertise but by the campaign contributions that they make,' she continues. Their political donations ensure that the politician's door is always open, and that open door also means the lobbyist can attract more clients and higher fees. 'Most lobbyists consider it a business expense,' Krumholz says, 'and a small one at that, relative to the profits they can reap or the danger of not participating, of not being at the table.' And she says the same lobbyists often act as campaign bundlers and introduce the Presidential candidates to even more people with deep pockets:

> They become the bagmen. Essentially, that's what these bundlers offer – the ability to tap their network quite easily and turn around and deliver hundreds of thousands of dollars simply by contacting their Rolodex.

Senator George McGovern admits that lobbyists have a role to play but says it should be limited:

> I'm not against lobbyists. It's perfectly fine for them to come to my office and say, 'Gee, Senator, I wish you'd vote to preserve the wetlands in my state', but they shouldn't have the unseen clout of large contributions that help finance your campaign.

Presidential candidates don't just have to go cap-in-hand to lobbyists; they also have to take money from a range of other business interests and individuals with money. Hollywood can provide a rich vein of cashed-up donors, and they are looking to get the ear of the candidates on issues as diverse as censorship, gay marriage, cigarette advertising and cerebral palsy.

But former Presidential hopeful Tom Vilsack told me of the difficulty he had extracting campaign contributions during his White House campaign in early 2007, even in tinseltown: 'They were always very polite, and they were always willing to write a cheque, but what they weren't willing to do was get their friends and neighbours to write a cheque.' He told me about one particular meeting he had with a wealthy Hollywood producer:

> I made my case about why I thought I would be a good candidate, and he looked at me and said, 'You're just terrific. I'd like to support your effort. Here's a cheque for $2300, but I should tell you that we're having fundraiser for one of your opponents and we're going to raise

$1.3 million tomorrow.'

Vilsack earned just over $2 million for his Presidential campaign in late 2006 and early 2007. His donors included James Donald, the CEO of Starbucks, who gave the maximum $2300, Gail Berman, the President of Paramount Pictures, who gave $2100, Norman Lear, the producer of *This is Spinal Tap*, who was tapped for $2100 and *Sex, Lies and Videotape* actress Laura San Giacomo, who gave $500. But it's hard to make that add up to enough:

> You have to have a group of individuals who are committed to helping you raise resources – these are individuals who not only go out and write a cheque themselves but have friends, business acquaintances, families, neighbours who will also write cheques. Part of the challenge with campaign finance laws the way they are written today is that no individual can write more than $2300 worth of support for a candidate – if you have to raise $50 or 60 or $100 million and you divide that by $2300, you have to have a lot of friends.

Without people prepared to act as bundlers, Vilsack says, he found it simply impossible to raise enough money via individual $2300-or-smaller chunks to keep his campaign alive. It took him three months to make what Barack Obama was making in a single night. 'It was fairly obvious,' Vilsack says, 'that I wasn't going to be able to close that money gap.'

Another 2008 Democratic Presidential hopeful, Senator Joe Biden, says he's a supporter of the full public financing of elections, and has been since 1973, early in his days in the Senate. 'You want to change the way these elections are done?' Biden asked a group of voters in Iowa in mid-2007. 'Have public financing of elections and don't allow special interest money into the process – and guess what? Your vote is as important as the Hollywood mogul's.'

Biden earned more than $12 million during his 2008 Presidential campaign, including $66,850 bundled from employees of Bank of America, almost $48,650 from the property developer The Adler Group, and a $2300 cheque from singer Barry Manilow. 'But I've come to this conclusion,' Senator Biden says. 'The only way we are going to get public financing of our elections is if a President of the United States makes it his or her number one priority domestically.'

⚑

Yet as it unfolded, the 2008 race brought about a potentially historic change in the way Presidential campaigns raise money – and may in the process have achieved more than three decades of campaign finance reform. The grassroots organisation built by Senator Barack Obama in particular, which was largely co-ordinated via the internet, proved a seemingly limitless source of money for his campaign.

Even his most successful rivals, including Hillary Clinton, maxed out most of their supporters for the full $2300, but Senator Obama maintained a broad base of over one and a half million individual contributors, all chipping in small amounts like $10 and $25 every week or two out of their pay cheques. As a result, his campaign raked in over a million dollars a day during the first three months of 2008 – a staggering total of $133 million, well ahead of Senator Clinton's $73 million. Clinton was forced to lend more than $11 million of her own money to her campaign just to try to keep up with Obama's massive TV 'ad-spend'.

Do the math, as Barry the lawyer at the Wellesley cocktail party might say: a million or so donors able to give up to $2300 little by little makes an available pool, in theory at least, of $2.3 billion – plenty to pay for a Presidential election costing about half a billion dollars for the top candidates. You just need to be a candidate with very broad appeal … and a website.

Tad Devine, who was chief political consultant to Al Gore in his 2000 White House campaign and a senior adviser to John Kerry's

Presidential bid in 2004, says:

> I think what Barack Obama is doing is revolutionising our politics.
> I think we've actually stumbled on a cure for the power of special
> interest politics in our country, which frees us from the influence of
> Washington lobbyists, insiders and the people who have exerted so
> much power over the political process because they've controlled it by
> virtue of their contributions.

Obama's online fundraising was certainly helped by the demograph-
ics of his supporters. Obama-voters were generally younger, better
educated and wealthier than Hillary-voters – and therefore statistically more likely to use the internet to buy things or make political
donations. The Obama campaign encouraged visitors to their official
website to register, and then sent them personalised daily updates
from the candidate, his wife Michelle, his campaign director David
Plouffe and others, all creating the impression that you were part of
the inside workings of the campaign. Other candidates did similar
things, but without the same effect.

'The amazing thing,' says Dennis Kanin, whom we'd spoken to
about Paul Tsongas' 1992 Presidential run, and who in 2008 acted
as an adviser to Obama's campaign, 'is that he's been able to raise the
resources even though he wasn't considered the most likely candidate
to win.' Kanin says Obama has built a core of donors among ordinary
citizens far more successfully than Hillary Clinton has: 'She's managed
to stay fairly competitive in terms of contributions, but most of her
money is coming in larger donations.'

Bob Shrum says he's been similarly impressed with Obama's
online fundraising effort: 'The internet is democratising fundraising
even as campaigns are getting more expensive.'

And according to David Weinberger, Howard Dean's internet
adviser in 2004, the Obama campaign has learned from what Dean's
campaign did four years ago, and taken it a lot further: 'Obama

has used the internet brilliantly to Get Out The Vote – taking a mass of people who are excited and turning that into a traditional campaign.'

The video-sharing website YouTube also created a new platform for the 2008 Presidential candidates, and again Senator Obama's campaign was the most active in recording and posting his campaign speeches within an hour or two of their being delivered. Obama's speech following the New Hampshire primary was even remixed into a song 'Yes We Can' by Will.i.am of the Rap/Pop/Hip-Hop group the Black Eyed Peas, and featured artists such as crooner John Legend, jazz great Herbie Hancock and actress Scarlett Johansson – it was watched by millions of people online within days. Obama's campaign, like that of a number of other contenders, also made use of social networking sites such as Facebook and MySpace to create a more personal connection between the candidate and his supporters.

Tad Devine says that through the internet Obama created a mechanism where his Presidential campaign could self-fund, and as a result, Senator Obama was able to significantly outspend all his rivals in each state in the first half of 2008 as the primary and caucus elections approached. As well as giving Obama the huge sums of money he needed to spend on TV advertising, it also allowed him to spend more time out on the campaign trail, rather than going to cocktail parties or being stuck in meetings with Wall Street bankers and Hollywood producers. 'We thought we'd need about $40 million to compete,' said Dave Contarino, Bill Richardson's campaign manager. 'Who knew Obama would raise that in a month?'

David Yepsen, back on the set of the TV show *The Iowa Press*, had an interesting theory:

If you look at the history of American Presidents, the most successful ones are the ones who have been able to use the dominant technology of their day – the Founders were big on the mail service and President Lincoln really understood the telegraph, Franklin Roosevelt and radio,

John Kennedy and television – and so there's a rule of thumb there that if you want to be President you first have to be able to master the various media you have to do it with.

If Yepsen is right, it could be Barack Obama's mastery of the internet, as much as anything else, that analysts will use to explain his victory.

The South and the North

South Carolina, 25 January 2008: Why is it statues of people in 20th century suits look strange whereas statues of men on horses wearing stockings, frilly coats and wigs don't? There's a modern statue in front of the State House in Columbia, South Carolina's capital, but what makes this larger-than-life statue eye-catching isn't the relatively dull contemporary attire – it's the name carved into the pedestal: STROM THURMOND. James Strom Thurmond started in politics in the 1920s and went on to serve in the US Senate for an extraordinary 7 years and 5 months; he retired at the age of 100 in 2002, just a few months before his death. But back in 1948, Thurmond, as Democratic Governor of South Carolina, was so opposed to a civil rights plank in the party platform that he and a group of other southerners split with President Harry Truman and Thurmond ran in that year's

Presidential election as a segregationist 'Dixiecrat'. He won the states of Alabama, Mississippi, Louisiana and South Carolina with rousing speeches that included lines such as these: 'There are not enough troops in the Army to force southern people to break down segregation and admit the negro race into our theatres, into our swimming pools, into our homes and into our churches.'

In the 1950s Thurmond switched to the more conservative Republican Party, and in his later political life he was seen as something of a living relic. But he remained a source of controversy – the Republican Senate Majority leader Trent Lott was forced to resign after making a speech at Strom's 100th birthday party suggesting that America would have been better off if Thurmond had won the Presidency in 1948. Given the local civic leaders' choice of statues, it's probably not surprising that there is also a Confederate flag flying in front of the State House in Columbia – to many, it signifies an adherence to the pre-Civil War order, including slavery. The state of South Carolina is crucial in any primary election campaign for the Presidency, because it is the first test of a candidate's support in the south.

Before heading to the south I'd met Dr Whit Ayers, a respected Republican pollster and campaign manager. Ayers ran former Tennessee Governor Lamar Alexander's 1996 Presidential campaign, and has close ties with key southern allies of Senator John McCain such as South Carolina Senator Lindsey Graham. I wanted Ayers to explain something that had been puzzling me about the American electoral map: 40 or 50 years ago, generally speaking, the Republican 'Red States' were in the north and the Democratic 'Blue States' were in the south, but since the 1960s that's almost reversed. What happened?

'Before 1960,' Dr Ayers tells me, 'very few blacks had the right to vote across the south. The Democratic Party was dominated by conservative white southerners. [However,] during the 1960s, as a result of the Voting Rights Act, a lot of blacks started to register and vote in southern elections.' He explains tactfully:

> Black and white southerners have very different opinions on the
> role of government, the level of taxation, the role of welfare, the
> death penalty – a whole host of issues separate black southerners
> and white southerners. It was very difficult to keep both groups in
> the same coalition, so as a result of blacks registering and voting in
> the Democratic primary, a number of white southerners became
> Republicans.

Like Strom Thurmond.

The economic development of the south, and a growing southern
white middle class, also helped generate support for the Republicans,
Ayers says:

> So you have these two forces of race and economic development that
> have led to the south becoming overwhelmingly Republican now.
> Conversely, the northeast, which used to be heavily Republican, has
> become heavily Democratic – so we have had a complete flip of the
> regional bases of the two major political parties.

Despite this new kind of political segregation, the south remains
very important to the outcome of Presidential elections. Since
1964, no Democrat has won the White House without being from
the south and using that home-town advantage to swing a couple
of southern states back into the Democrats' column. Georgia Governor Jimmy Carter did it in 1976, and Arkansas Governor Bill
Clinton did it in 1992 and 1996. But a series of northerners who
were effectively labelled 'liberal elitists' by conservatives – Hubert
Humphrey in 1968, George McGovern in 1972, Walter Mondale in
1984, Michael Dukakis in 1988 and John Kerry in 2004 – all lost.
Tennessee's Al Gore, though he won the majority of the popular
vote, is the only southern Democrat to have been beaten in a Presi-

dential bid (although President Carter failed to win re-election to a second term in 1980).

On the way to South Carolina, we'd stopped by the house of Jimmy Carter's long-time press secretary, Jody Powell. We talked at length about the Presidential nominating process as well as the pros and cons of being a southern candidate in the 1976 campaign. Powell observed that in the 1970s, much more than today, the American media was dominated by southerners. 'Perhaps it's the storytelling tradition of the rural south,' he mused. 'In some cases that was an advantage to us – they understood who he was.' But Powell says there was a downside too: 'There was a desire that he be almost perfect. They wanted this fellow, who might be the first President from the deep south since the Civil War, to make no mistakes, to have no warts, to have no shortcomings.'

There were other reporters, Powell says, who were not from the south, who admitted to having some prejudice against members of the Carter Administration:

> A young woman who covered the Justice Department told me – after a few drinks, I might add – that whenever she heard Attorney General Griffin Bell open his mouth, with that deep southern accent, all she could think about was the slaves being whipped up and down the rows of cotton fields!

Powell laughs.

Jody Powell remains very much a hospitable southern gentleman. After our interview he takes us for a bumpy ride in an off-road golf cart over the frozen paddocks of his property on Chesapeake Bay, pointing out the best spots for bird-watching. He is both a bird-lover and a hunter – hence the rifles and the duck decoys. He explains that he's heading down to do some shooting in Georgia the next day and invites us along. He also invites us to the NASCAR race at Indianapolis – he's friends with the guy who runs the PR for it. NASCAR is important to understanding the south, he tells us. Later, over a bottle of expensive bourbon, he talks a little more about the north–south divide and the legacy of the Civil War – which he's planning to write a book about someday – and how it still affects race relations and politics in America. Sadly, there's no time to take Jody Powell up on his offer of seeing a real southern shooting party, or a NASCAR race – there's an election to cover.

***

It's the day before South Carolina's primary. We take our camera to the campus of Benedict College, a historically black university in Columbia. Senator Hillary Clinton has been speaking to a large, mostly black, mostly young, mostly female audience. As the students file out of the auditorium into the cool morning sunshine, we gather a group of girls together to 'vox pop' for the documentary. They are all black, two are called Brittney, one is Akira, the other Alicia – all of them except one of the Brittneys are from South Carolina (she's come down to study from Maryland). They're all jostling and joking, flicking their hair and mugging for the camera, but they turn serious on cue when we ask who they plan to vote for and why – 'Hillary!' Why? 'Universal healthcare,' one Brittney says; 'Hillary's college loan scheme,' says the Brittney from Maryland, '… and ending the war in Iraq,' Akira ads before ducking back out of camera shot.

There is a bunch of media here, many looking for vox pops as well; an earnest-looking radio reporter with a microphone and a backpack has been grabbing people after we speak to them. Idling nearby is a flash-looking Fox News Channel van freshly painted with *You Decide 2008* and a camera taking pictures, but no journalist in sight.

Slouching down the front steps of the Benedict auditorium is

Marcus Shannon, a young African-American student, who says that while he came to hear Hillary speak today, he'll be voting for Barack Obama in the primary tomorrow. His reasons: 'universal healthcare and helping college students'. The issues are the same, as are most of the Democrats' policies; it's just the choice of candidate that differs. Another black male student at Benedict named Kevin Keene says he's supporting Obama too, because, Kevin says, he will bring change to the world and end the war in Iraq. But he says he likes Hillary too: 'It's a very, very tough choice this year.'

Martha Bray is black woman in her seventies; she's wearing a hat, and a heavy brown coat over a smart red dress, and she looks as if she could be coming from church. She explains that she's a retired schoolteacher, who was born and raised in Columbia, South Carolina, studied at Benedict College, and has lived in the same house for 50 years. Her late husband was in the military, she tells us, and her four boys all served in the US Armed Forces – one of them, she says with pride, was pinned a one-star General two weeks ago. Mrs Bray says she's a lifelong Democrat, and wants Hillary to win: 'I hope when they go to vote they look at strength and determination – not be a racial hypocrite.' Martha's daughter Filene adds, 'By not looking at colour, looking at who can do best for our country. She's a strong woman – they've been through a lot, she and her husband both.' Martha nods, 'Uh huh, they work together.'

Many older African-Americans still seem to think of Bill Clinton as 'America's first black President', as author Toni Morrison once described him because of the special empathy he showed on racial issues. And they have passed that loyalty on to Hillary. You also sense that a lot of women who have dealt with difficult times in their lives have an affinity with and respect for Hillary as well. Some African-Americans are wary of Obama – he may look black, they say, but he's not a descendant of slaves, he's the son of a Kenyan and a Kansan, and he wasn't around during the great battles of the civil rights movement in the 1950s and 1960s. They're not yet convinced that he deserves to stand on the shoulders of Dr King. Opinion polls reflect what we found on the streets of Columbia: younger black men tend to support Obama, older black and white voters and female voters in particular still tend to support Hillary.

Back at the State House, a reporter from a cable news channel is sitting rather imperially in a high director's chair, rugged up against the cool weather but under a shade sail to even out the lighting. She's been here all day, doing live crosses every 20 minutes or so with the State House as her backdrop. Because there isn't enough time between reports to leave this location, a team of field producers are gathering information about the latest exit polls and passing on colourful descriptions of things the reporter will never see. 'The turnout today is expected to be high, and the mood here in Columbia is one of eager anticipation …' Around the other side of the State House, near the Strom Thurmond statue, another female cable news correspondent is doing the same thing: reporting on a primary she's not actually been able to leave the camera long enough to witness.

A closer inspection of the Thurmond statue reveals a secret that the Senator they affectionately called 'Ole Strom' kept for 77 of his 100 years. After his death in 2003, a retired schoolteacher named Essie Mae Washington-Williams announced that she was the illegitimate daughter of the then 22-year-old Thurmond and a 16-year-old black house servant named Carrie Butler. He didn't like Negroes in swimming pools, theatres, homes or churches – his bed, however, was a different matter. Thurmond, Essie Mae said, had helped her financially throughout her life. He had even seemed surprised, she said, when she asked him why he was against racial intermingling – it was simply the custom of the south, Thurmond told his half-negro daughter, and no one man can change that. In 2004 Essie Mae's name was carved into the base of the statue of Strom Thurmond, along with the names of his wife and his 'legitimate' children. The memorial makes no mention of his 1948 segregationist Presidential campaign.

When the votes in South Carolina's primary are counted, John McCain has won the Republican primary, edging out Mike Huckabee by 33 per cent to 30 per cent and strengthening his claim on his party's nomination. A sweet victory for McCain, given that this was the scene of his brutal slandering in the 2000 campaign against George W. Bush – when he was accused of having fathered a black child. On the Democratic side, Barack Obama mobilised a record number of first-time voters to win a blowout 55.4 per cent to Hillary's 26.5 and John Edwards' 17.6. Obama won 80 per cent of the black vote, which made up about half of those taking part in the Democratic primary, but only 24 per cent of the white vote. It's a stunning victory – almost three times the margin tipped by most polls, but one that Bill Clinton immediately tried to play down by pointing out a black Presidential candidate had won here before.

'Jesse Jackson won South Carolina twice, in '84 and '88. Jackson ran a good campaign and Obama ran a good campaign here,' Bill told reporters. Jackson ultimately failed to win his party's nomination on both occasions. President Clinton was accused of 'playing the race card' and there were howls of protest. At that point, veteran Senator Edward Kennedy said, he decided to publicly endorse Senator Barack Obama.

New York City, 2 February 2008: So much for conventional wisdom. This was when the inevitable Hillary Clinton and the inevitable Rudy Giuliani would inevitably win their parties' Presidential nominations. Instead, Rudy was knocked out last week in Florida after donating the best part of $60 million to the college funds of the kids of TV station executives from Key West to Pensacola. As for Hillary, she's been playing catch-up for a month since Iowa, and as all her other rivals have dropped out, their supporters have been flocking to Obama – her 45 per cent support of 12 months ago is still about 45 per cent, but Obama has gone from less than 20 per cent to 45 per cent.

For the last six months, the TV pundits have been saying that the nominations would be all wrapped up by now – well they're half right. McCain has it in the bag, except he was the guy they said was finished last August. We had bought the 'inevitability' argument … and the plane tickets, too. We flew from Atlanta to New York City expecting Rudy and Hillary to claim the nomination in their home town on 5 February, Super Tuesday. But nobody counted on Barack Obama's remarkable rise and John McCain's remarkable resurrection.

We're in Chelsea in New York City, and I can't get that damn Joni Mitchell song out of my head – the same song that helped Bill and Hillary come up with a name for their daughter: *Woke up, it was a Chelsea morning, and the first thing that I heard was the song outside my window, and the traffic wrote the words.* Hillary is holding a rally around the corner in Chelsea tonight for just that reason, but we have other plans. We put our camera and sound gear into a backpack and I hoist the heavy tripod over my shoulder as we go in search of a 'phone bank' set up by local Obama supporters. We arrive at an apartment just off 10th Avenue that belongs to a 30-something film-maker and computer animator named Ethan. His contribution to the Obama campaign is to give his home and office over to whoever turns up to log on to a computer and start making calls. Many volunteers bring their own laptops and mobile phones, and then it's just a matter of finding a power plug, getting on to an internet database of Democratic voters in New York City and giving them a call. Just as the Obama campaign identified the internet as a powerful fundraising tool, it's also using web-based technology in an effort to Get Out The Vote.

Ethan's girlfriend, Lizzy, has an espresso machine working overtime making coffee for the 20 or so Obama volunteers, and there are baskets of bagels, plates of sandwiches and cakes to feed the workers. Every now and then Anthea, one of the volunteers, calls out reminding people to stretch – they sit for hours making calls. Ethan says that despite this being Hillary's home town they're finding a fairly even split: 'A girl was here before for two hours, and she spoke to 12 people – 5 were Obama, 5 were for Clinton and 2 were undecided, so I do think we're pretty close.' But they've also found, on a statistically small sample, which echoes a wider trend, that Hillary is still dominating among Hispanic voters.

Another of the volunteers, a white law student in her early twenties named Joanna, is perched in front of an iMac, working through a call list on her own mobile phone. She says this is the first time she's got involved with politics:

> I think he's a really exciting candidate … he represents a real
> distinction from 'politics as usual', and he motivates people to unify,
> and I really think we need someone to get people excited about the
> country again – which he does.

Across the room from Joanna, on her mobile phone at another iMac is Ashley. She's a girlish-looking black college student in a football T-shirt, with a pigtail and trendy black-rimmed glasses. Ashley's asking a New Yorker named Omar if he's planning to vote on Tuesday: he is, but for Hillary. 'OK, thanks,' she says brightly and hangs up. Ashley gets up to make herself a bagel, and explains that she's supporting Obama for a number of reasons:

> I think he would unite the country, and I think he's very inspirational
> and motivational and gets the young people out to vote – and people
> always say if the young people vote it changes the election – and I
> think that's going to happen … hopefully!

Ethan is sitting on a leather sofa next to a whiteboard on which Obama's trade mark 'YES WE CAN!' is written in red marker pen, and he's explaining to the latest volunteer to turn up that they aren't trying to convert any Hillary supporters – they are to just ask if people are planning to vote and if they know where their nearest polling station is. 'The people we are trying to talk to are the undecided voters,' Ethan explains to the Latino woman in her thirties. 'Some aren't going to want to talk about it. There will be others who will be more open – so you say, "Well, are there particular issues you're concerned about?" – just open the door.'

Lizzy interrupts to tell him he's needed in the front room because a couple of the computers have frozen and a few other volunteers can't get onto the Vote-Builder website that has the list of phone numbers. The technical problem looks like it's going to take a while, so Ethan suggests that maybe some of the volunteers should hit the streets and hand out Obama flyers and ask shopkeepers around the neighbourhood if they'll put up the black and white image of a smiling Obama with the single word – *VOTE* – on it.

Lizzy explains why simply getting people to vote on Tuesday is so important, and so difficult:

> There are just an enormous number of people who work two jobs or work and go to school, and voting, for them, is just another thing on their to-do list. In this election it really does matter; this is their opportunity not just to vote, but to change this country.

The computers still aren't working so we tag along with Joanna, another young white law student named Michael and a black woman in her fifties named Dianne who is a lawyer, and says she's glad for the walk because it means she won't have to go to the gym today.

As we walk along, I ask Dianne how she would feel watching Barack Obama take the oath of office as President of the United States. 'I never thought I would live to see it,' she says. 'I'm a child of the 1960s, I went to Berkeley, I marched, I prayed-in, I sat-in and now I feel proud of the country.'

But she thinks the African-Americans who are supporting Hillary have just become used to depending on whites for their survival. 'Hillary is part of the old master syndrome,' Dianne says. 'If your bread has been connected to a Hillary or a Bill for ten generations that's what you do – it's a mindset that has to be broken, and I think just having Obama run helps break it … just seeing it.'

As Dianne and I chat on the pavement on 23rd Street, Joanna and Michael head into a busy Chelsea Square 24-hour Italian diner and ask the owner if they can put up their Obama picture – sure, he says. They get the same response at the deli, the cleaners and the cigarette shop next door.

Dianne says that even though she's the fifth generation of her family to be college-educated, she's still amazed that so much has changed in her lifetime:

> When I was a child we went to visit my grandparents in the south and we couldn't use the same bathrooms on the way – and to go from not being able to use the bathroom to voting for such a qualified, well-educated black candidate is just mind-boggling. It's exciting: I never dreamed that this could happen.

Postscript: The New York primary saw a strong 17 per cent win for Hillary Clinton over Barack Obama. The results from the other Super Tuesday Democratic primaries and caucuses were split pretty evenly between the pair. In the weeks that followed, Obama won 11 primaries in a row, giving him a delegate lead that Clinton was unable to overhaul although she took her campaign to the final votes in South Dakota and Montana on 3 June – three days later she suspended her campaign and backed Obama.

Super Tuesday also confirmed John McCain's likely nomination as the Republican candidate, with the withdrawal of Mitt Romney. McCain became the first candidate to win his party's nomination after failing to come first, second or third in Iowa.

Senator Barack Obama formally accepted the Democratic Party's Presidential nomination on 28 August 2008 at the Democratic National Convention in Denver, Colorado – 60 years after Strom Thurmond quit the party to stand for the Presidency as a segregationist, and exactly 45 years to the day after Dr Martin Luther King Jr delivered the speech on the steps of the Lincoln Memorial in Washington DC which became known as 'I Have A Dream'.

Leadership

We've spent many weeks on the campaign trail, staying in a lot of $89-a-night motel rooms (breakfast buffet included), driving cheap rental Hyundais to rallies, house parties and interviews with candidates, campaign managers, volunteers, strategists, reporters, academics and hundreds of ordinary American voters. We've looked at the role of the media, the role of money, and even the role of plain old dumb luck in Presidential politics – how an election can turn on a slip of the tongue or a splinter in the candidate's eye. But a few questions remain in my mind: who are these men and, very occasionally, women, who seek the most powerful political office on earth? What motivates them, and why is it that some candidates succeed while others do not? Why do people follow some leaders and not others? Does this long electoral process deliver the best results – the best

Presidents? And what about that old article of faith in the US – that any American child can grow up to be President – is it true now? Has it ever been?

It's mild and overcast on Super Tuesday and we walk about 45 minutes from our hotel room in Chelsea to the campus of New York University in downtown Manhattan. The city is full of fans of the New York Giants, who two nights ago won gridiron's Super Bowl in a last-ditch, upset 17–14 win over the favoured New England Patriots. The Giants are being welcomed home today with a parade that has brought the bottom half of Manhattan to a standstill. It brings back memories of the last big sporting celebration we'd seen in the US – three days before the 2004 election, in Democratic Presidential candidate Senator John Kerry's home town, the Boston Red Sox had been given a tickertape parade after finally breaking the 'curse of the Bambino' and winning the Baseball World Series for the first time since they traded star Babe Ruth to the Yankees in 1919. Then, as now, there was a strange mingling of sport and politics on the streets – does that guy's red, white and blue T-shirt say *Red Sox* or *Vote Kerry – Go Hillary*! or *Go Giants!*?

<hr />

Thinking back to that late October afternoon in Boston in 2004, I realise that that was probably the day I first gained an appreciation of this peculiarly American form of democracy. Like many outsiders, I'd heard that at best, only about 50 per cent of Americans bother to vote, and I assumed that this was because of a deep sense of apathy. I was appalled that the few hundred million people who have the power to elect the single most important politician on the planet – a person whose decisions affect the wellbeing of billions – should seemingly take their responsibility so lightly. Hell's bells, America, if you don't want your vote, sell it on eBay!

But that autumn Saturday in Boston, with the Red Sox on parade, with wood smoke in the air and jack-o'-lanterns on brownstone porch steps for Halloween the next day, we followed the so-called Freedom Trail – a line of red bricks and red paint along the pavement, weaving past historic sites. Most of them are linked to the Revolutionary War: Paul Revere's House, Bunker Hill, the USS *Constitution*, Boston Common and a bunch of graveyards with famous inhabitants.

Several times along the way we met a modest white man in his forties who was campaigning for election to the Massachusetts Senate – it was on the same day as the Presidential poll. As we followed the red bricks and brass signs, weaving around old Boston, we found this man standing at various street corners with a sandwich board strung over his shoulders informing potential voters that his name was Robert Badham. Robert Badham explained that it was a bit lonely being a Republican in Democrat John Kerry's home town. He explained it was also a bit lonely being a gay man in the Republican Party. Yet here he was, a lonely gay Republican on this cool autumn afternoon, asking people for their vote, one at a time. All over Boston that day there were groups in matching candidate T-shirts – most for Kerry, some for Bush, others for various potential Senators and Representatives and other public office holders. There was something inspiring about such an open statement of a belief that they could 'make it' no matter what the odds – which in Badham's case seemed very long. But I realised, too, that the notion of competition is embedded in that dream – I'll make it, but I'll have to beat a few people to get there.

In the US, it seems, everything is competitive. Elections are a part of life, from voting for class president in the 5th grade, to the Homecoming Queen and 'most likely to succeed' in the high school yearbook, through to electing Sheriffs and District Attorneys. It's also a country with beauty pageants for 3-year-olds, spelling bees, honour rolls and prizes for the fattest pig.

The same competitive dream is on display today on the streets of Manhattan. After skipping the free breakfast buffet, I'm taking particular interest in the hot dog vendors with their steaming carts of brightly coloured frankfurts. Every one claims to have the 'Best hot dogs in New York!' And I have no doubt most dream that someday they may trade that hotdog cart for a van, then maybe trade the van for a store, then maybe a chain of stores – who knows, somebody started Wendy's, right? Of course most will never make it beyond their hot dog cart. Maybe it's their hotdogs, maybe it's their cart, their ketchup or sauerkraut – or maybe it's because they need a shave and just ashed in the bun basket.

In the same way, some politicians just don't make it: Robert Badham, the gay Republican, didn't win a Senate seat, John Kerry didn't win the White House in 2004, and Dennis Kucinich never got much more than 1 or 2 per cent in the 2008 primaries. Yet it's fundamental to the American dream that they all believe it is *possible*, that they could go from 2 per cent in Iowa to the White House or from a hotdog cart on a street corner in Manhattan to a global day-glo frankfurt empire. And every now and then someone comes along to reaffirm their faith in that dream. That freedom of opportunity – real or imagined – is, after all, what they fought for on Bunker Hill. And every American child is taught that while that first battle of the Revolutionary War there in 1775 was lost, it paved the way for victory over their oppressors.

〜〜〜

We're due at NYU at 10.30 am to meet Bob Shrum, who has worked for Democratic candidates on every Presidential campaign since 1972, without ever actually winning the White House. He was running John Kerry's campaign in 2004 when the Red Sox came marching home in glory – and hopes were high that Kerry would soon do the same. Shrum is technically retired from Presidential politics and is lecturing now, but he's still regarded as one of America's top political strategists and a pretty fair speechwriter into the bargain. He's just back from London, where he's been trying to help out Labour Prime

Minister Gordon Brown.

We arrive early and set up our tripod, camera, lights and sound gear in a conference room. Bob Shrum bustles in right on time, but like a man who is always late. He's all apologies, overcoats and mobile phones. He has a plane to catch, so we get right down to it: who are these people who run for the Presidency of the United States?

> All kinds of people – but I don't think there are any of them who aren't ambitious and who don't have a very strong sense of self. One of Ronald Reagan's great strengths was that he knew what he believed. He went out there and said what he believed, and I think that's when you do your best. Presidential candidates who have beliefs and are willing to state their beliefs do better than those who don't – and I would apply that to both the left and the right.

Bob Shrum worked on Edward Kennedy's 1980 insurgent run against President Carter, and as a speechwriter for President Bill Clinton. He was also Al Gore's campaign manager in 2000. Does he see anything in common among all the Presidential candidates he's known?

> Some are shy, and politics for them is an act of will. I think in many ways Al Gore is a sort of shy and self-contained person and he taught himself to be political. Some people are complete political naturals – Bill Clinton is a complete political natural, Ted Kennedy is a complete political natural.

Yet naturals or otherwise, Shrum believes that when the difference between electoral success and failure can be measured in a handful of votes, winning can easily come down to a single blunder or badly phrased comment. Certainly he says that may be true of Senator John Kerry's 2004 Presidential campaign against George W. Bush, when the Democrat tried to explain why he voted against an appropriation Bill for the troops in Iraq: 'He said, "I voted for the $87 billion before I voted against it." And the Republicans instantly had the piece of film they needed to make the flip-flop argument.' Kerry was seen as indecisive, cynical and unpatriotic in one fell swoop. The point was underscored by TV ads which showed the Senator from Massachusetts sailing one way and then another on his sailboard – going whichever way the wind was blowing.

Shrum says that while firm beliefs are important, so is being prepared to accept that they aren't always right: 'One thing that marks really good candidates out from candidates who aren't so good is whether or not they are open to criticism – internally.'

Some would argue that that's been one of George W. Bush's failings. Certainly Democratic Party County Commissioner Tim Hagan says the 43rd President has inspired a lot of politicians to think they may be up to the job: 'Many people – on the Republican side as well – have questioned the credibility of Bush, and his ability to be President, and a lot of people say, "I'm not as bad as that guy! Let me take a shot at it."' He says that at one time or another most of the 50 Governors and 100 Senators in the US will contemplate a tilt at the White House: 'Presidential ambition is an occupational hazard for most of these people, and all of them think that they could be President.'

But what are those would-be presidents thinking? It is, after all, a pretty big deal to say that you want the top job. In 1992, Pat Buchanan challenged incumbent President George H.W. Bush for the Republican Presidential nomination. Buchanan did surprisingly well in the New Hampshire primary, getting within 17 per cent of Bush, but his campaign soon faded due to lack of money and patchy support. Even so, there are many, including George W. Bush, who believe that Buchanan helped pave the way for Bill Clinton's defeat of a weakened President Bush in November of that year.

Buchanan ran again for the Republican nomination in 1996 but lost out to Senator Bob Dole. Finally Buchanan stood as a Reform Party candidate in 2000, when, as fate would have it, he was the accidental recipient of enough of Al Gore's votes on a confusing 'butterfly ballot' in Florida to cost Gore the Presidency and win the election for George W. Bush.

I asked Buchanan about the thought process – was there any soul-searching when deciding to run for the Presidency of the United States?

> I wouldn't have run if I didn't think I had it in me to do it. I've known all of the Republican Presidents since Eisenhower, and I've known their strengths and weaknesses and their abilities, and I had no doubt I had abilities in many cases equal or superior to theirs.

Charles Bierbauer spent longer in the White House than any of the four Presidents he reported on for CNN, and he says the one thing all the prospective American Presidents had in common was ego: 'There is a desire to lead, there is a sense that you have a capacity to lead, and then there is what has to be this enormous ego that says, "I'm better than anyone else at doing this job."'

Senator George McGovern agrees. 'I think you have to be a bit of an egomaniac to think that out of a country of 300 million people, you're the best person qualified to be President,' he says. This is a man who ran for the White House in 1972, sought the Democratic Party's Presidential nomination unsuccessfully in both 1968 and 1984, and put out feelers again as recently as 1992. McGovern admits he still thinks about running for the White House, even at the age of 85. 'I still get the urge every four years,' he laughs. 'I hear that fire bell ringing every four years – I resist it, but I hear it!'

'When I look at the Presidents in my lifetime,' says former Carter White House spokesman Jody Powell, 'other than all being boys, I don't know what the common thread is. Obviously you have to feel like you can do something important and worthwhile.'

Of course why the candidates seek office and what they bring to the table is only half of the equation. At election time, what's on offer needs to match up with what voters are looking for.

John F. Kennedy famously said that in politics, 'victory has a thousand fathers, while defeat is an orphan'. Still, some defeated candidates have a pretty good idea why their campaign was unsuccessful. Maxine Isaacs, Presidential candidate Walter Mondale's Press Secretary in the 1984 campaign, says her former boss concluded that he lost simply because he wasn't telling voters what they wanted to hear:

> The day after the election I sat down with Mr Mondale ... and I said, 'What do you think the election was about?' and he said, 'I think it was about Reagan selling them Morning in America – and I was selling them a root-canal.' He just felt his message looked very grim, very pessimistic, and Reagan looked sunny and optimistic.

It seems that for would-be Presidents, simple timing can also be very important. How strong is the field of candidates they are up against? Is the economy strong? Is the nation at war? Many elections are a reaction to what has come before, and often the selection of the President seems to be very much a response to the predecessor. As Jody Powell says:

> There is no doubt that 1976 was suited to a candidate like Jimmy Carter, and Jimmy Carter was ideally suited to that year and that time. We were really in the afterglow of Watergate ... and people were quite disgusted with 'business as usual' in Washington and actively looking for someone who was not a creature of that process.

Likewise, in the 2000 election, a nation weary of scandals during the Clinton years turned to another candidate who presented himself as being above the partisan bickering of Washington – Texas Governor George W. Bush.

Certainly, timing worked against Iowa Governor Tom Vilsack

during his short run for the White House. By his own admission, he wasn't what the electorate was looking for heading into 2008: 'They were looking for a rock star, and I was offering rock solid.' He was selling simple, old-fashioned hotdogs; they were buying ones with the works. Arguably, early frontrunner Hillary Clinton's timing was also out: the electorate was in the mood for change, and she was perceived as part of the political establishment. Despite having not dissimilar policies, Clinton didn't win enough delegates and Super Delegates to take the nomination away from Barack Obama.

Pollster John Zogby says picking a Presidential candidate comes down to a gut instinct with many voters:

When push comes to shove, Americans really have to love the
candidate. They really came to love Jimmy Carter, they really
came to love Ronald Reagan and George H.W. Bush – these were
fatherly guys who each brought something to the mix. Even in his
darkest hours, America really liked Bill Clinton, and then George
W. Bush … we want to know that our President is 'everyman' or
'everywoman'.

That desire for an 'everyman' or 'everywoman' is possibly why so many wealthy candidates, including Ross Perot, Steve Forbes, John Kerry and Mitt Romney, have failed to win the hearts of the American public.

Mike Glover, from Associated Press in Iowa, says the way Americans pick their President is simple:

American people sit down and make a decision on 'Who would I
like to look at on the evening news for the next four or eight years?'
In 2004 I think the American people saw a flinty, crusty, reserved,
nuanced New Englander in John Kerry – because that's what he is
– and I think they saw a brash, self-assured, maybe even arrogant

Texan in George W. Bush, and by about 50,000 votes in Ohio they liked the Texan better. That's what it boiled down to.

I suspect he's right, and wonder what will ultimately decide the election of 2008. Will John McCain, a Republican with a reputation as a maverick and a compelling life story as a former POW be best suited to the national mood of America? Or will the pent-up demand for change after eight years of an increasingly unpopular President and more than five years of bloodshed in Iraq sweep the fresh-faced yet inexperienced Barack Obama into office? Will the decisive issue be experience or race?

≈≈≈

We're in Washington DC exactly a year to the day from when either Barack Obama or John McCain will be sworn in as America's 44th President. It's painfully cold and windy as we take in the famous sites: the Capitol, the Lincoln Memorial, the Washington Monument. The story of President William Henry Harrison now makes complete sense to me: he caught a cold while making his inaugural address in 1841, the cold developed into pneumonia, and he died just over a month after he'd taken office.

Over the road from 1600 Pennsylvania Avenue in Washington DC is a public park called Lafayette Square. We're there to film some external footage of the Executive Residence, as it was officially known until 1903, when President Teddy Roosevelt called it what it was: the White House.

Lafayette Square has been used as a zoo, a racetrack and even a slave market – all within sight of one of the world's most famous buildings. We set up our camera on a tripod next to a reassuringly traditional statue of President Andrew Jackson on horseback in that rampant equestrian style that brings to mind the Lone Ranger. As Rebecca focuses in on the stars and stripes fluttering in the icy winter wind from the top of the White House's gold-tipped flagpole, I notice several flocks of sparrows darting in and out of the hedging plants that form a low wall around the statue of President Jackson.

When you're not the one looking through the viewfinder of a camera, adjusting focus and checking for light, there's a fair bit of time for looking around, noticing things and annoying the person who is pulling focus by saying, 'Hey, look at that, look over there!' This is exactly what I do as the sparrows fly in a dense swarm which suddenly and simultaneously changes direction like a school of fish and then just as quickly drops down onto the hedge as if they are playing a party game and the music has stopped.

Were Norwegian Zoologist Thorleif Schjelderup-Ebbe still alive, and here in Lafayette Square in Washington DC, he could have explained his pioneering work into the pecking order of chickens, which forms the basis of much of our understanding of the social ordering of birds. He could have told me how birds of different species assert their dominance, and, having done so, how they effectively become leaders and have their pick of the food and the mates. Unfortunately, Thorleif is long dead … and anyway, I don't speak Norwegian. But it's a fairly good bet that were he alive, and had he witnessed these sparrows over the road from the White House, he would have approved of the potential visual metaphor I was now telling Rebecca to point the camera at.

Of course all animals instinctively know when you want to film them doing something, and immediately stop doing it. Not having any breadcrumbs, I try to trick them by throwing leaves. This works at first, until the lead sparrow, which Thorleif would have called the 'alpha bird', got wise and stopped taking his flock to dried leaves – it would presumably have damaged his reputation and 'alpha-ness' among the rest of the sparrows.

Back in the 1930s, by spending more time around chickens than most men care to, Schjelderup-Ebbe determined that the pecking order was worked out by fighting between birds, but once established, it led to peaceful barnyards. Everyone knew their place, and as long as they stayed in that place they all got fed and the farmer got to sleep in.

In other species, such as sparrows, the pecking order extends to flight formations, where the lead bird does the thinking about where to go to eat tonight, and the rest just follow, looking at its tail-feathers. In most species, males tend to dominate – but some scientists discovered that if you give a female European Chaffinch or a Japanese Quail male hormones and dye her plumage to look masculine, she rises in the pecking order.

The metaphor is obvious and may look kind of dopey in the documentary, but I do wonder how and why we choose to follow the leaders we do.

It's a question Presidential aspirant Tom Vilsack clearly gave some thought to:

> There are some people who decide [who to follow] on an issue.
> Iraq is a very good example. Some people gravitate toward a person
> simply because they like a candidate; [they have] an emotional
> reaction and response to the person. Some like the idea of supporting
> an underdog – certainly in the Democratic Party that's a prevalent
> feeling – so they look for the candidate who maybe is not as well
> known and they decide to support that candidate. And for some
> it depends on who their friends and neighbours are supporting
> – people they trust locally and who they look to for support and
> assistance. So it's a very interesting dynamic.

Ah ha! Democrats are just like the Song Sparrows of British Columbia, Canada, Thorleif would exclaim: they are as likely to follow a smaller bird as a larger one, and again just like the Democrats, the smaller birds often get beaten up.

But is the two-year barnyard fight we've witnessed through places like Ames, Iowa and Manchester, New Hampshire the best way to establish the 'Presidential pecking order'?

Conservative Pat Buchanan is doubtful that the whole process comes up with the best candidate. But then someone who has run three times without being elected President might well say that. 'I don't think politics automatically brings to the top the toughest, wisest, best, most knowledgeable people,' Buchanan told me. 'It brings to the top the best politicians.'

John F. Kennedy once said, 'Mothers all want their sons to grow up to be President, but they don't want them to become politicians in the process.'

I doubt the sparrows in Lafayette Square give two tweets about whether any sparrow can grow up to be their leader, male or female, large or small, but certainly many of the hotdog vendors on the streets of Manhattan believe anyone can grow up to start the next Wendy's. It is no coincidence that one of the most popular expressions of the American dream is that they believe anyone can make it to the White House. Under British rule the colonials rebelled against the fact that no American could lead their own nation (and a bunch of other stuff, some of which involved tea), but in an independent United States, the founders believed, any American child could grow up to be President.

Historically, that's been more theory than practice, of course. The first 42 individuals to hold the office were all white men, and all but Catholic President Kennedy were Protestants. In 2008, Hillary Clinton was heavily favoured to become the first woman nominated for the Presidency by a major party, but in the end the party opted for another male. Yet, according to a study conducted by the Pennsylvania-based IRC research organisation, more girls than boys think they can grow up to be President – 64 per cent compared with 61 per cent – and more than half of all American parents believe their child can be President. (If you are confused about why the 44th President will be elected in 2008 but it's an office previously held by 42 individuals, not 43, it's because one of them, Grover Cleveland, was President on two separate occasions, making him both the 22nd and the 24th President.)

So despite 220 years which would suggest otherwise, the idea that any child can be President remains very much an article of faith – and not just in the aspirations of the parents and children of America. Perhaps encouraged by the diversity of the 2008 field of candidates, which has included a woman, a black man, a Latino, an Italian-American and a Mormon (not to mention Kucinich the vegan), many people who have run for the office, and helped others to run – perhaps more than ever before – also believe it to be true.

Former CNN White Bureau Chief Charles Bierbauer says there are stories of unlikely candidates on both sides of politics:

> John McCain's father was an admiral, his grandfather was an admiral, but the thing we remember most is those nearly six years spent as a prisoner of war – not exactly privileged. And Barack Obama – if there was an unpredictable and least-predictable story ... African father, American mother, grew up in Hawaii and Indonesia. That's a terrific story.

Republican campaign manager and pollster Dr Whit Ayers agrees that the old axiom may be truer now than ever before. 'It is a fundamental part of the American dream and the American ideal that any American child can grow up to be President,' he says, and he adds that Barack Obama has certainly reinforced that dream:

> This is the son of a white woman from Kansas and a black African from Kenya – normally the thought that that kid could be President

of the United States would be dismissed out of hand ... I don't share his party and I don't share many of his political beliefs, but it's a good thing for America.

Senator George McGovern also believes there are examples in the past that support the ideal:

> I think so. Jimmy Carter in a sense came pretty close – born in Plains, Georgia, son of a peanut farmer. Barack Obama came out of rather humble circumstances, and so did Bill Clinton – Hope, Arkansas, parents that were in difficulty and so on. I think it's still possible in this country to rise from the low ranks to be President.

But, McGovern warns, while social status, gender and race may no longer be major barriers, money is: 'As campaigns have become more and more expensive, it's probably less and less likely that an ordinary citizen can rise to the top of a Presidential contest.'

Maxine Isaacs, former Vice President Walter Mondale's Press Secretary, thinks the 2008 field of Democrats proved that today there is a much more diverse range of candidates who are considered potential Presidents:

> I think the system is now wide open. I think it's because people are prepared to fish in a broader pool. Part of it is that they don't like what they have been given so far – they want change. I think anybody truly can be President in this country and I think it's going to send a powerful message to the world.

Shrum says the nomination of Barack Obama reaffirms that in America in the 21st century it is possible for any child to aspire to the highest office:

> Obama as President ... the day he raised his hand and was sworn in,

America's image would go up in the world very substantially. But do I think all American children should [aspire to the office of President]? I'm not sure it would make for a happy life.

A Warm Bucket of Ambition

Democracy means that anyone can grow up to be President – and anyone who doesn't grow up can be Vice President.

Tonight Show host Johnny Carson

The Vice President of the United States is just a heartbeat, criminal indictment or reasonably well-aimed bullet away from the most powerful political office on earth. The VP needs to be ready to lead at a minute's notice, although historically only a third of them have ever been called on or eventually elected to the Presidency. Every Presidential candidate, once they have secured the nomination of their party, must pick a Vice Presidential running mate whose name appears on the ballot under theirs, and as George McGovern found out in 1972, the wrong choice can be a real bummer.

Ever since the 'Eagleton Affair', the two major American political parties have been a lot more careful when they vet the potential Vice Presidential candidates, who are usually past or present state Governors or members of the US Congress. According to Mickey Kantor, who was chairman of the successful 1992 Clinton–Gore campaign, and who later served as US Secretary of Commerce and Trade Representative in the Clinton Administration, the modern vetting process is long and intrusive, as it hunts down any possible skeletons in closets:

> It gets as personal as you can get without having any governmental authority. You generally will enlist the services of a number of lawyers or people who have been involved with politics ... and each will take one, two or three people on your list and they will look at public records, financial reports, talk to friends and relatives, and you get a pretty good picture of the person by the end of the process.

Kantor says the first test in whittling down a typical list of 20 or 30 possible VPs is to determine whether the individual is qualified to assume the Presidency if required. 'That will narrow your list to some degree,' Kantor says. 'And the second is "Do no harm" – they should not cause you a problem that will put the campaign off the tracks.' And finally, Kantor says, you look at what the candidate brings to the ticket: 'Who can help you, how can they help you and what they symbolise.'

Sometimes that 'help' comes in the form of the Vice Presidential nominee being a popular politician from a key state, a state that could make the difference in a tight election. Also, often the VP is a 'ticket balancer' – an older, more experienced Vice Presidential candidate can make up for a Presidential candidate's perceived youth and inexperience: 43-year-old Senator John F. Kennedy ran for the Presidency with 52-year-old Senate Majority Leader Lyndon Johnson as his VP in 1960. It also helped that Johnson was from Texas, in the

Deep South; that supplied geographical balance to Kennedy, who was from the northern state of Massachusetts.

'If you do the process right,' 1988 Democratic Presidential nominee Mike Dukakis told me, 'it will inevitably lead you to the right choice.'

Those who favoured a 'unity ticket' of Barack Obama and Hillary Clinton pointed out that in 1980, the partnering of former rivals for the nomination Ronald Reagan and George H.W. Bush helped bring the Republican Party together after a sometimes acrimonious nominating contest.

On a number of occasions, just as 72-year-old John McCain did through biological necessity in 2008, the Presidential candidate has picked a more youthful heir apparent as his running mate. It worked fairly well for 62-year-old Republican Dwight D. Eisenhower and 39-year-old Richard Nixon in 1952, but less so when another Republican, George H.W. Bush, selected Senator Danforth Quayle in 1988. The Vice Presidential candidates' debate that year between Dan Quayle and veteran Democratic Senator Lloyd Bentsen is remembered for one brief but devastating exchange.

The handsome 41-year-old Quayle, having served just seven years as US Senator from Indiana, answered a question about his relative lack of experience by stating correctly that he'd served as long in the Senate as John F. Kennedy had when he won the White House in 1960. The 67-year-old Bentsen look across the stage to Quayle and replied, 'Senator, I served with Jack Kennedy, I knew Jack Kennedy, Jack Kennedy was a friend of mine. Senator, you are no Jack Kennedy.'

Those 23 words have gone down in US political history as the greatest ever 'slam dunk' in a televised debate, something every candidate wants to both replicate and avoid happening to them. 'It was an electric moment, and the thing I remember most was the spontaneous uproar from the audience,' Bentsen's campaign manager, Joe O'Neill, recalls. 'Senator Quayle had been making a lot of references to Kennedy in his stump speeches, and we were aware of that,' O'Neill says. But he denies that the knockout line was scripted in advance.

Mike Dukakis, the Democrats' Presidential nominee, was watching the VP debate at home on television:

> I picked up the phone right after and I said, 'You did good' – and he did. His performance in that debate was terrific. But it was more than that – he was thoughtful, he was mature and I don't think anybody doubted if anything happened to me, Lloyd Bentsen would have been an excellent President.

The same could not be said for Dan Quayle. In that single 30-second exchange in an otherwise forgettable debate, Dan Quayle had spectacularly failed the first of Mickey Kantor's Vice Presidential tests – he didn't look ready to be President. Ironically, O'Neill says, he was later told by Roger Ailes, Bush's media adviser and Fox News founder, that Quayle had only been chosen as Bush's Vice Presidential running mate because they were convinced he would make the silver-haired Bentsen look old.

Dukakis says Quayle became a serious liability for George H.W. Bush's Presidential bid, but reflecting on the campaign 20 years later, he told me:

> I don't think I exploited it as fully as I should have – we had good polling information saying had the race ended up much closer, Lloyd Bentsen could have made the difference. He turned out to be a terrific running mate and had I run a better national campaign he could well have made the difference because the contrast with Dan Quayle was so clear.

But just like George McGovern 16 years earlier, and John Kerry 16 years later, Mike Dukakis says his biggest problem in 1988 was his failure to effectively respond to Republican attacks on his record. 'It was just a terrible mistake,' he says now. During the campaign, Dukakis was criticised for a prisoner furlough program he'd presided over as Governor of Massachusetts, through which a convicted murderer named Willie Horton was freed – he later committed a rape and an assault:

> I'm a positive guy and I thought I could somehow brush it off, but you can't if they are coming at you with this stuff. After my experience and Kerry's experience, I don't think any Democratic nominee will ever let that happen again, and Obama certainly isn't.

The team of Bush and Quayle comfortably won the 1988 election against Dukakis–Bentsen, by an almost 8 per cent margin, carrying 40 states. But Vice President Quayle gained a reputation for bungling and misspeaking, claiming on one occasion that man could breathe on Mars. Another time the hapless VP corrected a 12-year-old student's spelling, insisting that the word 'potato' should be spelt 'potatoe'. The 6th grader, William Figueroa, later told amused reporters that the Vice President 'is an OK guy, but he needs to study'.

Quayle's embarrassing gaffes may not have lost the 1988 election, but they did provide TV comedians with plenty of material, and they certainly didn't help President Bush's failed re-election effort four years later, when Quayle was again on the ticket. Some observers joked that Quayle made Bush 'impeachment-proof', because nobody would want Dan Quayle as President. But when President Bush collapsed during a state dinner in Japan in early 1992, the joke seemed a very serious possibility – however, it turned out just to be the flu.

In that year, the Democrats went for an unconventional ticket to try to oust President Bush and Vice President Quayle from the White House. Once 46-year-old Arkansas Governor Bill Clinton had sealed the party's presidential nomination, attention turned to who would be his running mate. In 1976, another southern Governor seeking the Presidency, Jimmy Carter, had chosen Walter Mondale – a Senator from Minnesota, well north of the Mason-Dixon Line – as his VP in a classic piece of geographical 'ticket balancing'. Dukakis and Bentsen in 1988 also fitted that North–South (or Boston–Austin) model.

But Clinton's team decided on an unusual option: pick another young southerner, Al Gore, (he was two years younger than Clinton) to run with their young southern Presidential candidate. Clinton's campaign chairman Mickey Kantor says:

> The campaign we were running was about the future. It was about change, about moving in a different direction, and about America creating hope again. And it became clear [that] Al Gore was the perfect option. It defied the way in which, historically, Vice Presidents were chosen, but we didn't believe we needed balance – we needed to emphasise what this effort was about, and that's what Al Gore did.

And of course it worked.

Still, all that VP vetting can seem like a lot of fuss for somebody who doesn't really have much to do except hang around waiting for the President to die or resign. As far the Constitution of the United States is concerned, as Presiding Officer of the US Senate, the Vice President can be called in to break a tie in the 100-member chamber and has a duty to oversee and certify the official count of the Electoral College which votes for the President. Otherwise, that's pretty much it for four years – the Vice President's job is to do as much or as little as the President asks of them. Being the political equivalent of an understudy led Founding Father Benjamin Franklin to describe the

Vice President as 'His Superfluous Excellency', and Vice President Thomas Marshall once described himself as 'a spare tyre to be used only in the case of emergency'.

≈≈≈

Unlike Al Gore, who had run unsuccessfully for the Presidency himself in 1988 as well as 2000, his Vice Presidential successor, Dick Cheney, never seemed to want the top job – although you could well argue that he got it at times. Richard B. 'Dick' Cheney was a senior White House adviser to President Gerald Ford (1974–77), and then spent five terms as a Congressman from Wyoming before being appointed US Defense Secretary under President George H.W. Bush. It was Cheney who was set the task of putting together a list of potential Vice Presidential running mates for Texas Governor George W. Bush in mid-2000. Turns out George didn't think much of the list of VPs but liked the guy who put it together. That was despite the fact that Cheney had a less than distinguished military record, having successfully sought six deferments after becoming eligible for service in the Vietnam War – Mike Dukakis describes him as 'the biggest draft-dodger in American history'. Cheney also had a number of serious health problems, having suffered at least four heart attacks before having a defibrillator implanted in 2001.

Cheney's lack of personal Presidential ambition was part of the reason he managed to redefine the role of the Vice President, becoming what David Frum, former speechwriter and Special Adviser to President Bush, describes as the most influential VP in history:

> He has maybe taken his job to the limits. Historically, Vice Presidents were completely unimportant people, the subject of political humour, but starting with Jimmy Carter's Vice President (Walter Mondale) in the 1970s, each Vice President has become more important to policy-making than the last.

The only exception to that rule, Frum says, is Dan Quayle, whom he diplomatically refers to as 'more like a typical Vice President of the past'. Err ... quite.

In the moments following the two attacks on the World Trade Center towers in New York City and the Pentagon building in Arlington, Virginia on September 11, 2001, President Bush was famously reading a book called *The Pet Goat* to students at the Booker Elementary School in Sarasota, Florida. After it became clear that the US was facing a co-ordinated terrorist strike, President Bush spoke by telephone to Dick Cheney, who was in his office in the West Wing of the White House in Washington DC, then boarded the Presidential plane *Air Force One*. In that telephone conversation, President Bush would later tell the 9/11 Commission, he authorised the shooting down of any other hijacked planes which threatened Washington. Minutes later, when a military aide told Vice President Cheney that United Flight 93, a Boeing 757 with 7 crew, 33 passengers and 4 hijackers on board, was heading for Washington, and possibly the White House itself, it was Vice President Cheney who technically issued the order to shoot down the plane.

The funny part is, the 9/11 Commission established that there was no evidence that the call from President Bush on *Air Force One* to Vice President Cheney in the White House ever took place, or that Cheney had the President's authority to issue the order to shoot down a civilian airliner. Questions were asked at the commission about whether in fact the Presidential authorisation came *after* the Vice President issued the order. That suggestion was denied. Still, whatever really happened, and in what order, Dick Cheney's role in responding to the extraordinary events of September 11, 2001, was unlike that of any other Vice President in history.

Having seen Cheney in action inside the White House in 2001

and 2002, David Frum believes the power of future VPs will inevitably diminish:

> We've probably taken this about as far as we can go, and it's still true that the Vice President has no institutional power and only has as much power as the President chooses to accord him – and it's doubtful the next Vice President will be as powerful as Dick Cheney because George Bush relied on Dick Cheney so much.

But as luck would have it, most people won't remember Dick Cheney as the most influential Vice President ever; instead they'll probably just recall that he shot someone in the face. In February 2006, Dick Cheney shot 78-year-old millionaire attorney Harry Whittington in the head, neck and chest with pellets from a shotgun while hunting for quail on a Texas ranch. To make matters worse, Whittington then suffered a minor heart attack after a pellet lodged in the outer layers of that ageing organ, and was rushed to hospital. Cheney admitted to having had 'a beer at lunch', but denied that alcohol had anything to do with his lousy aim (he was never breathalysed). Wittington was discharged from hospital six days later and may well be the only lawyer in history to be shot in the face and not sue. In fact he apologised to Dick Cheney for all the fuss … now that's power. But perhaps Harry Whittington was a student of American political history and knew things could have been much worse.

In 1804, Vice President Aaron Burr shot and killed a man who had thwarted his political ambitions once too often. That man was one of the Founding Fathers of the United States, Alexander Hamilton, who'd backed Thomas Jefferson over Burr in a tricky 1800 election when electoral votes were tied. Hamilton had also blocked Burr's bid to become Governor of New York four years later, and that was the final straw. A very cranky Vice President Burr challenged Hamilton to a pistol duel where he gained satisfaction – Hamilton was shot dead. But Burr still never became President.

If Dick Cheney enjoyed power, if not marksmanship, that far exceeded that of any other Vice President, Thomas R. Marshall (the 'spare tyre') shunned greater responsibility at just about every turn. A small, simple man with a slightly-too-large moustache, it was Thomas Marshall who famously quipped during a long Senate debate, 'What this country needs is a good 5 cent cigar' (although some argue the line was taken from the funny pages of the time). Vice President Marshall was in office from 1913 to 1921, and was by all accounts a very modest man. He enjoyed a good smoke and a pithy story, and lived quite cheerfully in the long shadow cast by President Woodrow Wilson.

Wilson hadn't wanted Marshall as his Vice Presidential running mate, and once lumbered with this folksy fellow from Indiana by party officials, he proceeded to largely ignore him. He described Vice President Marshall as 'a small calibre man', and for his part, Marshall was self-deprecating to the point of insecurity: 'The American people may have made a mistake in setting me down in the company of all the wise men in the land.'

Vice President Marshall seemed to spend a good amount of time with his feet up on his desk, growing his moustache and puffing on a cigar that cost more than 5 cents. After he and Wilson were elected, Marshall attended a few Cabinet meetings, but found himself out of his depth, overlooked and irrelevant. He mused, 'I do not blame proud parents wishing that their sons might be President of the United States, but if I sought a blessing for the boy I would not pray that he becomes Vice President.'

Yet for all his modesty, Vice President Marshall was becoming something of a Washington celebrity. His line about the 'good 5 cent cigar' struck a chord with American smokers, and cigar-makers used it in their advertising and sent boxes of cheap cigars to the Vice President's office. Marshall also used his homespun wit to great effect as an after-dinner speaker – so much so that Wilson had no choice but to keep Marshall on the ticket in the 1916 election, which saw the Democrats returned and Marshall become the first Vice President in eight years given a second term.

The US entered World War I in April 1917, and President Wilson became the key architect of the Treaty of Versailles, signed in June 1919, which established the postwar order and set out plans for the ill-fated League of Nations. That international work forced Wilson to spend months away from the US, and he decided that Vice President Marshall should put out his cigar, get his feet off his desk and preside over Cabinet meetings. It was Marshall's chance to show that he had what it takes. He duly attended a few Cabinet sessions, but then thought better of it, apparently concerned that deputising in this way compromised his duties to the Senate. So he went back to his desk, lit another cigar and left it to others to run the affairs of state in Wilson's absence.

Opportunity knocked again for Marshall in October 1919, when Woodrow Wilson suffered a paralytic stroke. While First Lady Edith Wilson and Presidential physician Cary Grayson hushed up the extent of the President's infirmity, it soon became clear that Wilson could die at any time. But Vice President Marshall was stunned at the prospect of leading the US. According to the diary of Agriculture Secretary David Houston:

> The Vice President expressed the view … that it would be a tragedy for him to assume the duties of the President, at best, and that it would equally be a tragedy for the people; that he knew many men who knew more about the affairs of the government than he did.

So again Marshall deferred to other Cabinet members when Wilson was unable to work. He spent the last 18 months in office dreading the idea that he might become President at any tick of the clock. President Wilson clung to life and, technically, power, but his illness meant that he failed to get the Treaty of Versailles ratified by the US Senate. Thomas Marshall left the office of Vice President in January 1921 a very relieved man.

John Nance Garner was no Thomas Marshall – he really wanted to be President, not Vice President. The prickly Texan known as 'Cactus Jack' Garner served 30 years in the US House of Representatives, rising to the influential position of speaker, and in 1932, with America in the depths of the Great Depression, decided it was his time to run for the White House. The sitting President, Republican Herbert Hoover (1929–33), was about as popular as the economic downturn he'd failed to prevent, so Cactus Jack liked his chances of winning the White House.

Unfortunately, he found himself fighting the wealthy and popular New York Governor Franklin Delano Roosevelt for the Democratic Party's nomination. Garner lost, but was given the Vice Presidency as a consolation prize in return for backing Roosevelt. So while FDR is now remembered as one of the greatest Presidents ever, Garner is remembered for ruefully observing that the Vice Presidency was 'not worth a warm bucket of spit'. In fact he's not even remembered too well for that, because others quote Garner as saying that the Vice Presidency wasn't worth 'a warm pitcher of piss'. Either way, his feelings on the subject are apparent.

Unlike 14 other Vice Presidents, Jack Nance Garner never got the number one job. He waited around for eight years, and began running for the Presidency himself in 1940, when it was assumed that Franklin Roosevelt would step down. Ever since America's iconic first President, George Washington, had declined a third term, the convention was that no President would stay in office for more than two four-year terms. But FDR couldn't let go – after all, there was a war in Europe which threatened to embroil the US any day. 'Cactus

Jack' stood for election in 1940 against FDR anyway, but lost on the floor of the Democratic Party convention ... and lost the Vice Presidency to boot, though that troubled him less.

Franklin Roosevelt's next Vice President was his former Agriculture Secretary, Henry A. Wallace, a rather enlightened man who was decades ahead of his time on issues like the racial desegregation of the southern states. But Henry Wallace had an inclination towards what would now be described as 'new age mysticism' and he was also rather more pro-Soviet Union than was considered wise. Wallace was the Dennis Kucinich of his day.

Roosevelt's health wasn't great: in fact he'd been paralysed from the waist down since 1921 after an illness thought to have been polio but now suspected of being the autoimmune disease Guillain-Barre Syndrome. Remarkably, Roosevelt's ongoing infirmity was largely kept from the American people, most of whom never knew their President was unable to actually walk. He was propped up and supported by aides during public speeches, and was hardly ever photographed or filmed in his wheelchair.

But by 1944 FDR's heavy smoking and the pressures of office were adding significantly to his health problems: he had advanced heart disease. Democratic Party powerbrokers decided that slightly wacky old Henry Wallace shouldn't be the one to inherit the Presidency should Roosevelt die during his fourth term. Wallace had to go. And so it was Senator Harry S. Truman of Missouri who became FDR's third Vice President.

Harry Truman was a short, bespectacled man, and he had been an Army captain and a haberdasher from Independence, Missouri before becoming a Senator. He was made head of a Senate committee which was set up to make sure Defence contractors weren't ripping off the American taxpayers, and that was enough to win him the nomination for the Vice Presidency in 1944 over Wallace, as FDR stood for an unprecedented fourth term ... and won.

It was just 82 days after being sworn in as Vice President that Harry Truman was taking another oath – as the 33rd President of the United States. In those 82 days, Harry Truman had hardly seen President Roosevelt, and he had never had a briefing on the atomic bomb which within months he would order to be used against Japan. When Roosevelt suddenly died, at the age of 63, while receiving treatment for his paralysis at Warm Springs in Georgia, Truman told reporters he felt 'the moon, the stars and all the planets' had fallen on him.

President Truman famously had a small wooden sign on his desk in the Oval Office of the White House inscribed with the motto 'The buck stops here!', reflecting the ultimate authority and responsibility fate had given him. Less well known is the fact that on the side of the sign facing the President was written 'I'm from Missouri', a contraction of the expression 'I'm from Missouri – you've got to show me.' The saying was initially coined in the 19th century to suggest that folk from Missouri were kind of slow and needed to be shown something before they'd believe it, but the meaning changed over the years to suggest instead that people from Missouri were canny, not easily fooled or misled. Despite being seen as something of an 'accidental President', Harry Truman's steady hand during the final months of World War II and his firm line with the Soviet Union in the early stages of the Cold War won him a place in history few would have predicted. While he was never particularly popular in office, Truman's reputation has grown considerably since, and he's been ranked among the top ten Presidents of the United States by numerous surveys of political scientists.

George W. Bush, during his unpopular second term, often told reporters that he expected history would be kind to him and his handling of the 'war on terror' and the wars in Afghanistan and Iraq, just as it had been to President Truman.

Lack of ambition was never an issue for Richard Milhous Nixon. Vice President under General Dwight D. 'Ike' Eisenhower from 1953 to 1961, Nixon's rise through Republican ranks was meteoric. He was elected to the US House of Representatives in 1946, and became a leading anti-communist crusader in the notorious House Un-American Activities Committee (HUAC). He rose to national prominence for his questioning of a former State Department official named Alger Hiss, who was accused of spying for the Soviet Union. Nixon launched a bitter but successful bid for a Senate seat in 1950, and in 1952 the 39-year-old was named as Eisenhower's Vice Presidential running mate.

Richard Nixon became the first of a new breed of Vice Presidents, travelling widely, meeting world leaders and generally preparing for his own time as President. His time almost came in 1960, when he narrowly lost to John F. Kennedy in one of the closest Presidential elections in history. But on that occasion TV proved to be his undoing: a shifty, sweaty-looking Nixon with a five-o'clock shadow, who refused to wear makeup for the cameras, couldn't match the youthful, tanned good looks of Senator Kennedy.

People listening to the candidate's four Presidential debates on the radio awarded them to Nixon, but TV viewers were sure Kennedy had won. So it wasn't until 1968, after the assassinations of JFK, his brother Robert Kennedy and civil right leader Dr Martin Luther King Jr, that Nixon was finally elected to the Presidency over the Democratic candidate, Vice President Hubert H. Humphrey. In August 1974 he became the first President in US history to resign to avoid impeachment for 'high crimes and misdemeanours' – over the cover-ups surrounding the Watergate scandal. Nixon's Vice President, Gerald R. Ford, became President, but only because Nixon's first Vice President, Spiro Agnew, had resigned 10 months earlier in the face of charges that he had taken bribes – Agnew later pleaded no contest and repaid the money.

※

Four American Presidents have been assassinated, all of them shot: Abraham Lincoln in 1865, James Garfield in 1881 (although it took him a couple of months to die from his wounds), William McKinley in 1901 and John F. Kennedy in 1963. This means that four Vice Presidents – Andrew Johnson, Chester Arthur, Theodore Roosevelt and Lyndon Johnson – came to office suddenly and amid tragedy.

When Lyndon Baines Johnson took the Presidential oath of office on 22 November 1963 onboard *Air Force One* on the tarmac at Love Field in Texas, former First Lady Jacqueline Kennedy was by his side, with the blood of her slain husband drying on her jacket. Five days later, President Johnson addressed a joint sitting of Congress, saying, 'All I have I would have given gladly not to be standing here today. The greatest leader of our time has been struck down by the foulest deed of our time.' Johnson vowed to continue the policies of the Kennedy Administration, and in doing so he reaffirmed America's commitment to 'South Viet-Nam' and to be 'unceasing in the search for peace'. Johnson led the US deeper into a war that effectively cost him the Presidency and dominated American politics for a decade.

※

The first woman to be nominated as a Vice Presidential candidate on a major party ticket was Democratic Representative Geraldine Ferraro – a mere 196 years after the nomination of the first male Vice President, John Adams. Mrs Ferraro was the running mate of Walter Mondale, former Carter Vice President, in his unsuccessful 1984 bid for the White House. I spoke to her during the early weeks of the primary election campaign, in February 2008, at a 'Hillary Clinton for President' call centre in a Teachers' Union building in New York City.

Along with dozens of other volunteers, Ferraro was calling potential voters from a printed list. 'I just got a guy with a heavy Irish accent – he said it was the wrong number.' So far she'd had lots of answering machines and lots of wrong numbers. 'It's like my bingo cards,' the 72-year-old Ferraro deadpanned, 'never the right numbers.' She dialled again … another answering machine. She left a message:

> Hi, this is Geraldine Ferraro calling for Lisa Dalden. Miss Dalden, I'm calling for Hillary Clinton and urging you to please come out and vote for her. As someone who has run for national office, I've been waiting for a long time this opportunity to campaign for someone like Hillary for President.

I asked Ferraro, when she finds someone at home, do they remember her, and do people think it's a joke when a former Vice Presidential candidate calls them up on the phone? She laughed:

> They say, 'Is this *the* Geraldine Ferraro?' I say, 'Yeah.' It happens all the time when I'm paying a bill: they say, 'Is this *the* Geraldine Ferraro!' But get somebody who is 22 – they wouldn't have a clue who I am.

I wanted to know if Mrs Ferraro was surprised that almost a quarter of a century after she ran for the Vice Presidency, gender is still seen as an issue in politics:

> As soon as a woman runs for politics, gender is an issue; as soon as a black person is running, their race is an issue. When I ran, being the first Italian-American was also an issue – in fact it was a worse one.

She freely admitted that if she hadn't been a woman she would never have been selected as Walter Mondale's Vice Presidential nominee in 1984. A high point of that campaign came when she took on George H.W. Bush in the Vice Presidential debate. It was declared a draw by most pundits, but George was overheard boasting that he'd 'kicked a little ass'. It got worse; after the debate, when future First Lady Barbara Bush was asked what she thought of Mrs Ferraro, she said she couldn't say it on television, but it rhymed with 'rich'. Mrs Bush later called Ferraro to apologise, saying the rhyming word she meant was 'witch'. Even if the gender barrier had been broken, the flipside of the sexism coin – the idea that female politicians had to be treated differently, and had to act differently – was still there.

Ferraro created quite a media flap herself in March 2008 when she said Obama wouldn't be where he is today if he weren't black. Like Bill Clinton, she was accused of playing 'the race card', and she stood down from further public involvement in the campaign. 'It's OK to be sexist in this country,' she told me, 'but it's not so good to be racist. I personally think it's not good to be either one.' And with that she was back to her call sheet. 'This is driving me nuts! I haven't got a single real person today!'

Ironically, the selection of Geraldine Ferraro as the Vice Presidential candidate for the Democrats in 1984 is the reason Walter Mondale's former Press Secretary Maxine Isaacs says she didn't see the need to support Hillary in 2008: 'Walter Mondale said to the world, "I'm choosing a woman and I believe she's qualified to be President."' As a result, Isaacs says she doesn't think gender is an issue any more. 'I believe the country dealt with that question. They're past it; we dealt with it 24 years ago.' She put her considerable influence and ability to help generate financial support behind Obama.

Naturally enough, once Barack Obama had won enough delegates and Super Delegates during the caucuses and primaries in the first five months of 2008 to secure the Democratic Presidential nomination, attention immediately turned to who he would pick as his Vice Presidential running mate. In the dying days of her campaign, Hillary Clinton none-too-subtly let it slip in a conference call with financial backers that she would be open to an invitation to be Obama's Vice Presidential nominee. A number of prominent Hillary supporters argued that after such a long and close nominating contest the best way to bring the party together and ensure victory over McCain in November was with a 'unity ticket'. When I spoke in July 2008 to Mickey Kantor, who acted as an informal adviser to Senator Clinton throughout her campaign, he was convinced that the pairing of the former rivals would create huge excitement:

> She has enormous experience, particularly in the foreign policy and
> defence area; it would be a perfect blend of two people who between
> them have received 36 million votes in the primaries.

Obama established a committee to conduct what amounted to an executive search for the Democratic VP, and that search was to be headed by Maxine Isaacs' husband, the multimillionaire businessman Jim Johnson. Johnson, a former chairman of mortgage lender Fannie Mae, had headed the 1984 search for Mondale's VP that came up with Geraldine Ferraro (Johnson and Ferraro got engaged in November 1984). Johnson also ran Senator John Kerry's VP vetting process, which picked John Edwards, in 2004.

While the final decision always rests with the Presidential candidate, it is a huge responsibility for the VP search committee members, as they may also, in effect, be shortlisting or ruling out a future President of the United States. 'Clearly Jim has great stature,' says Joe O'Neill, who counts Johnson as a friend. 'He's widely recognised in Washington as one of the really smart guys. He's also very methodical, meticulous, and keeps his own counsel, which is very important – and he has a network of lieutenants to do the vetting.'

Also on Obama's VP search committee in 2008 were President John F. Kennedy's daughter Caroline and former Clinton Administration Deputy Attorney General Eric Holder. As well as considering an Obama–Clinton ticket, the search team looked at a list of about 20 potential VPs, believed to include former NATO commander General Wesley Clark, who had campaigned himself for the Democratic Presidential nomination in 2004 and supported Hillary Clinton in the 2008 nominating contest. A number of other former Obama rivals, including Senator Joe Biden, Senator Chris Dodd, former Senator John Edwards and Governor Bill Richardson, were all reportedly considered for the VP slot.

Indeed some pundits suggested that even when we'd seen Bill Richardson shaking hands and sweating it out at the Iowa State Fair back in August 2007, he had really been running for the Vice Presidential spot, not the Presidential one. But Dave Contarino, his campaign manager, denied it when I spoke to him during the 2008 VP search process. 'Bill Richardson believed, and still believes, that he was the best person running to be President,' Contarino said. 'We never had a discussion about running for the Vice Presidency – that never entered Bill Richardson's mind.' But after Richardson dropped out and endorsed Obama, Contarino told me, he was definitely interested in the job. 'Certainly if you think you are qualified to be President you think you're qualified to be Vice President. If Senator Obama wanted to talk about that he'd be honoured and he would certainly entertain those discussions.' Joe Biden also stated openly that if asked, he would be happy to serve as Obama's Vice President. John Edwards maintained that he'd run for the Vice Presidency before in 2004 and didn't want to do it again.

Obama's VP committee hit a snag when Jim Johnson was criticised in the *Wall Street Journal* for accepting what it called a 'favourable' $2 million loan from Countrywide Finance, a firm which had become caught up in America's sub-prime mortgage crisis. Johnson immediately resigned from his post to avoid damaging Obama's candidacy. 'Quite frankly it was unfortunate, and it was a bit of a loss for Senator Obama not to have Jim's input into the process this time around,' says Joe O'Neill.

The McCain campaign claimed that with Johnson's resignation, Obama had failed in the first real test of his judgment. Meanwhile, the VP search and the speculation continued. Would Obama go for Hillary after all? Or maybe another woman – Governor Kathleen Sebelius of Kansas, who gave the State of the Union reply in January 2008 and then endorsed Obama? Or maybe he would opt for Vietnam veteran-turned-novelist-turned-Senator Jim Webb, who had also served in the Reagan Administration. The name of Virginia Governor Tim Kaine was also mentioned often during the weeks leading up to the announcement.

In late July it became clear why John Edwards didn't want to face the vetting process for the Vice Presidential slot. After being chased by a tabloid reporter into the men's room of the Beverly Hilton Hotel in the early hours of the morning of 22 July, Edwards later admitted he had been in the room of a former campaign employee named Rielle Hunter. After a series of reports in *The National Enquirer* claiming Edwards had fathered her 'love child', the former Presidential candidate confessed to having had a brief affair with Ms Hunter in 2006 while she was filming him on the campaign trail, although Edwards denied he was the father of her child. Many Edwards supporters just shook their heads, feeling sorry for Elizabeth Edwards, and wondering what would have happened if Senator Edwards had actually won the nomination for the Presidency.

In the end, Barack Obama's choice of Joe Biden as his Vice Presidential running mate, just three days before his party's National Convention began in Denver, was an attempt to counter claims the Democratic nominee lacked experience – particularly when it came to foreign policy. Biden, despite having questioned Obama's preparedness to lead America while campaigning for the Presidency just a year earlier, and for all his verbal gaffes (including his unfortunate description of Obama as being 'clean') and the chance another slip could damage the Obama campaign, the Senator from Delaware was still seen to have the gravitas required to take on John McCain. Those thirty-six 'ears of experience' finally paid off for Joe Biden. Ironically, of all recent Presidential tickets, with their mix of youth and experience Obama–Biden probably most closely resembled Bush–Cheney – although Democrats understandably preferred the comparison with the Washington outsider Governor Clinton and the insider Senator Gore in 1992.

On the Republican side, David Frum had worked for Rudy Giuliani in his spectacularly unsuccessful 2008 Presidential run, so it was not surprising that he favoured a McCain–Rudy team:

> John McCain needs to be thinking, if he wins, [that] his running mate is a future leader of the party. Given McCain's age, the VP could be running as soon as 2012. Who do you want that person to be and what is your vision of the kind of Republican Party you leave behind?

Frum says the same planning for the ideological future of his party applies even if McCain loses.

The day after Senator Obama accepted the Democratic Party's Presidential nomination with another widely praised speech in front of 84 000 delirious supporters at Invesco football Field in Denver, John McCain celebrated his 72nd birthday with a Vice Presidential pick that took most pundits completely by surprise. In a move described as 'bold and brilliant' or 'insane' (depending on whether you watched Fox News or CNN), McCain announced conservative Alaskan Governor Sarah Palin would be his running-mate.

The 44-year-old mother of five had been in office only 20 months, and became just the second woman nominated for the Vice Presidency on a major party ticket after Geraldine Ferraro 24 years earlier. In her first appearance on the campaign trail, Governor Palin paid tribute to Ferraro and Hillary Clinton, no doubt hoping to woo disaffected female Democrats – but in the media there were as many comparisons being drawn between Palin and Dan Quayle as Palin and Ferraro or Hillary Clinton. Did she pass Mickey Kantor's first test: was she qualified to assume the Presidency, if required? Would Palin undermine McCain's own argument that Obama wasn't ready to lead?

As well as being McCain's birthday, 29 August 2008 was also the third anniversary of Hurricane Katrina hitting New Orleans. To many, the Bush Administration's inept response to that disaster, which claimed nearly two thousand lives, came to typify their failures. As fate would have it, as McCain stepped on stage to introduce Sarah Palin to supporters in Dayton, Ohio, another major storm was brewing in the Caribbean. Forecasters said Hurricane Gustav could make landfall around New Orleans within three days – the first day of the Republican National Convention in St Paul, Minnesota.

And so, with the running-mates announced, the stage was set. Eighteen months after embarking on what he described as 'an improbable quest' in Lincoln's home town of Springfield, Illinois, Senator Barack Obama prepared for the final nine weeks of a marathon Presidential campaign that had already made history and promised to make more. His ability to motivate and inspire grassroots supporters had seen off all comers, including the formidable Clinton political machine – in the process ending two decades of two-family rule in the US. But the polls were close – much closer than many Democrats had expected.

Now, just one man stood between America and its first black President: John McCain, a man whose journey, from five and a half years in a military prison in Hanoi to his party's Presidential nomination, after being vilified and defeated in 2000 and almost bankrupted in mid-2007, had been just as improbable and, for millions of Americans, just as inspiring.

11 The Fall

Hurricane Gustav churned its way through the Caribbean with winds gusting up to 240 kilometres per hour, killing more than 50 people in Haiti alone before raging into the Gulf of Mexico. It was announced that both President Bush and Vice President Cheney would cancel their speeches on the first day of the Republican National Convention to oversee the emergency response. John McCain headed straight to the Gulf States, declaring: 'It wouldn't be appropriate to have a festive occasion while a near tragedy or a terrible challenge is presented in the form of a natural disaster.' The Convention was suspended except for some minor procedural matters and a brief address by Cindy McCain and first Lady Laura Bush. But as the hours passed, Gustav steadily lost intensity, weakening from what New Orleans Mayor Ray Nagin called 'the mother of all storms into the mother-in-law of all storms'.

The worst of it was felt in places like Cocodrie, Louisiana, and while Gustav was no Katrina, dozens of people were killed in the storm, in road accidents or from heart attacks during the evacuation.

Meanwhile, another major storm was brewing. Not the four named Atlantic low-pressure systems queuing up behind Gustav, any one of which could potentially have turned into another Hurricane Katrina, but a whirlwind of news reports and a torrent of internet rumours about Sarah Palin.

First it was revealed that Palin was under investigation for dismissing an Alaskan Government official: Public Safety Commissioner Walt Monegan. Monegan had refused to sack Palin's former brother-in-law, a State Trooper who had been involved in a messy divorce from Palin's sister, and had admitted using a stun-gun on Palin's nephew. All true, said the McCain campaign, but she did nothing improper and it wasn't about her brother-in-law; she had 'other reasons' to dismiss the official. (A later inquiry would find that while Palin abused her authority and violated Alaska's ethics laws, she had had other reasons to sack Monegan.)

Then the same tabloid that got the scoop on the John Edwards affair, *The National Enquirer*, reported that Sarah Palin had had an affair with her husband Todd's former business partner – completely untrue, said the McCain campaign. There were also reports, fuelled by blogs, that Governor Palin's fifth child, a son named Trig, who was born in early 2008 and who has Down's syndrome, was really the son of her 17-year-old daughter Bristol – untrue, said the McCain campaign. The internet scuttlebutt continued. Photos of Palin as a swim-suited 21-year-old Miss Alaska entrant surfaced and were splashed across TV screens around the world. More pictures emerged, of Palin in a Stars-and-Stripes bikini toting a hunting rifle – they proved to have been digitally altered, but many Americans believed they were real.

The *Washington Post* then reported what many observers now suspected: Palin had been a last-minute decision and hadn't been properly vetted. Does she even have a passport? Yes, she got her first passport in 2006. Former Reagan speechwriter and conservative *Wall Street Journal* columnist Peggy Noonan was discussing the Palin selection on the NBC TV network, and when they went to an ad break she was picked up saying, ruefully, 'It's over' on a live mic.

The mainstream media were alternately fascinated and appalled by Palin; the polls said voters were intrigued, and had yet to make up their minds. Then it was announced, during Day 1 of the Republican National Convention, that Bristol Palin was in fact pregnant to her ice hockey jock boyfriend Levi Johnston, who described himself on his MySpace page as a 'fucking redneck' who didn't ever want kids. No longer was the name 'Dan Quayle' being muttered darkly; now the word was 'Eagleton'. Things were beginning to unravel for McCain's 'maverick' Vice Presidential pick.

Thomas Mann is a respected political analyst and senior fellow at The Brookings Institution, one of the oldest Washington DC public policy organisations or thinktanks. (It describes itself as non-partisan, although it is generally regarded as centrist or centre-left politically.) He was in St Paul for the Republican National Convention as 'Hurricane Sarah' hit:

> Controversy was swirling, rumours were around, and it sounded like a soap opera in many respects. It wouldn't have been that important had it not been for the bewilderment over how John McCain – who emphasises national security – could have selected someone who is, frankly, patently unqualified to assume the responsibilities of the Presidency, and someone who is under investigation for abuses of power to settle a personal score.

As far as Tom Mann was concerned, the issue became John McCain's decision-making:

> It raises questions about John McCain's judgement and about the vetting process. When you select a Vice President, your running-mate,

it's your first executive decision ... [she's] certainly not ready for the White House at this time and so John McCain finds himself in serious difficulties, and this isn't going away.

After all but cancelling the first day of the Republican Convention in Minneapolis-St Paul because of Hurricane Gustav, the major speeches finally got under way on Day 2. They included an address from President Bush beamed live into the hall from the White House. He was still too busy overseeing the federal response to what was now heavy precipitation to attend in person. As for Dick Cheney, nobody could really remember when he had last been seen anywhere.

Former Presidential candidate Mike Huckabee, who had recently signed on with Fox *News* to host his own chat show, roused delegates on Day 2 by quipping that the media flap over Sarah Palin's family situation was 'tackier than a costume change at a Madonna concert'. He also said he was sick of claims that Palin lacked experience, especially compared with the Democratic VP candidate. 'She got more votes running for mayor of Wasilla, Alaska, than Joe Biden did running for President of the United States.' Ouch! (Not actually true.)

Six days of intense media scrutiny since being named as McCain's running mate had created huge interest in Sarah Palin's speech on Night 3 of the Convention. More than 40 million American television viewers tuned in to see the Alaskan Governor speak for herself, just 2 million fewer than watched Senator Obama's Democratic Convention speech a week earlier. Despite being thrust into the national media spotlight before what was by far the largest audience of her career, and despite a faulty teleprompter which meant she was forced at times to read off a scrawled-on early draft of the speech that had been folded up in a campaign aide's back pocket, Sarah Palin gave an outstanding and confident performance that delighted and reinvigorated the conservative base of the Republican Party. She countered claims of her lack of political experience by highlighting her real-life experience. The self-described 'hockey-mom' also quipped, 'You know the difference between a hockey-mom and a pit-bull? Lipstick!' Palin ripped into Obama as a man who had 'authored two memoirs but not a single major law or even reform'. The hall at the Xcel Energy Centre erupted into applause. Doubts and despair instantly turned to elation.

The speech was a huge hit. Sarah Palin's large all-Alaskan family – including her husband Todd and an awkward-looking Levi, who was conspicuously holding hands with Bristol throughout the address and wearing a suit in the unfamiliar way of a footballer at an awards night – looked on proudly. The young couple, it was gushingly announced, was engaged to be married. But for all the stage-management, there hadn't been such a 'star is born' moment in US politics since Barack Obama's keynote Democratic Convention speech in 2004. Suddenly nobody was muttering 'Quayle' or 'Eagleton' … it was 'the conservative Obama' or in even more reverent tones, the deified 'Reagan'.

John McCain's own nomination acceptance speech the following night was largely overshadowed, but the post-Convention poll bounce put McCain-Palin in front of Obama-Biden for the first time since the Illinois Senator sealed the nomination in June. The 5-day conflict between Russia and Georgia over the breakaway provinces of South Ossetia and Abkhazia had played to McCain's strength of foreign affairs and national security and helped him get back into the contest in August, and now with the Palin selection he moved from an 8 per cent deficit to a 5 per cent lead over Obama in the Gallup daily tracking polls of early September. Another poll, from *USA Today* on 5 September, had McCain surging to a 10 per cent lead. Mac was back – yet again.

Democrats grew nervous. Could they yet find a way to lose this election? Was it a mistake to overlook Hillary even for the Vice Presidential nomination? A growing number of former Hillary supporters said they were now switching their votes to McCain because of Sarah Palin. Suddenly women were asking for the Sarah Palin Hairdo – a swept-up bun with a Scotty terrier fringe – and there were reports of optometrists selling out of her designer 'Kawasaki 704' spectacles.

Dr Lynette Long is a Maryland psychologist, feminist and author. She was a vocal backer of Hillary Clinton during the primaries, but after it became clear that Senator Obama would be the Democratic nominee she had a meeting with Senator McCain and his senior adviser, Carly Fiorina, and said she implored him to select a woman as his VP. When he did, Long endorsed McCain and made several appearances at campaign events. I ask Dr Long why she changed party allegiance in the middle of an election. She concedes that it was as much a protest vote as anything else:

> Hillary Clinton was treated appallingly in the primaries by the Democratic party and the media. Women are very angry. Hillary got more votes than Obama ... she got 19 million votes – more than any other candidate in history in the primaries – and she wasn't given a spot on the ticket.

Washington Republican pollster Dr Whit Ayers explained the surge in support for the GOP in September:

> The excitement that Sarah Palin has brought to the ticket is quite remarkable. White women have really been energised by the Palin pick. There has been enormous excitement because Sarah Palin is not only a woman but a working mom with whom a great many women can identify.
>
> If Barack Obama had picked Hillary as his running mate John McCain would have had far less incentive to have picked a woman and Sarah Palin might not even be on the ticket. On the other hand, Barack Obama didn't want to have to try to govern with Bill Clinton whispering in Hillary's ear in the office next to his for the next 4 years.

So I understand why they did not pick Hillary, but it has opened the door to the Palin phenomenon.

I wanted to know how Lynette Long and other Democratic women, who are usually staunchly in favour of a woman's right to choose whether or not to have an abortion, could decide to support an anti-abortion Presidential ticket: Sarah Palin says she'd like to overturn the landmark 1973 Supreme Court ruling *Roe v Wade*, which effectively legalised abortion in the US, and opposes abortion in all instances, including cases of incest and rape. Dr Long tells me:

> I am vehemently pro-choice, but nobody has touched *Roe v Wade* in 35 years and if President [George W.] Bush didn't reverse it, who would? And I can work with Palin and McCain because they are honest and straightforward ... I don't like Barack Obama at all – I don't like his lack of experience, I don't like his church and Reverend Wright, and I don't like the way he was disrespectful of Hillary Clinton.

As well as predicting a McCain win in 2008 because of the support of disaffected women – women make up 52 per cent of the population and 60 per cent of Democrats – Lynette Long expects that the 2012 election will see Hillary Clinton against Sarah Palin because John McCain will be too old to run for re-election – he'll be 76. If that happens, Dr Long says, she isn't sure who she'd vote for.

Barack Obama had proved himself to be a remarkably gaffe-proof candidate during more than 18 months on the campaign trail, apart from his use of the word 'bitter' to describe some working-class voters during the primaries. But comments he made at a campaign stop in Lebanon, Virginia, in September 2008 added to his problem with disaffected female voters. Obama, speaking off the cuff, was likening

John McCain's policies to those of President Bush on a range of issues – the economy, taxation, healthcare, education and foreign policy – saying McCain didn't represent any real change, but he went further: 'That's not change … you know, you can put lipstick on a pig, it's still a pig.' His comment was a reference to an old-style saying, 'You can put lipstick on a pig, but you can't call it a lady', meaning you can pretty something up as much as you like, it doesn't alter what it is. But use of the word 'lipstick' so soon after Sarah Palin's 'lipstick' quip had some Republicans convinced he was in effect calling Sarah Palin a pig. The 'lipstick on a pig' controversy dominated several 24-hour news cycles. Obama accused his critics of expressing 'phoney outrage'.

Despite the defection of some female 'Hillary-crats', the doubts over Palin's readiness to lead should anything happen to John McCain grew. First there came media criticism that the Alaskan Governor was unavailable for interviews; she was being shielded from the press, not even taking any questions from journalists when making campaign appearances. The McCain campaign was asked, had Governor Palin ever actually met a world leader? No, she hadn't. Then came an almost farcical series of 'photo opportunities' during the UN General Assembly in New York in late September where Palin met for 10 minutes or so with a string of world leaders in what amounted to diplomatic 'speed dating' – an impression heightened when first the Pakistani Information Minister Sherry Rehman asked her, 'And how does one keep looking that good when one is so busy?' and then the new Pakistani President, Asif Ali Zardari, shook her hand for a bit too long, and described her as 'Gorgeous … now I know why the whole of America is crazy about you.' He seemed to have gotten over Benazir real fast.

Whit Ayers didn't believe Palin's lack of experience would be a major issue, because of the vulnerability of Barack Obama to similar claims: 'What are the Democrats going to argue, that the Republicans' Vice Presidential candidate is as inexperienced as the Democrats'

Presidential candidate? I don't think that's going to be a compelling argument.' And indeed whenever Obama was asked about Palin's inexperience he skirted around the subject.

After a fortnight's intense cramming on foreign and domestic policy with McCain advisers, including Richard Nixon's former Secretary of State, Henry Kissinger, Sarah Palin was deemed ready to make her debut with the news media. It didn't go well. First, Charlie Gibson on the ABC's *World News* looked like a dubious college professor quizzing a party-girl college student on her missed coursework.

He peered over his half-glasses and asked, 'Do you agree with the Bush Doctrine?'

Governor Palin paused, blinked, and replied, 'In what respect, Charlie?'

Gibson wasn't going to help: 'The Bush ... well, what do you interpret that to be?'

'You mean his world view?' the Governor asked.

'No, the Bush Doctrine enunciated in September 2002 before the Iraq War.'

Sarah Palin licked her carefully painted lips, but her answer was more hockey-mom than pit-bull: 'I believe what President Bush has attempted to do is ... [sigh] ... rid this world of Islamic extremism, terrorists who are hell-bent on destroying our nation. There have been blunders along the way though ...'

Professor Gibson wasn't buying the fudge. Peering again over the top of his half-glasses, Gibson explained to the Governor in a condescending tone: 'The Bush Doctrine, as I understand it, is that we have the right to anticipatory self-defence; that we have the right to make a pre-emptive strike against any country that we think might attack us.'

To many Democrats the exchange proved Palin wasn't on top of her brief, that she didn't really understand the guiding principle of post-9/11 US foreign policy. But to most conservatives she did just fine and Gibson was indulging in cheap 'gotcha journalism'; they said it was a game of 'stump the candidate', just like when then Governor George W. Bush was given a pop quiz on world leaders by a reporter in late 1999.

On that occasion, Bush was asked by Andy Hiller of Boston's WHDH-TV if he could name the General who was in charge of Pakistan, to which Bush replied: 'The new Pakistani general, he's just been elected – not elected, this guy took over office. It appears this guy is going to bring stability to the country and I think that's good news for the subcontinent.' It wasn't really an answer, but it didn't really hurt Bush, and maybe the whole Bush Doctrine thing wouldn't hurt Palin.

As the campaign entered its final eight weeks, and the three Presidential and one Vice Presidential debates loomed, several major Wall Street hedge funds and investment banks started to falter as credit markets froze. In early September, the federal government took control of the publicly traded mortgage giants Fannie Mae and Freddie Mac, who between them had written or guaranteed half the household mortgages in America.

The number of Americans defaulting on their home loans grew as introductory low-interest rates expired, and the number of mortgage foreclosures averaged a staggering 10,000 per day. Suddenly, the banks had all but stopped lending to anyone – including each other. Facing collapse, investment bank Lehman Brothers put itself on the market in what amounted to a fire sale – five days later the firm was declared bankrupt. Merrill Lynch & Co. hurriedly found a buyer in Bank of America Corp., aiming to avoid a similar fate. The next domino to start wobbling was insurer AIG, which needed an emergency transfusion of US$85 billion in government funds to stop it flat-lining. Stockmarkets around the world went into freefall, losing 5 per cent … 8 per cent … even 10 per cent of their value in a single trading session. The Dow fell below 10,000 points, then below 9000 for the first time in 5 years. A ban was imposed on so-called short selling, whereby investors profit from stocks that fall in value, which tends to force sliding markets further down. Former chairman of the Federal Reserve Alan Greenspan said the Wall Street meltdown was a 'once in a hundred years event'. Those comments hardly calmed frayed investor nerves. Another $200 billion was pumped into equity markets by the US and European governments to stem the tide of value vanishing from stocks.

Treasury Secretary Henry Paulson, himself the former Chief Executive of investment bank Goldman Sachs, announced an unprecedented bailout package, worth around $700 billion, whereby the government would use taxpayer funds to buy up bad loans and free up the market. The plan had the backing of President Bush, but before it could be enacted into law it had to pass in the US Senate and House of Representatives.

Sarah Palin's next interview, with the right-wing radio talk show host and Fox presenter Sean Hannity, was something of a make-over exam. He covered similar ground to that covered by Charlie Gibson a week before, but this time there were no condescending explanations or 'gotcha' questions.

There was no such luck for Palin with her following network news outing, however: her interview with Katie Couric on CBS was disastrous. As concerns grew about the credit squeeze on Wall Street, which had begun with the meltdown in the subprime mortgage sector in late 2007, Couric asked Palin for examples of when her running mate, John McCain, had worked to reform Wall Street in all his years as a Senator. Palin answered by talking about McCain being a maverick, who had stood up to his own party. Katie Couric pressed for specifics:

Couric: I'm just going to ask you one more time — not to belabour the point – [for] specific examples in his 26 years of pushing for more regulation [of Wall Street banking practices].

Palin: I'll try to find you some and I'll bring them to you.

Governor Palin then became so tangled in her own words that when comedian Tina Fey on NBC's *Saturday Night Live* impersonated the Republican Vice Presidential pick that week, she wasn't using a script from a professional comedy writer – she was quoting Palin verbatim:

Palin/Fey: Ultimately what the bailout does is help those who are concerned about the healthcare reform that is needed to help shore up our economy ... to help um ... it's got to be all about job creation too.

The nonsensical linking of the credit squeeze, healthcare and job creation had *SNL*'s audience in stitches, but some conservative commentators, including Kathleen Parker from the *National Review*, called for the real Palin to drop out of the race for the good of the Republican Party. Fellow conservative columnist David Brooks of the *New York Times* described Palin as 'representing a fatal cancer to the Republican Party' and stated that she was 'absolutely not' ready to be President or Vice President of the US.

It was clear that the next President of the United States, whoever that was going to be, would be facing probably the greatest economic challenge in 70 years. And now there were real doubts that Sarah Palin was ready to become that President should anything happen to John McCain. Opinion polls saw McCain-Palin slipping back behind Obama-Biden as the financial situation became grimmer by the hour.

The first Presidential debate between McCain and Obama was due to be held on Friday, 26 September, at 'Ole Miss' – the University of Mississippi. With the Paulson bailout plan before the Senate, and yet to go to the House for a vote, John McCain stunned observers by announcing that he would suspend his campaign to return to Washington to steer the rescue package through Congress. He also called for the Presidential debate and the following week's Vice Presidential debate to be postponed until the Paulson plan was passed. Senator Obama refused to delay the debate, saying the next US President must be able to 'deal with more than one thing at once'.

With Senators McCain, Obama, Biden and Clinton all in attendance, the bailout package comfortably passed the Senate, stewarded through by the Chairman of the Senate Banking Committee Senator Chris Dodd, who we'd last seen during his brief Presidential run in Iowa in mid-2007. The House of Representatives would continue to look at the plan, and would vote within a couple of days.

The first Presidential debate went ahead as planned. Obama called McCain's bluff and said he would be attending the debate whether the Republican was there or not. With the deal half-done on Capitol Hill, McCain decided he'd better be at the debate after all.

The format and the focus – on foreign policy and national security – had been agreed to by the parties more than a year earlier, but with the US economy collapsing it was decided that domestic affairs could not be ignored and would take up the first 30 minutes of the 90-minute forum. The debate was unremarkable, with Obama named the winner by independent and undecided voters polled by Gallup and CNN, and McCain named the winner according to 86 per cent of the viewers of Fox *News*.

Meanwhile, back in Washington DC, the 435 members of the House, elected from congressional districts across America, had other ideas. Whereas only 35 of the 100 US Senators were up for re-election in November 2008, all of the House would have to face voters on the same day as the Presidential ballot, and the Paulson plan was proving very unpopular in middle America. The general sentiment seemed to be, why should 'Main Street' American taxpayers bail out Wall Street bankers who have been living high on the hog for years?

Despite having bi-partisan support, when the Bill came to a vote in the House, the Paulson rescue package was narrowly defeated, by 228 votes to 205 – about one-third of Democrats opposed the deal and two-thirds of Republicans were against it. The result was a strange alliance of ideological opposites such as Democratic Congressman Dennis Kucinich on the left and conservative Iowa Republican Congressman Steve King on the right. I called Congressman King on the evening of the vote to ask why he had opposed the Bill, putting him at odds with both John McCain and George W. Bush:

> We say 'not this deal' because it's not a free-market solution, it's a government solution, a government takeover of the private market – even a government takeover of the speculators' market. That's $700 billion to bail out Wall Street speculation at the expense of mainstream America. It came to the floor [of the House for a vote], take it or leave it; we decided to leave it.

Economist Dean Baker, from the Centre for Economic Policy Research, was on Capitol Hill advising several members of the House in the lead-up to the vote. He says the Congressmen and Congresswomen from both sides of politics who opposed the bailout plan were just listening to their constituents:

> This is incredibly unpopular. Of course we have an election coming up in 5 weeks, so that makes it much harder for members of Congress, but the vast majority of the public are saying, why should we be taxed to help out these Wall Street bankers who didn't know what they were doing and brought down the economy with them?

But Baker admits that, like investors, he was surprised by the 'nay' vote: 'I frankly thought this would pass. I talked to many members and the view was that this was going to pass.'

The Dow plummeted 777 points after the vote – its largest ever points decline in a single trading day.

Barack Obama had stood on the sidelines of the process, but John McCain had gambled on being the deal-maker, so when the deal fell through, he was left looking ineffective. Congressman King was more forgiving:

> If it hadn't been for John McCain injecting himself into this process, this Bill would have passed, and $700 billion in taxpayer dollars – a blank cheque – would now be on its way to Henry Paulson, our Secretary of the Treasury.

It was back to the drawing board. The Bill went back to the Senate, which tinkered and sweetened the deal by adding billions of dollars' worth of seemingly unrelated pork-barrel 'earmarks' into the 451-page Bill, including $192 million in excise rebates for rum producers in Puerto Rico and the Virgin Islands, $148 million in tax breaks for wool-fabric producers and $2 million in tax benefits for the makers of wooden arrows for children (the bow-makers would just have to manage on their own). All those Hollywood moguls who hosted so many generous fundraisers weren't forgotten either – they got a tax break of $48 million just to encourage them to make their films in Hollywood rather than someplace like Toronto or Tijuana ... or even Sydney. John McCain, Barack Obama, Joe Biden and 71 other Senators voted in favour of the heavily 'earmarked' amended rescue package, which again passed the Senate.

It was German Chancellor Otto von Bismarck who said, 'Laws are like sausages – it's better not to see them being made.' On Capitol Hill in the weeks leading up to the 2008 election those sausages were 100 per cent pork. It was now up to Steve King, Dennis Kucinich and the 433 remaining members of Congress to decide if the Wall Street bailout would pass the House at a second attempt. But first, attention returned to the Vice Presidential candidates ahead of their one-off debate.

〰〰〰

Jack Antaramian is a long-time Republican and was a strong supporter of George W. Bush in 2000 and 2004. In fact, he helped raise so much money for the Bush re-election campaign that he earned himself a coveted invitation to the Presidential inauguration. This multi-millionaire property developer from Naples, Florida – a very well-heeled, and usually very Republican town – has the white hair and chestnut tan that you can only get sunning yourself on the deck of a very expensive yacht. He strikes me as the kind of self-made man who has probably left instructions that Frank Sinatra's *My Way* should be played at his funeral, though I suspect he intends to never die – his life is too good.

Yet even in Naples, Florida, property prices have been falling over the past year, and Mr Antaramian is concerned. If the Republicans win and something happens to John McCain, he feels Sarah Palin just isn't up to the task:

> I just can't see Governor Palin having the capability to handle the stress and demands of suddenly being President – I can't see her being Vice President, let alone President, in the case of Senator McCain suddenly leaving or something happening to him … she may be a great hockey-mom, but I think that's the end of it.

In contrast, the Florida millionaire says he sees Barack Obama as another JFK, and if necessary, Joe Biden as another Lyndon Johnson: that is, a VP well qualified to take over the burdens of the Presidency. He now describes himself as 'a reformed Republican'.

Antaramian has hung a large vinyl Obama-Biden banner over the entranceway to his neo-classical mansion (which has the same arched windows and heavy white Romanesque columns as 1600 Pennsylvania Avenue). He also hosted a fundraiser at the local yacht club where about 300 friends, neighbours and business associates paid hundreds of dollars each to hear Joe Biden speak for 15 minutes; 40 of the guests paid a staggering $10,000 each to meet Joe, shake his hand and get a photograph. The days when you could just wander up to Joe Biden and chat for free at the Iowa State Fair are long gone.

In the space of a couple of hours, Antaramian helped raise over half a million dollars. The donors are still only allowed to give a maximum $2300 to Obama-Biden; the rest of the $10,000 is split between the Democratic National Committee, the State Democratic Party and various State candidates. Antaramian tells me he was very impressed with Senator Biden, whom he describes as 'very charming, very knowledgeable about foreign policy' and 'undoubtedly ready to be President'.

But for all his success in helping win over the likes of Jack Antaramian, Joe Biden is still Joe Biden – he's made a few gaffes along the way. Biden was thanking local supporters at a rally in Columbia, Missouri, in early September 2008 when he called on state Senator Chuck Graham to stand up: 'Chuck, stand up, let people see you!' Trouble is, Senator Graham can't stand up – he is a paraplegic. 'Oh God love ya, what am I talking about?' Biden said. 'I tell you what, [let's all] stand up for Chuck', which the crowd did.

The Vice Presidential debate isn't usually a ratings winner, but with huge amounts of attention being focused on Sarah Palin, and the very real possibility that either candidate could say something very stupid, record numbers of Americans tuned in on 2 October. The TV networks were running an endless loop of that clip of Lloyd Bentsen destroying Dan Quayle's career in a single sentence. Nearly 70 million Americans tuned in to watch the one Palin-Biden match-up at Washington University in St Louis – an astonishing 17.5 million more than watched the first McCain-Obama encounter a week earlier.

The question was, who would be playing the part of Lloyd Bentsen? In fact, there were plenty of other questions too: would Joe Biden say something terribly inappropriate to Sarah Palin? Would he be able to resist showing off his undoubtedly superior grasp of foreign affairs? Would he look like a bit of a bully as George H.W. Bush had against the only other woman to run for the Vice Presidency, Geraldine Ferraro in 1984? Or would his hair plugs come popping out of his scalp with the effort of trying to resist all of the above? And what about Sarah Palin? Which Sarah would it be – the folksy hockey-mom from the Republican Convention or the floundering novice of the Gibson and Couric interviews?

As it turned out, both Vice Presidential candidates rose to the occasion. Biden was the perfect gentleman, attacking McCain and not patronising Palin. As for the Alaskan Governor, she again exceeded expectations and even silenced some critics. From the first introductions, when she asked Biden chirpily, 'Can I call you Joe?', it was clear, for better or worse, that Palin would be defiantly Palin. Joe said a few things off the cuff that weren't quite correct: that the US drove Hezbollah from Lebanon (they are still very much there), and that FDR calmed the nation during the Great Depression by going on television (there was no television in the 1930s except in a few labs). But those were two slips in thousands of facts and nobody really noticed. Overall, if Biden won on substance, Palin more than held her own on style.

Meanwhile, Wall Street continued to stagger from one dismal trading session to another, until Congress finally agreed on a revised version of Henry Paulson's bailout plan, the day after the VP debate. There was enough political pressure and 'pork' to make the House vote a comfortable 263–171 this time around. President Bush wasted no time signing it into law and the taxpayer bailout of Wall Street was under way. Meanwhile the Labor Department announced that the US economy had shed a massive 159,000 jobs in September. A recession seemed inevitable, and as more Americans became concerned about losing their jobs and their homes, they turned away from the ruling Republican Party. They blamed George W. Bush and by association John McCain for the lack of financial regulation and irresponsible lending practices which had ultimately helped burst the housing bubble.

The second Presidential debate was billed as a 'Town Hall' style of meeting, held on 7 October at Belmont University in Nashville, Tennessee. Unlike the format at 'Ole Miss', where the candidates were anchored behind rostrums, at Belmont they were seated on stools and free to roam the stage with a handheld mic like duelling Vegas nightclub crooners. The format favoured Obama, as his lithe 47-year-old frame sauntered across the stage in front of the hand-selected audience of undecided voters. McCain looked old and stiff, like a nuggetty old pug at best, but at times he looked more as if he was scanning around for a walking frame. McCain seemed cranky with Obama, who was extending his lead in opinion polls, and noticeably failed to make eye contact with his Democratic rival. At one point McCain couldn't even mention his opponent by name, just referring to him oddly as 'that one'. The rules of the debate limited follow-up questions and replies, and effectively stifled any real debate between the candidates. Again, the majority of viewers deemed Obama the winner; the viewers of Fox, however, again gave the debate to McCain by a three-to-one margin.

The Presidential candidates kept up their hectic schedules during October, criss-crossing the nation and appearing in countless rallies, with and without their running mates. Biden made a few more gaffes, including the Quaylesque statement that he had 'three words' for what America needs: 'J-O-B-S.' But it didn't make much news;

it was just 'Joe being Joe'. There was a brief media flap over Sarah Palin's claim that Obama had been 'palling around with terrorists' – a reference to his association with William Ayers. Ayers had been a founder of a radical anti-Vietnam War group called the 'Weather Underground' in the late 1960s and early 1970s; the group bombed targets including a statue commemorating police deaths in an 1886 labor riot in Chicago (the statue was rebuilt, and blown up a second time by members of 'The Weathermen'). Ayers went on to become a Professor at the University of Illinois and an expert on educational theory. He and Obama were appointed to a number of the same community boards during the 1990s. Obama described the association as distant, just 'some guy in my neighbourhood'. The Republicans said the relationship was closer than Obama was letting on.

The final three weeks of the 2008 campaign saw the third and last debate between McCain and Obama, at Hofstra University in New York. It will probably be remembered as the 'Joe the Plumber debate', although John McCain will do his best to forget about it. The polls were looking increasingly bad for the Republicans: traditionally 'red' states such as Virginia, which hadn't voted for a Democrat since Lyndon Johnson in 1964, looked like swinging to Obama. Jack Antaramian's state of Florida drifted from 'too close to call' to 'leaning Obama', with the Democrat moving 5 per cent clear of McCain in a state the pundits said Republicans had to win to have any realistic hope of retaining the White House.

The state of Ohio decided the 2004 election, and was again a battleground in 2008. During a campaign stop in Toledo on 12 October, Senator Obama spoke to a 34-year-old man named Samuel J. 'Joe' Wurzelbacher, who asked the candidate if he (Joe) would pay higher taxes under Obama's tax plan if the plumbing business he hoped to buy generated an income of over $250,000 a year. Obama explained that more than 90 per cent of Americans would pay less tax under his plan, but also said he wanted to 'spread the wealth around, because that's good for everybody'.

The McCain campaign saw an opening. To them, 'Joe the Plumber' represented the aspiration at the heart of the American dream – the Republican-American dream in particular: a plumber wanting to buy a plumbing business and get ahead in life without the government getting in the way, just like those hotdog vendors on the streets of Manhattan. But 'spreading the wealth around' sounded a little like socialism to some folks – it was bad enough that the government was buying into Wall Street banks. Senator McCain used 'Joe' to attack the Obama plan during the Hofstra Presidential debate, and the Toledo plumber was mentioned more than two dozen times during the 90-minute encounter. Both candidates looked into the camera and addressed him directly when explaining their tax plans. Again, most polls awarded the contest to Obama, by a narrower margin, but afterwards McCain said that 'Joe the Plumber was the real winner of the debate.' Joe was booked to appear on Fox *News* that weekend.

Joe was an overnight sensation. He appeared the next day with Katie Couric on CBS, he was invited to appear at a rally with John McCain but begged off because of his scheduled appearance on Mike Huckabee's Fox *News*. Huckabee predicted on air that Obama's 'spreading the wealth around' answer to Joe's question could swing the election to McCain in the final fortnight. More than 100 reporters camped outside Wurzelbacher's Toledo home, and *Tonight Show* host Jay Leno joked, 'This plumber has done more interviews in one day than Sarah Palin since she was chosen.'

Hastily made McCain campaign ads aired featuring Joe – even after it was revealed that he wasn't quite what he seemed. First of all, he wasn't technically a plumber ... Sure, he fixed drains and things for a living, but he didn't have a plumbing licence. Worse for McCain, it turned out that Joe hadn't been paying his taxes, owed money for unpaid medical bills and was in no position to buy his plumbing firm – Joe was making about $40,000 a year. In fact, it turned out that 'Joe the Plumber' would have been much better off under Barack Obama's tax plan.

But if John McCain had 'Joe the Plumber' in his corner, Barack Obama had another endorsement: former Republican Secretary of State, General Colin Powell. Like many others, Powell cited the choice of Sarah Palin as McCain's running mate as one of the reasons he was backing Obama for the Presidency: 'I don't believe she is ready to be President of the United States, which is the job of the Vice President of the United States,' Powell told NBC's *Meet The Press*. Powell's backing of Obama came despite his 25-year friendship with McCain and wasn't because he was black.

Over on Fox *News*, Bill O'Reilly said General Powell endorsed Obama because, 'Powell remains bitter over the way he was treated by the Bush Administration and some rank-and-file Republican stalwarts.' When I spoke to former Presidential candidate Gary Bauer, who ran against John McCain and George W. Bush for the Republican nomination in the year 2000, he went even further:

> I wonder if Colin Powell's choice wasn't more about race … I don't
> know what was in his mind, but he has supported a number of
> Democratic candidates who were black … it wasn't about Sarah Palin
> or experience.

These days Gary Bauer is head of a Christian Conservative advocacy group called 'American Values'. He says race isn't a decisive factor for him, and if Barack Obama was a conservative and opposed abortion, same-sex marriage, high taxes and large government, he would have no problems supporting him: 'I look forward to voting for a black candidate who shares my values.' In fact, if anything, Bauer says, the colour of Obama's skin has been an advantage: 'Barack Obama's race has won him more votes than it has cost him.'

The Powell endorsement came the day the Obama campaign announced that they had set a new fundraising record – over $150 million for the month of September alone, with more than 3 million active donors chipping in an average of $86 each. John McCain was limited to spending a total of $84 million in the general election campaign after accepting public financing. The difference officially gave Barack Obama the largest money advantage for one Presidential candidate over an opponent since a cashed-up Richard Nixon beat George McGovern in 1972.

⚜

In the final days of the Presidential election campaign, Obama enjoyed a seemingly solid 5–7 per cent lead in most national polls, and strength in states such as Virginia. One of the great, though usually unspoken fears re-emerged about the potential dangers facing a black Presidential candidate – the spectre of assassination. A campaign already resonating with the echoes of the murdered Jack and Bobby Kennedy and Martin Luther King was put on edge by the arrest of two self-described white supremacists in Tennessee who bragged online that they would go on a killing spree targeting more than 100 African-Americans, beheading some and culminating in a bizarre plot to don tuxedos and drive their car at Obama at top speed, firing shotguns. As outlandish as the plan seemed, the pair were placed under arrest and appeared in court charged with making threats against a Presidential candidate.

It wasn't the first threat against Obama's life. A similar plot had been uncovered during the Democrat Convention: to shoot the candidate during his acceptance speech. A 32-year-old named Nathan Johnson was arrested along with three others in possession of drugs, two high-powered scope rifles, bulletproof vests and wigs. Johnson told arresting officers, 'He don't belong in political office. Blacks don't belong in political office. He ought to be shot.'

The End of the Road

Late October 2008: The spruikers of the new 450-seat Airbus A-380 superjumbo say it's the way of the future for aviation. It's bigger, quieter and more fuel efficient than any passenger aircraft ever built. They won't tell you the best bit for the US politics junkie: on that little flat screen built into the headrest of the person in front of you there's access to updated news from the Associated Press news wire. So here, about 35,000 feet above Hawaii, I'm happily getting a US election fix, reading a story filed only half an hour ago from a McCain rally in Pennsylvania. It's a state Senator McCain probably has to win if he's to find what's looking like an increasingly narrow path to the Presidency next Tuesday. It sounds as if he's still pounding the 'Joe the plumber' anti-taxation theme – and some polls show it's gaining traction in places like Pennsylvania and Ohio.

The pilot keeps coming in loudly over the PA during the re-run of the 2007 *Extras* Christmas Special I'm watching. The captain gushes with information about the plane, sounding like an excited dad in a brand-spanking-new sedan that turned out to have a bit more under the bonnet than he expected. 'Welcome aboard our wonderful new state-of-the-art Airbus A-380. We're a little late leaving Sydney, but in this terrific plane we should be able to make up the time along the way.' ('Buckle up, kids, we're late – I'm going to open her up a bit on the highway and see what she's got!')

We land at the Tom Bradley International Airport in Los Angeles – it's named for the former Mayor of the city who is now best remembered for losing an election he looked like winning. Tom Bradley was a popular African-American Democrat who ran for the Governorship of California in 1982 against Republican State Attorney-General George Deukmejian. In the weeks leading up to the ballot, Bradley enjoyed a significant lead in opinion polls. The pundits agreed: California was about to elect its first black Governor. But come Election Day, a funny thing happened – despite exit polls showing the black Mayor was ahead, Bradley lost. The opinion polls were wrong … or were they?

The discrepancy between the opinion polls, exit polls and the result gave rise to what became known as the 'Bradley Effect' – the idea that white voters will tell pollsters they will be voting for the black candidate, but come the moment to cast their actual ballot in the privacy of the booth, they can't quite overcome some latent racism that has them make a furtive switch to the white candidate. The 'Bradley Effect' was also cited as the possible reason for the lower-than-expected winning margin for black democrat Doug Wilder when he ran for the Governorship of Virginia in 1989. Some commentators even dusted off Bradley after Obama's loss to Hillary in the New Hampshire primary in January 2008, and it's been back in the news this week as pundits ponder whether Obama's poll lead in the final days of the campaign is real or not.

Rebecca and I planned a night in LA to catch up on some sleep before heading back to the mid-west. Waiting for our bags to trundle past on the airport's baggage carousel, I do a double-take when an appalling-looking figure walks by. He's at least six and a half feet tall, with a terrible deathly white face, ghoulish black-rimmed eyes and wearing strange long black robes. My God, why isn't anyone doing something? And there's a man in an ice-hockey mask. What's going on here? Then it gradually dawns on my jet-lagged brain: ahhh … it's Halloween.

After checking in at our airport hotel and locking our camera and laptop in the hotel safe, we hop into a rented Pontiac G6 and hit one of the worst LA traffic jams of the year. Moms and dads are all leaving work early to get home and take the kids 'trick or treating', so at 4.30 pm the freeway is hardly moving at all. Sorry, kids.

The 20-minute drive to Santa Monica Boulevard for dinner takes the best part of 2 hours. A guy jumps out of the back seat of a white SUV and gets his workout by jogging alongside, except that he has to slow to a walking pace to not get too far ahead. Finally the traffic fumes get to him and he flops back into the vehicle. The delay gives us time to flip through the different talk radio stations to get a sense of what reporters are saying about the Presidential campaign: McCain says he's going to win, Obama says he hasn't won yet, the polls say Obama will win, the pundits ask, 'What about the Bradley Effect?'

By the side of La Cienega Boulevard there's a group of 20 young Obama supporters waving banners at passing traffic, including a large sequinned 'Honk for Obama' sign. Given that this state's 55 electoral votes are certain to go to the Democrat by a 20 per cent margin, there are surprisingly few honks – maybe the number of road-rage-related shootings hereabouts keeps people off the horn unless it's really necessary. Our straw poll of bumper stickers gives Obama-Biden a two-to-one lead over McCain-Palin in Los Angeles.

Everyone in LA this evening, except us, seems to be dressed up for Halloween. The waiters and waitresses at our restaurant are all in costume – a black girl in a witch's outfit, a white youth in the grape-coloured T-shirt and matching yellow shorts and headband (oh right, we realise, he's meant to be the boyfriend from the indie film *Juno*). Our waitress, Darlene, is dressed like a vampire bumble-bee (of course) with fake blood dripping out of her mouth – I have to think twice when she asks if I want ketchup with my burger and fries.

The funny thing about a town like LA, which I think it is fair to say has more than its share of 'colourful' characters, is that some of the people out tonight leave you unsure if they are dressed for Halloween or not. Has that person in a hospital gown just wandered out of Cedars Sinai down the road? Is she really a cop? And it must be nice for the genuinely eccentric or deranged to have at least one night of the year when people say, 'Cool hair-do, dude' and, 'Where did you get that straitjacket? It's so real!'

Another, smaller group of Obama supporters are standing on the side of Santa Monica Boulevard chanting, 'Four more days! Four more days!' – a different take on the traditional encouragement given to Presidents seeking re-election, 'Four more years!' What appears to be a same-sex couple crosses the road up ahead carrying a cardboard sign opposing 'Proposition Eight', which seeks to define marriage as between only a man and a woman and effectively bans same-sex marriage statewide. In 2004, propositions banning gay marriage attached to the Presidential ballot boosted voter turnout among conservative evangelical Christians and helped win the election for George W. Bush. The number of evangelicals saying they'll vote for the Democrats has jumped from 17 per cent in 2004 to 33 per cent this year. Almost 20 per cent of people who describe themselves as 'conservative' say they'll be voting for Barack Obama. But if the 'Bradley Effect' is real, they would say that, wouldn't they?

Iowa, Sunday, 2 November 2008: Fifteen months after seeing John

McCain making bad jokes at the Iowa State Fair, chatting with Joe Biden about the importance of grassroots campaigning, and watching the first debate where Obama and Edwards ganged up on Hillary, we're heading back to where the long road to the White House began.

The Iowa roads surveyor must have been able to go to lunch early the day he did Route 80. Iowa is so flat it's pretty much just one ruler-line running east–west across the state. It's so straight that as we cruise along in our rented Buick 'Lucerne' we pass a woman who, I kid you not, is reading a magazine propped on the steering wheel of her silver Honda *while she's driving at 75 mph!*

We pass a Winnebago mobile home as big as a bus, hauling a full-sized SUV like a dinghy behind a motor launch. Countless tankers transporting ethanol made from subsidised Iowa corn hurtle past, heading back east; so do three semi-trailers, each carrying a single 40-metre-long blade for a massive wind turbine.

When we stop off at a *Kum&Go* service station to fill the Buick's fuel tank, the 'Unleaded Plus' containing 10 per cent ethanol is down to $1.93 per gallon – about half the price of just 4 months ago – so the tank of the large car is full for less than $30.00. The American love affair with big cars may have to end someday, but it seems last summer's oil shock was just a trial separation, and for now they've managed to patch things up.

It's very mild for autumn, with the temperature rising above 20ºC, and a misty fog hangs over the stubble of dried corn stalks. The harvest is almost over. To the side of the highway just outside Des Moines a massive John Deere combine harvester cuts its way slowly and rhythmically along one of the remaining rows of corn like a Marine Corps barber shearing a new recruit. The machine's powerful blades slice through the head-high stalks, sending ears up a conveyor into a smaller wagon that tags alongside like a hungry calf.

Iowa was the scene of Barack Obama's first great electoral triumph, winning the caucus one day shy of 10 months ago. The day after tomorrow he may be elected America's 44th President. Like a number of 'battleground states' that voted for President George W. Bush 4 years ago, Iowa is expected to swing from Republican 'red' to Democrat 'blue' on Election Day. The front page of this morning's *Des Moines Register* reports that Obama's national lead has slipped to 6 per cent, but that he has stretched his lead over John McCain in Iowa to 15 per cent – it's now 52 to 37. Senator Obama paid tribute to the role Iowans have played in his campaign's success when he made a whistlestop swing through Des Moines last Friday: 'This campaign began here. You helped launch this campaign, so the people of Iowa – I will always be grateful to all of you.'

One person who can claim some of the credit for Obama's lead in Iowa is Nancy Bobo. Nancy is a white woman in her mid-fifties who walked into the Obama campaign office in Des Moines in January 2007, and became their very first Iowa volunteer:

> They had this tiny little office downtown, a folding table and two
> folding chairs and two laptops and they were the first staff in the state
> and I signed on. A week later I got to meet him [Obama] personally
> and started working for him right away.

And Nancy has been working 10 hours a day most days for the 22 months since then, making phone calls, knocking on doors and organising campaign events. Her efforts earned her an invitation to be an Obama delegate at the Democratic National Convention in Denver, where she was seated with her fellow Iowans in the third row. 'It was obvious that he was a once-in-a-lifetime leader … we don't see many like this in our lives, we just don't,' Nancy says, her eyes shining with emotion.

Nancy is making calls today from another volunteer's house – on Foxhound Circle in Des Moines – and sending more helpers out with boxes of 'door-hangers': they look like hotel 'Do Not Disturb' signs except they remind people to vote on Tuesday. The first election Nancy got involved with was George McGovern's in 1972, when she was a college student. Like McGovern himself, she sees some similarities between the two campaigns.

'McGovern was considered so liberal back then, and a lot of the ideals he had are mirrored by Barack Obama. And so at his age, to see this happen ...', she shakes her head. 'I just wish there were more older people who worked so hard to see this happen – those from the civil rights movement and those who changed the Democratic Party – I wish they could see it too.'

I was reminded of what another former Democratic Presidential candidate, Mike Dukakis, had told me: the key to Obama's success hasn't been the vast sums of money he has raised for his campaign, it's been his ability to inspire and organise volunteers like Nancy Bobo at the grassroots level:

> Obama did not win that nomination because he had a lot of money
> – he won the nomination because he understood that grassroots
> organisation, especially in the caucus states, was very important. That
> doesn't cost money – the internet is a wonderful fundraising tool
> but it's also a wonderful organising tool. That's why volunteer-driven
> grassroots campaigning is so effective and inexpensive. McCain doesn't
> have that – he's raising money, but it's mostly from Republican fat cats.

But Governor Dukakis doesn't think all future Presidential candidates will be able to replicate the Obama campaign. 'He's extraordinary – I'm not quite sure that all of us have that,' the sometimes rather dour Dukakis say, laughing self-deprecatingly. 'But he's got it and it's made a huge difference, especially with the remarkable number of young people. It's a rare quality – a lot of us like to think we are good on our feet but he's almost in a class by himself.'

≈≈≈

Iowa, Monday, 3 November 2008, 10 am: We're due to leave Des

Moines and head back east towards Obama's home town Chicago for Election Day tomorrow, but first we need some more footage at the Volunteer Centre on Locust Street. We want to get some 'B-roll' pictures of Obama campaign workers on the phone and handing out voter information cards – the kind of images you see illustrating things a volunteer like Nancy Bobo will be saying in the documentary. While Rebecca takes the camera inside, I stay in the Buick and do a couple of radio reports over the mobile phone. The Obama office, like so many others we've seen around the United States in the past year, is in a rundown retail district in Des Moines. The shop looks like the kind of place that would suit a mattress warehouse – there's a faded FOR SALE sign outside that looks like it's been there quite a while. I lock the car doors.

Rebecca is still inside filming Obama volunteers on the phone – probably waiting for them to actually find someone at home. I pass the time by flipping through the Monday edition of the *Des Moines Register*. It seems that just like voters in California, Iowans have a proposition to consider on tomorrow's ballot. But, the paper tells me, it's not about gay marriage; it's about Iowa's 'Idiot clause'. Section 5 of Article 11 of the Iowa State Constitution proclaims: 'No idiot or insane person, or a person convicted of an infamous crime, shall be entitled to the priviledge (sic) of an elector.' The constitutional amendment would strike out the words 'idiot or insane' and replace them with the term 'mentally incompetent'. Funnily enough, the 'Idiot' proposition was supposed to be put in the 2006 election for the Governorship, the *Register* says, but there was a mix-up at the Secretary of State's office and they failed to give proper notice. Still, the gaffe didn't stop the Secretary of State, Chet Culver, succeeding Tom Vilsack as Iowa's governor.

The Buick also has satellite radio, and right now there is a whole channel dedicated to the Presidential election: it's called POTUS 08 (POTUS being short for President of the United States). On POTUS I find that pollster John Zogby, whom we met back in January in upstate New York, now has his own radio show. He's being asked by his co-host, Fritz Wenzel, what he thinks about the 'Bradley Effect'. Zogby lets out a deep sigh: 'There is no Bradley Effect; we are getting the truth. Voters tell us if they don't like Barack Obama.'

Time to hit the road again. We've decided to push on all the way to Chicago tonight – about 7 hours' drive away. But we have one more stop to make. I want to catch up with Professor Dave Redlawsk, who conducts and analyses opinion polls, at the University of Iowa in Iowa City. What does he think of the 'Bradley Effect' – will it affect tomorrow's result?

'Can't we talk about this on Wednesday?' Redlawsk laughs. But he does answer:

> While I think in fact there was a real effect at the time Tom Bradley
> ran for the governorship, that was a long time ago and things have
> changed. There is some sense that race still matters, but the real
> question is: is it already reflected in the polls or not? And speaking the
> day before the election, we really do not know. But we do know people
> have unconscious biases that can affect the decisions that they make
> and they may not be aware of it.

Chicago, Monday, 3 November 2008, 11.15 pm, Election Eve: After checking in to the Hilton Chicago we decide to wash away the dust of the long road from Iowa with a drink in the downstairs lobby bar. On a gilt-framed plasma screen TV CNN's Larry King is quizzing some of the pundits who have been popping up daily on news programs like this for the past 18 months. One of them, Paul Begala, was part of Bill Clinton's legendary 'War Room' in 1992 – they ran what was then the slickest and nimblest Presidential campaign that had ever been seen. Tonight Begala can't stop grinning. The national polls are holding above 50 per cent for Obama – something Bill Clinton never achieved in either of his wins. Jimmy Carter was the last Democrat to crack the big 'five-oh', and that was in 1976. 'It is looking good for the Democrats tomorrow,' Begala says, 'as long as everyone turns up to vote.'

We order another round of drinks from the Latino waiter. The negative ads are running on high rotation on CNN tonight, including one that brings back Jeremiah Wright's infamous sound-bite: 'Not God Bless America, God Damn America!' The ad attacks Obama's failure to condemn his preacher's firebrand ranting for 20 years, until he was running for the Presidency. The second part of 'god damn' has been bleeped out, implying that he may have used an even worse word than 'damn', and the punchline holds nothing back: 'Barack Obama, Too Radical, Too Risky.'

It's been a long day, and tomorrow is going to be even longer; Rebecca has lots of footage to shoot and I have more than a dozen live reports to do for radio stations back in Australia. We hop into a lift to the Hilton's 25th floor and Larry King and his guests are being piped in there as well, on a small TV set. A tired-looking man in his mid-twenties with short-cropped hair, casual clothes and cigarettes on his breath is in there too. He nods towards the endless election analysis on TV and says, 'It's almost over.'

'Yeah,' I say. 'What are we all going to do the day after tomorrow?'

He laughs mildly.

Rebecca asks if he's here in Chicago for the election, thinking he may be a journalist or campaign worker. He says he's with the secret service and that he's been working on Obama's 'security detail' for three months. We're rather surprised: isn't that supposed to be, well, a secret?

'I'm going to be posted to the Transition Office,' he says matter-of-factly as the old lift slowly grinds up to our floor.

The location of that Obama 'Transition Office' remains a secret, but transition planning has been under way on both sides for months. Just as the Vice Presidential candidates had to be vetted and selected, there are hundreds of senior Administration appointments, including Cabinet officials, that need to be made so that the new Administration can hit the ground running on 20 January 2009. For Obama that transition effort draws on the experience of a lot of former Clinton officials; John Podesta, who was President Clinton's Chief of Staff, has been heading the preparations, working out of his office at the left-leaning Washington thinktank, The Centre for American Progress. And Obama's close ally Rahm Emanuel, the 48-year-old former Clinton aide and Illinois Representative who masterminded the Democratic takeover of Congress in 2006, has been offered the job of White House Chief of Staff if Obama wins.

Understandably, given his lead in the polls, Obama is much further advanced in his transition planning than his Republican opponent. McCain says he's superstitious about such things. The Arizona Senator has also accused his rival of being over-confident and 'measuring the drapes in the Oval Office'.

'Goodnight folks,' the young Secret Service man says wearily, almost slumping against the wall of the lift as he holds the door open for us. 'Big day tomorrow.' We agree.

<hr />

Chicago, Tuesday, 4 November 2008, Election Day: The Hilton Chicago was built in 1927. In those days it was the biggest hotel in the world, and it's still bigger than most, with 1544 rooms on 27 floors and taking up a whole city block. It is right over the road from Grant Park on South Michigan Avenue, and next door to the Blackstone Hotel. It was from a 4th floor suite at the Blackstone that Senator George McGovern witnessed the bloody battle between police and anti-war protesters during the Democratic Convention of 1968. Mayor Daley's over-zealous police beat and urinated on a youth who had lowered an

American flag in the park. Then, the Walker Report of Inquiry later found, the police themselves rioted, attacking the peace protesters, and spraying mace indiscriminately in front of the hotels. Protesters stormed into the lobby of the Hilton to escape the tear gas, but the police followed – guests had to be locked in their rooms for their own protection. The 17-minute 'battle of the Hilton' was waged in front of dozens of reporters who were staying at the hotel, and like many bystanders, they too were maced by Daley's men. The whole thing was carried live on TV. Those were the 'Gestapo tactics' Abe Ribicoff condemned when he nominated George McGovern for the Presidency on the floor of the Convention.

Just as it was in August 1968, today Michigan Avenue and Grant Park are swarming with hundreds of police and thousands of ordinary people from all over America. But instead of reading 'End the War in Vietnam', their placards read *Obama-Biden* and *Change*. The crowd in the park and surrounding streets is expected to exceed half a million later tonight. Sometime this evening Barack Obama and Joe Biden will take to the temporary stage erected behind several inches of bullet-proof glass, and if the polls are right, they will claim victory in this historic election. But what if he loses? That's why the riot police are here.

Forty years after the assassinations of Bobby Kennedy and Dr Martin Luther King, and the Chicago riots that led to the democratisation of the Presidential candidate selection process, there is a feeling in Chicago today that things have come full circle. Everyone seems conscious that this is history happening before their eyes, an election they will be telling their children and grandchildren about. As the city's famous wind blows in off Lake Michigan, the canyons of stone, steel and glass seem to echo with the ghosts of the past.

We walk a few blocks to get coffee from a place that boasts about its espresso, not its restroom, and pass a wiry old black man with bowed legs and a worn dark overcoat. He's easily 80 years of age and hobbling in the direction of Grant Park with a younger companion who may be his son – they are both wearing brand new black OBAMA baseball caps. The old man's white teeth beam a broad smile from behind his shaggy grey beard and I fancy I see a little skip in his step, although it could just be that he has arthritis.

Last night in North Carolina, Senator Obama told a crowd of about 90,000 supporters that his grandmother had died that morning of cancer, at the age of 86. A white woman from Kansas, who worked on bomber-assembly lines during World War II and worked her way up to become Vice President of a local bank, Madelyn 'Toot' Dunham had raised Obama in the years he lived in Hawaii while his mother was studying in Jakarta.

Standing alone on a stage in the misty evening rain in Charlotte, Obama shed a tear over which there was no doubt and no discussion: 'She's gone home, so there is great joy as well as tears. She was one of those quiet heroes we have all across America.'

Like Dr King and Bobby Kennedy, Toot Dunham didn't live to see if America would elect its first black President today.

As polls begin to close, the first results start coming in from the east coast. With 1 per cent of the vote counted McCain is leading in states Obama was meant to win. What's happening? But then the exit polls start revealing what was on voters' minds as they left polling places around America today. Overwhelmingly they confirm that it is Obama who has more successfully tapped the profound mood for change and anxiety about the economy. They also confirm that 60 per cent of voters don't think Sarah Palin is qualified to be Vice President.

Grant Park is filling up fast with groups of mostly college-aged kids, running for the best positions near the stage. Chicago's population of around 3 million is almost evenly divided between whites, blacks and other races, mostly Hispanics and Latinos. It's noticeable just how racially diverse these groups of friends are – evidence, perhaps, that these 'millennials' are as post-racial as the sociologists have observed them to be. CNN is being shown on a massive outdoor television screen and doing something weird with a hologram of their reporter in Chicago looking like something R2D2 projected in *Star Wars*. More results flash on the big screen; a huge roar comes from deep down in 100,000 throats as Obama takes Virginia and Ohio … Pennsylvania now looks like staying in the Democrats' column. Mathematically, things are getting very difficult for McCain and Palin.

Every state in America is allocated a certain number of Electoral College votes, very roughly on the basis of their population – a smaller state like Iowa gets just 7 votes, a larger state like Florida has 27, and California has the most, with 55. Those votes will be cast by delegates who are pledged to either Obama or McCain, depending on who wins the most votes in their state. The delegates will vote when the parliament-like Electoral College sits – just once, to formally vote for the President – in January. So technically, America isn't electing a President today, just delegates to the Electoral College, which will elect a President … not that anyone really cares about that distinction.

With Obama winning in Pennsylvania I tell a radio program in Melbourne the election is over: Obama has won. Then immediately I wish I hadn't. I remembered at 7 pm in Boston on election night in 2004 when the exit polls put John Kerry in front, and at midnight in 2000 when the TV networks projected Al Gore the winner in Florida and President-elect. Oops! That could be a tape that follows me for a while.

Just about everyone in Grant Park, and those spilling out onto Michigan Avenue, is talking excitedly, many shouting into their mobile phones, 'I can't believe it! I can't believe it! Look at *Florida*!' Florida is looking good, and as polls close in California at 10 pm Chicago time, California's swag of electoral votes immediately puts Obama over the magic 270 Electoral College votes he needed to win. There is no Bradley Effect tonight. The opinion polls gave Obama a 7 per cent lead, and that's about how it's working out.

'A black man is President! A black man is President!' shouts a middle-aged black man, dancing in a circle like an excited child, punching the air.

'He did it, he did it!' cries another.

An older black woman in a fur-collared jacket stands perfectly still in the lobby of the Hilton, frozen, as if she's just remembered she left something important at home and doesn't know whether to go back for it or not. She shakes her head and says, 'My Lord.'

It's a happy riot on the street: white people and black people are hugging and crying, a fire engine sounds its powerful horns, rows of Secret Service people and State Troopers are on standby and a Chicago Police chopper hovers low overhead. Rebecca is using a handheld camera to film the euphoria but there is so much noise that I won't be able to hear the mobile phone for my next radio report, so I head back into the hotel. It's no better inside the lobby. Everyone is shouting out to friends, and the word 'Obama!' keeps rising up from the crowd.

All the elevators are packed with dressed-up people going to the dozens of official election night parties in the hotel. There are Obama campaign officials, local politicians, business figures and hordes of reporters and camera operators. Five black women in their forties are chanting sassily, 'Obama – he done it – Obama – you know it!' As I edge past an important-looking black man in an expensive suit he says to a friend, 'I just don't believe it.' I can't help but notice, though, that unlike the racially diverse groups of young people in Grant Park, here in the hotel the groups of whites and blacks are standing in separate huddles waiting for the lift, and the only Latinos seem to be hotel workers.

Back in our room on the 25th floor I open up the window to let in the evening air, full as it is with cheering from the park and more sirens and horns. I turn CNN on and they've crossed live to Arizona, where McCain is conceding the election. It's a gracious speech spoiled by the booing from the disappointed Republican crowd when he says he's just called Senator Obama to congratulate him on becoming

President-elect of the United States. There are celebrations in LA, in New York, and Obama supporters have taken to Pennsylvania Avenue right in front of the White House – nobody has seen an election night like it before. Outside, the Democratic crowd in Grant Park is also watching CNN, and their cheer rolls across Michigan Avenue like thunder. All the mobile phone cells are down, and I realise no emails have been coming through on my laptop for a couple of hours. The hotel switchboard is also in meltdown and I can't get a line to call through to Australia for my next report. Finally I get a line to Sydney, and I stick my head out the window so they'll pick up the atmosphere.

'It's a remarkable scene here in Chicago,' I report.

It's sinking in to the hundreds of thousands of people gathered in Grant Park and downtown Chicago this evening that America – a nation built on slavery – has made history and elected its first black President. There are people on the streets of every colour – they are wearing Obama T-shirts, caps and badges ... hugging and cheering. It's like every New Year's Eve and rock concert you've seen rolled into one. Security is incredibly tight with police out in force, and three inches of bullet-proof glass will screen Senator Obama when he speaks in a moment. This is still a divided nation: while tens of millions of Americans voted for Obama, only a few million less voted against him. He has offered his followers hope; he's told them together they can change the world. Now as President, he has to deliver on that promise.

As I'm speaking, I start to think about the enormous task ahead of President Obama. Like Jimmy Carter in 1976, he's been elected on a wave of change after a failed presidency, where his relative inexperience in Washington served as an advantage, if anything. But just like President Carter, Obama inherits a nation wearied by war, facing major economic problems at home and a world of trouble abroad.

He also confronts issues like global warming and climate change that were largely unknown 32 years ago.

The optimists will see Obama becoming another Franklin Roosevelt or Abraham Lincoln helping to lift a nation from its knees. The pessimists will fear another time of 'malaise' and the sort of 'crisis of confidence' that Carter identified during his single term in the White House, but could do nothing about. Tonight in Chicago there are plenty of optimists – and why not? Obama's candidacy was, in his own words, 'improbable' and his campaign has been almost flawless. The currents of history and winds of political fortune that propelled him to this point will surely abate. Yet there is a cool self-assurance and calm that inspires hope for his Presidency. Obama has survived the gauntlet of a marathon two-year contest, resisted the attacks over Jeremiah Wright and Bill Ayers, seen off all comers, including Hillary Clinton and John McCain. Maybe that long road from Iowa to Washington isn't such a bad preparation for the Presidency after all.

Another huge cheer comes from across the road in Grant Park, then from across the room on the TV and a second later down the phone line, where the audio is being carried on the Australian radio station I'm about to speak on. President-elect Barack Obama, soon-to-be First Lady Michelle Obama, Vice President-elect Joe Biden and his wife Jill have appeared on stage, smiling and waving. The Reverend Jesse Jackson is among the VIPs in a fenced-off area of the park. Jackson was standing next to Martin Luther King on that hotel balcony in Memphis in 1968 when the assassin's bullet hit. Jackson ran unsuccessfully for the Democratic Presidential nomination himself twice in the 1980s, and tonight he is watching the first black man win the Presidency of the United States. Tears are streaming down his cheeks.

Obama begins:

> If there is anyone out there who still doubts that America is a place
> where all things are possible; who still wonders if the dream of our

founders is alive in our time; who still questions the power of our democracy, tonight is your answer ...

It's been a long time coming, but tonight, because of what we did on this day, in this election, at this defining moment, change has come to America.

I was never the likeliest candidate for this office. We didn't start with much money or many endorsements ... our campaign wasn't hatched in the halls of Washington – it began in the backyards of Des Moines and the living rooms of Concord and the front porches of Charleston.

It was built by working men and women who dug into what little savings they had to give $5 and $10 and $20 to this cause.

It drew strength from the young people who rejected the myth of their generation's apathy; who left their homes and their families for jobs that offered little pay and less sleep; from the not-so-young people who braved the bitter cold and scorching heat to knock on the doors of perfect strangers; from the millions of Americans who volunteered, and organised, and proved that more than two centuries later, a government of the people, by the people and for the people has not perished from this Earth. This is your victory.

I realise Obama has just provided us with the answer to the question we first posed almost a year and a half ago: Can a candidate do as George McGovern tried to do and Jimmy Carter did – win the most powerful political office on Earth from relatively humble beginnings in a small state like Iowa?

Yes, he can.

Postscript: On 4 November 2008, Senator Barack Obama of Illinois and Senator Joe Biden of Delaware received 52.6 per cent to Senator John McCain of Arizona and Alaska Governor Sarah Palin's 46.1 per cent of an estimated 130 million votes cast nationally. It was the largest proportion of the popular vote for a Democratic ticket since the election of President Lyndon Johnson and Vice President Hubert Humphrey in 1964.

It was also the first time since the mid-1960s that Virginia, once home to the capital of the old Confederate South, had voted for a Democratic Presidential candidate. Other traditionally Republican states like North Carolina and Indiana were won narrowly by Obama-Biden. Battleground states won by President Bush in 2004 – including Florida, Ohio, Iowa and New Mexico – turned from Republican Red to Democrat Blue. Obama became the first African-American elected to the Presidency and Biden the first Catholic elected to the Vice Presidency.

Meanwhile, voters in California supported Proposition Eight banning gay marriage, with active encouragement from members of the Mormon Church and the African-American community; and Iowans supported the state constitutional amendment to remove the word 'idiot' from the list of people disqualified from voting.

After Election Day, it was revealed that the McCain campaign had serious concerns about Sarah Palin's lack of general knowledge after her selection as his running mate. Fox *News* reported the Alaskan Governor thought Africa was a country, not a continent. Nevertheless, speculation had already begun that Palin would run for the Presidency against Obama in 2012. She was due to make her first appearance in Iowa at a Governor's Association meeting two weeks after the 2008 election. Fellow Republicans Newt Gingrich, Mitt Romney and Mike Huckabee were all expected to visit the state before year's end.

Chicago, Thursday, 6 November 2008, 10 am: A black businesswoman in her thirties wearing a smart dark skirt-suit is sipping coffee in the breakfast room of our hotel. Oprah Winfrey is on the flat-panel TV mounted on the wall near her table. Oprah is very excited. She was in Grant Park for Obama's speech and is excitedly asking her guest, the African-American actor Will Smith, 'Did you cry? I cried. Did you cry?'

A hotel worker, also a black woman in her thirties, stops in front of the TV and leans on her upright vacuum cleaner. Oprah, America's highest paid TV star, and Will Smith, one of the most popular actors in Hollywood, are sharing more memories of the historic night. 'This is big,' says Oprah. Yes, Smith agrees. He says he also shed a tear. Oprah throws to a break, and the businesswoman turns to the hotel cleaner and says, 'Wasn't that election something?' The second woman nods, 'It sure was something!'

'Wow,' says the businesswoman, putting down her cup.

'Wow,' says the cleaner, getting back to her work.

★ Index

abortion policy 46
African-Americans 20, 153–4
Agnew, Spiro 195–6
Ailes, Roger 184
Albright, Madeleine 78
Ames, Iowa 13–14
'Anthea' (Obama supporter) 161
Arthur, Chester 196
'Ashley' (Obama supporter) 161
assassinations 49, 114, 196
Associated Press 50
'Audacity of Hope' speech 74
Ayers, Whit 132, 153–4, 178–9

Badham, Robert 167–8
'Barry' (lawyer) 136–7
Bell, Griffin 155
Benedict College, South Carolina 156–8
Bentsen, Lloyd 183–4
Berman, Gail 147
Biden, Joe
    as running mate for Obama 200,
        201–02
    at Drake University 50, 53
    at Iowa State Fair 18–20
    fundraising by 57, 147–8, 220
    loses Iowa Caucus 86–8
    supporters 45, 81–2
Bierbauer, Charles 55, 171, 178
'Big Boars' 16–17
black voters 20, 153–4
blue and red states 153
Bonior, David 108
Boston, 2004 Presidential campaign
    166–9
Boston Red Sox 166
Bradley Effect 228, 235, 240
Bray, Filene 157
Bray, Martha 157
Broder, David 120

Brown, James 25–7
Buchanan, Pat
    challenges George Bush Sr. 170–1
    on Barack Obama 133
    on candidates 177
    on fundraising 142
    on George McGovern 124–8
    on media 58
bundlers 137–8
Burr, Aaron 189
Bush, Barbara 198
Bush, George Sr.
    as running mate for Reagan 183
    collapse in Japan 185
    debates Ferraro 198
Bush, George W.
    2000 campaign 172
    Cheney and 187–9
    failings of 170
    view of history 194
Butler, Carrie 158

campaign itinerary 96–7
candidates for President 168–80
candidates for Vice President 181–202
Canuck letter 119, 128
'Carol' (Kucinch supporter) 37–40, 42
Carson, Johnny 181
Carter, Jimmy (James Earl)
    1976 campaign 172
    as possible running mate for McGovern
        122, 186
    background of 154–5, 179
    campaigning for 10
    UFO sighting 68
Carter Printing 31
Caucus – The Musical! 77
caucus vs. primary-style elections 2–3
Center for Responsive Politics 145–6
Chappell, Lori 12

Cheney, Dick 187–8
Clark, Wesley 78, 200
Cleveland, Grover 178
Clinton, Bill
    African-American support for 157–8
    as Presidential candidate 91–3, 169
    at Coralville Conference Center 77–8
    background of 154–5, 179
    introduces Hillary 78–9
    loses voice campaigning 70
    on South Carolina primary 159
    running mates for 186
    Shirley MacLaine on 65–6
Clinton, Hillary
    2008 campaign 173
    African-American views of 157–8, 163
    as running mate for Obama 199
    at Coralville Conference Center 77–8
    at Drake University 48, 53
    at Iowa State Fair 20–2
    at Nashua school gymnasium 94–6
    fundraising by 57, 140–1, 148
    George McGovern endorses 132–3
    loses Iowa Caucus 86
    loses South Carolina primary 159
    registration cards 31
    supporters 44–5, 156, 196–7
    tears in New Hampshire 129
    Tom Vilsack on 62–3
    votes to support Iraq war 60–1
    wins New Hampshire primary 108
    wins New York State 163
    withdraws from contest 159–60
Colson, 'Tex' 127
Committee to Re-Elect The President 128
Contarino, Dave 150, 200
Coralville Conference Center 73–7
CREEP 128
Cuyahoga County Commission 141–2

Danson, Ted 78
Dean, Howard
    'Dean Scream' 4
    failure of campaign 76–7
    on media 63
    on role of Iowa 8–9
DeLauro, Angela 106–7
Democrats 57, 153–4
Denton, James 98, 108
Des Moines, Iowa 1–2

Devine, Tad 149–50
'Dianne' (Obama supporter) 162–3
Dodd, Chris
    at Iowa State Fair 32–4
    fundraising by 57
    supporters 45–6
    withdraws 88
Dole, Bob 125
Donald, James 147
Douglas, Michael 110
Drake University, Iowa 43–50, 52, 58–64
Dukakis, Michael
    Northern background 154
    on Dick Cheney 187
    on Lloyd Bentsen 184
    running mates for 183

Eagleton, Thomas F. 123–4, 126
Eastwood, Clint 66
Edwards, Elizabeth 29–30, 62, 71, 108–9, 201
    New Hampshire campaign 97–8
Edwards, John
    as running mate for Kerry 199
    as possible running mate for Obama 200, 201
    at Drake University 49–50
    at Iowa caucus 69–73
    campaign office 105–6
    Dave Redlawsk on 34–5
    fundraising by 57, 140–1, 143, 144
    Iowa campaigning 25–31
    loses South Carolina primary 159
    New Hampshire campaign 96–100
    supporters 46, 105–6
    withdraws from contest 109–10
Ehrlichman, John 127
Eisenhower, Dwight D. 183, 195
endorsements 29
Estrada, Joseph 66
'Ethan' (Obama supporter) 160–2

Fair Elections Now Act 142
Fairfield, Iowa 36–40
Federal Communications Commission 63
Feingold, Russ 138
Ferraro, Geraldine 196–9, 202–03
Figueroa, William 185
financial crisis 213–14, 216–18, 221–22
Florida polling dates 9

Flynt, Larry 110
foot-in-mouth disease 20
Ford, Gerald R. 127, 195
Ford, Robert John 80–1, 83–6
Franklin, Benjamin 186–7
Frum, David 187–8, 202
fundraising 56–7, 137–44

Garfield, James 196
Garner, John Nance 192–3
gender issues 196–7
geographic voting patterns 153–4
'Getting Out the Vote' campaign 90–1
Giuliani, Rudy
    as possible running mate for McCain
        202
    at Iowa State Fair 23–4
    avoids Ames Straw Poll 13
    fundraising by 57, 140
    loses Iowa Caucus 88
    withdraws from contest 159–60
Glenn, Rebecca 3
Glover, Mike 50–1, 173–4
Gore, Al
    as Presidential candidate 169
    as running mate for Bill Clinton 186
    media image 54–5
    Southern background 154–5
Graham, Lindsey 153
Gravel, Mike
    excluded from debate 68
    fundraising by 57, 140–2
    interview with 61–2
    lack of support for 53
    oldest candidate 59
    Vice Presidential nominee 123
Grayson, Cary 191

Hagan, Tim 141–2, 170
Haldeman, Bob 127
Hamilton, Alexander 189
hand-shaking 2
Harkin, Tom 92
Harrelson, Woody 110
Harrison, William Henry 174
Hart, Gary 6, 61
healthcare policy 100
Heaney, Seamus 18, 88
Hensley, Jim 102
Heston, Charlton 66

Hiss, Alger 195
Hoffman, Abbie 115
Holder, Eric 200
Hoover, Herbert 192
Horton, Willie 185
House Committee for Un-American
    Activities 195
House parties 70, 97
Houston, David 191
Hoyt, Ron 31
Huckabee, Mike
    supports Sarah Palin 207
    fundraising by 30, 58
    loses South Carolina primary 159
    wins Iowa Caucus 88
Hughes, Joey 94
Humphrey, Hubert H. 114, 116
    as possible running mate for McGovern
        122
    Nixon defeats 195
    Northern background 154
Hunter, Rielle 201
Hurricane Gustav 204

image, importance of 54, *see also* media
Internet campaigning 148–51
Iowa City, Iowa 5–6
Iowa Caucuses 1–34, 69–87
Iowa State Fair 11–12
Iraq policy 104
Isaacs, Maxine 55–6
    on candidates 179
    on failed campaigns 172
    on gender issues 198

Jackson, Henry 'Scoop' 118
Jackson, Jesse 159
Jackson, Tiffany 81
'Joanna' (Obama supporter) 161
'Joe the Plumber' 223–25
Johnson, Andrew 196
Johnson, Jim 199–201
Johnson, Lyndon Baines 113–14, 182–3,
    196

Kaine, Tim 201
Kanin, Denis 91–3, 149
Kantor, Mickey 182, 186, 199, 202
Keene, Kevin 157
'Ken' (reporter) 47

Kennedy, Caroline 200
Kennedy, Edward 'Ted' 33, 118
  as candidate 169
  endorses Barack Obama 159
  McGovern invites to be running mate
    122
Kennedy, John F. 172, 177
  assassination of 196
  Nixon loses to 195
  running mates for 182–3
Kennedy, Robert
  assassination of 49, 114
  dog owned by 112–13
  opposes Johnson re-election 113
Kennedy, Robert Jr. 26
Kerry, John
  Dennis Kucinich and 35
  loses in 2004: 168–70
  Northern background 154
  running mates for 199
Kimmel, Edward 96
King, Martin Luther Jr. 75
Kinnock, Neil 18
Klein, Mike 36, 61
Krumholz, Sheila 145–6
Kucinich, Dennis 35–42
  at Drake University 60–1
  fundraising by 57
  loses in 2004: 168
  on gay marriage 59
  supporters 64–8, 83
  UFO sightings 67–8
  withdraws from contest 110
Kucinich, Elizabeth 36, 38

Lafayette Square, Washington DC 174–5
Lear, Norman 147
Leber, Bill 72–3
Lincoln, Abraham 196
'Lizzy' (Obama supporter) 160–1
lobbyists 145–6
Loeb, William 119
Lott, Trent 153
Lynch, John 135, 138–9
Lynch, Susan 138–9

MacLaine, Shirley 64–8
Manilow, Barry 148
Marshall, Thomas 187, 189–93
'Matt' (Edwards supporter) 105–6

McCain, Cindy 101–2, 204
McCain, John
  at Exeter Town Hall 100–4
  avoids Ames Straw Poll 13–15
  concedes 241
  fundraising by 57–8
  loses Iowa Caucus 88
  proposes fundraising bill 138
  supporters 100
  wins Republican nomination 160,
    163–4, 202
  wins South Carolina primary 159
McCarthy, Gene 113, 118
McGovern, Eleanor 117
McGovern, George 111–18
  1972 campaign 118–24
  dirty tricks against 124–5
  endorses Barack Obama 134
  endorses Hillary Clinton 132–3
  Gary Hart campaigns for 6
  nominated for President 115
  Northern background 154
  on candidates 171, 179
  on fundraising 140, 142–3
  on lobbyists 145–6
  running mates for 181–2
  Shirley MacLaine backs 65
McKinley, William 196
McLean, Don 17–18
media
  accessibility to 56–8
  candidates on 173–4
  Howard Dean on 63
  importance of 54–5
  role in primary nominations 121
  spending on 144
Michigan polling dates 9
Miller, Dennis 131–2
Miller, Judy 94
Mitchell, South Dakota 111
Mondale, Walter
  as running mate for Carter 186
  as possible running mate for McGovern
    122
  failed campaign 172
  media image 55–6
  Northern background 154
  running mates for 196, 198
Mudd, Roger 33
Muskie, Edmund 118–19

Nashua, New Hampshire 93–6, 105–6
Nelson, Willie 110
New Hampshire 6, 89–110, 131–2
New York City 159–64
New York State primary 159–64
New York University 166
Nixon, Richard Milhous
    1972 campaign 118, 127
    as running mate for Eisenhower 183
    rise and fall of 128, 195–6
Norris, Chuck 98
Novak, Robert 126

Obama, Barack
    African-American support for 157–8
    as candidate 178–80
    assassination fears 226
    at Coralville Conference Center 73–7
    Colin Powell endorses 225
    election night speech 243–44
    fundraising by 57, 140, 142, 225
    George McGovern endorses 134
    Internet campaigning 148–51
    Jeremiah Wright 236
    Jim Spencer on 91
    Joe Biden on 20, 201–02
    John Edwards endorses 109–10
    New York supporters 160–2
    Oprah Winfrey endorses 99
    Pat Buchanan on 133
    Rahm Emanuel 237
    running mates for 198–201
    Secret Service protection 48–9, 236
    supporters 45, 81, 85, 232–33
    wins Democratic nomination 134,
        163, 201
    wins Iowa Caucus 86
    wins South Carolina primary 159
O'Neill, Joe 184, 199, 201
online campaigning 148–51

Palin, Sarah 202–03, 205–12
    diplomatic 'speed dating' 211–12
    doubts about 215, 219, 225, 245
    interviews 212, 214–15
    Republican National Convention
        speech 207–08
    rumours 205–06
    style 209
Patterson, David 78

Patterson, Tom
    on fundraising 57–8, 144–5
    on media 54–5
    on pork barrelling 15–16
    on primary nominations 121
Paul, Ron 14, 88, 93
Penn, Sean 98, 110
Pentagon Papers 61–2
Peron, Eva 66
Perry, Mary 106
Petrzelka, Bob 69, 71–2
Plouffe, David 149
Political Action Committees 141
pork barrelling 15–16
Powell, Jody
    in Iowa 10–11
    on 1972 campaign 122
    on 1976 campaign 172
    on voting patterns 155–6
Presidential candidates 168–80
Presidential debates 215–16, 222–23
primary-style vs. caucus elections 2–3
Proposition Eight 230, 245
push-polling 14

Quayle, Danforth 183–5, 203

racialism 198
Reagan, Ronald
    acting background 54, 64, 66
    running mates for 183
    strengths of 169
red and blue states 153–4
Redlawsk, Dave 32, 34–5, 98–9, 235
Republican National Convention 204,
    206, 207–08
Republicans 57–8, 153–4
retail politics 5
Ribicoff, Abe 115
Rice, Donna 6
Richardson, Bill
    as possible running mate for Obama
        200
    at Iowa State Fair 1–2, 7, 11
    baseball cards 31
    fundraising by 57
    loses Iowa Caucus 86, 88
    supporters 83–4, 107
    withdraws from contest 110
Romney, Mitt

campaigns in Iowa 13–14
  fundraising by 57
  loses Iowa Caucus 88
  withdraws from contest 163
Roosevelt, Franklin Delano 192–3
Roosevelt, Theodore 196
Rove, Karl, push-polling by 14
Rubenstein, Marcos 39
Rubin, Jerry 115

San Giacomo, Laura 147
Schjelderup-Ebbe, Thorleif 175–6
Schwarzenegger, Arnold 66
Secret Service protection 48–9
Sensible Iowans 27, 47
Shannon, Marcus 157
Shriver, Sargent 124
Shrum, Bob 120–1
  on candidates 168–71, 179–80
  on fundraising 144, 149
  on George McGovern 122, 127
  on primary nominations 116
Sibelius, Kathleen 201
soft money contributions 138
South Carolina 152–9
South Dakota 111–18
sparrows in Washington DC 175–6
Spencer, Jim 90–1
Squire, Peverill 5–6
Standel, Harry 106, 143
Stephanopoulos, George 52–3, 59
'Strength Through Peace' 39
Sununu, John H. 6
Super Delegates 117
Super Tuesday 166
'Swift Boat' claims 126

tax policy 47
Temple, Shirley 66
terrorism policy 104
Tezak, Deborah 81–2
'The Audacity of Hope' speech 74

This Week With George Stephanopoulos 44
Thompson, Fred 64, 66, 88
Thurmond, Strom 152–3, 158
ticket balancing 182, 186
Truman, Harry 193–4
Tsongas, Paul 91–3

UFO sightings 67–8
Union Leader 119
United Flight 93: 188
Ursa (dog) 112
Utica, New York 130–2

Vice Presidential candidates 181–202
Vice Presidential debate 220–21
Vilsack, Tom
  2008 campaign 12–13, 173
  at Coralville Conference Center 78
  Hillary Clinton and 21, 62–3
  on candidacy 51
  on fundraising 146–7
  on Iowa polling 71
  on leadership 176
Vote-Builder website 162
Voting Rights Act 153–4

Wallace, George 49
Wallace, Henry A. 192
Washington-Williams, Essie Mae 158
Watergate scandal 127, 142
Webb, Jim 201
Weinberger, David 149–50
Wellesley College, Massachusetts 135–45
Whittington, Harry 189
Wilson, Woodrow 190–3
Winfrey, Oprah 99
Wright-Penn, Robin 110

Yepsen, David 53–4, 58, 150–1
YouTube 150

Zogby, John 91, 130–2, 173